DC

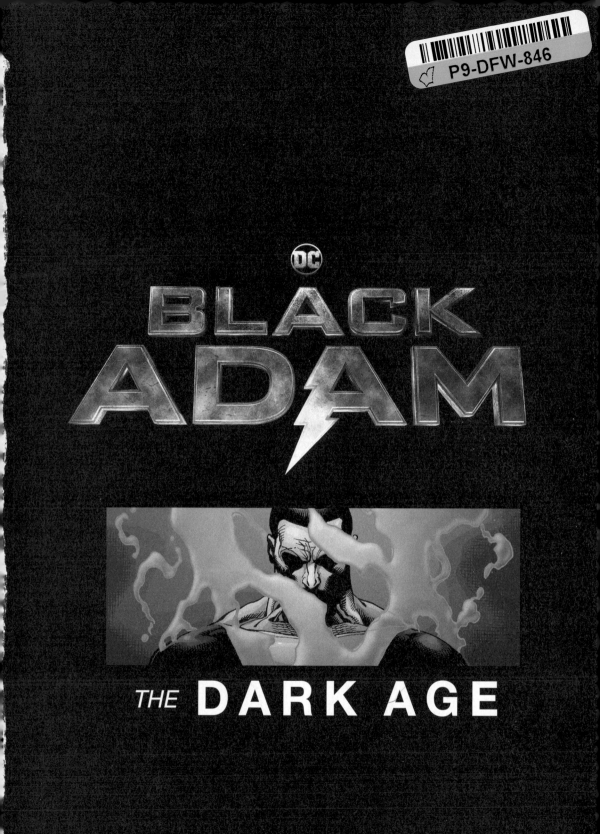

BLACK ADAM

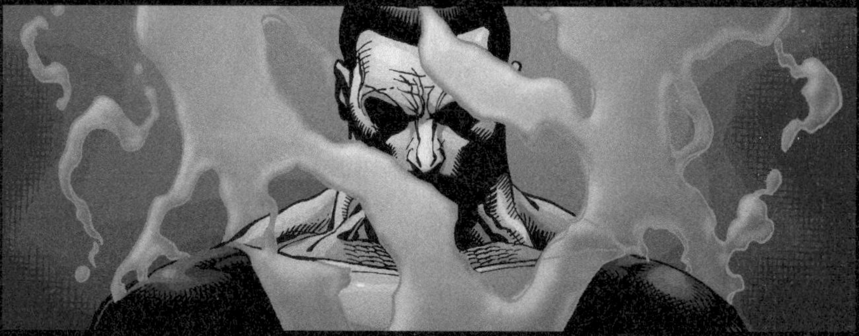

THE DARK AGE

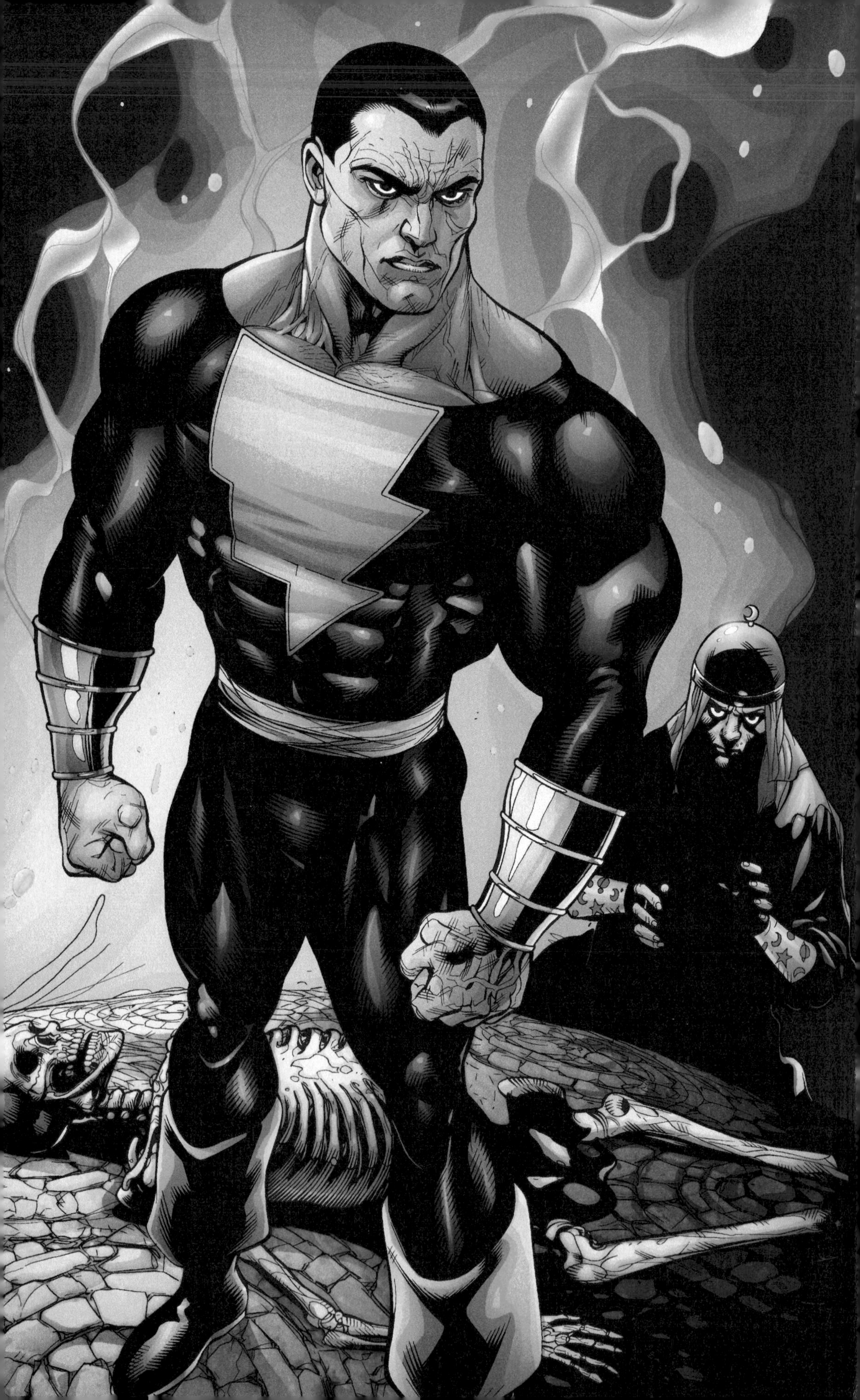

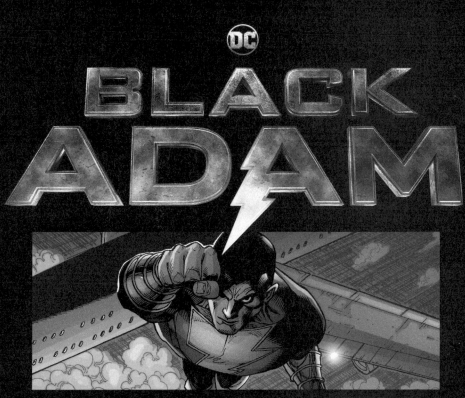

BLACK ADAM

THE DARK AGE

Peter J. Tomasi
Writer

Nathan Eyring
Colorist

Doug Mahnke
Penciller

Nick J. Napolitano
Rob Leigh
Letterers

Christian Alamy
Norm Rapmund
Rodney Ramos
Inkers

Series covers by
Doug Mahnke

Michael Siglain Editor – Original Series
Harvey Richards Assistant Editor – Original Series
Bob Harras Editor – Collected Edition
Steve Cook Design Director – Books
Amie Brockway-Metcalf Publication Design
Evin Vanover Publication Production

Marie Javins Editor-in-Chief, DC Comics

Anne DePies Senior VP – General Manager
Jim Lee Publisher & Chief Creative Officer
Don Falletti VP – Manufacturing Operations & Workflow Management
Lawrence Ganem VP – Talent Services
Alison Gill Senior VP – Manufacturing & Operations
Jeffrey Kaufman VP – Editorial Strategy & Programming
Nick J. Napolitano VP – Manufacturing Administration & Design
Nancy Spears VP – Revenue

BLACK ADAM: THE DARK AGE

DC Comics, 100 S. California Street, Burbank, CA 91505
Printed by LSC Communications, Owensville, MO, USA. 8/5/22.
ISBN: 978-1-77951-538-4

PEFC Certified
This product is from sustainably managed forests and controlled sources
PEFC
PEFC/29-31-337
www.pefc.org

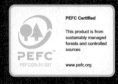

Chapter One

This chapter inked by Christian Alamy and Norm Rapmund

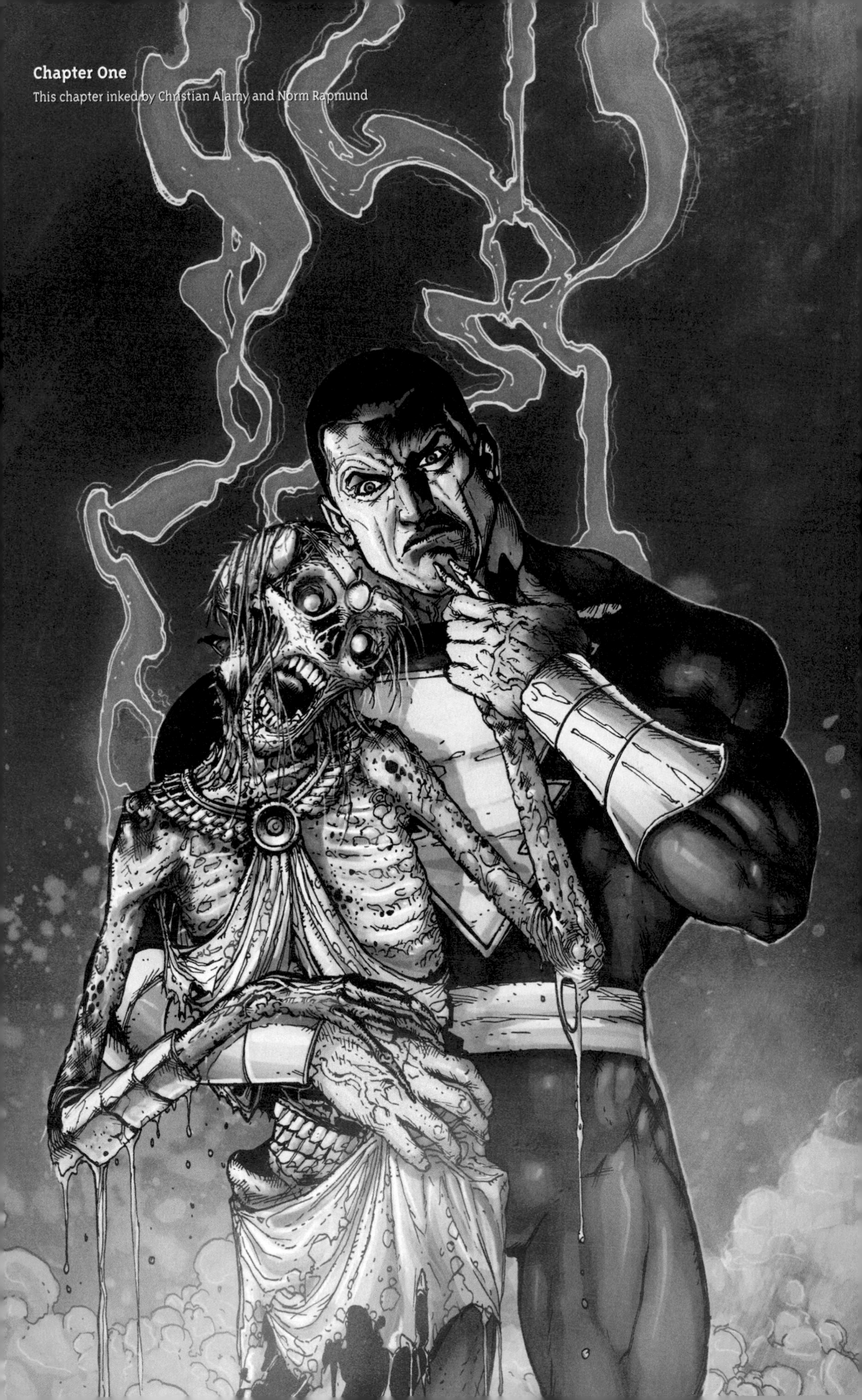

Variant cover to BLACK ADAM 1
Art by Alex Ross

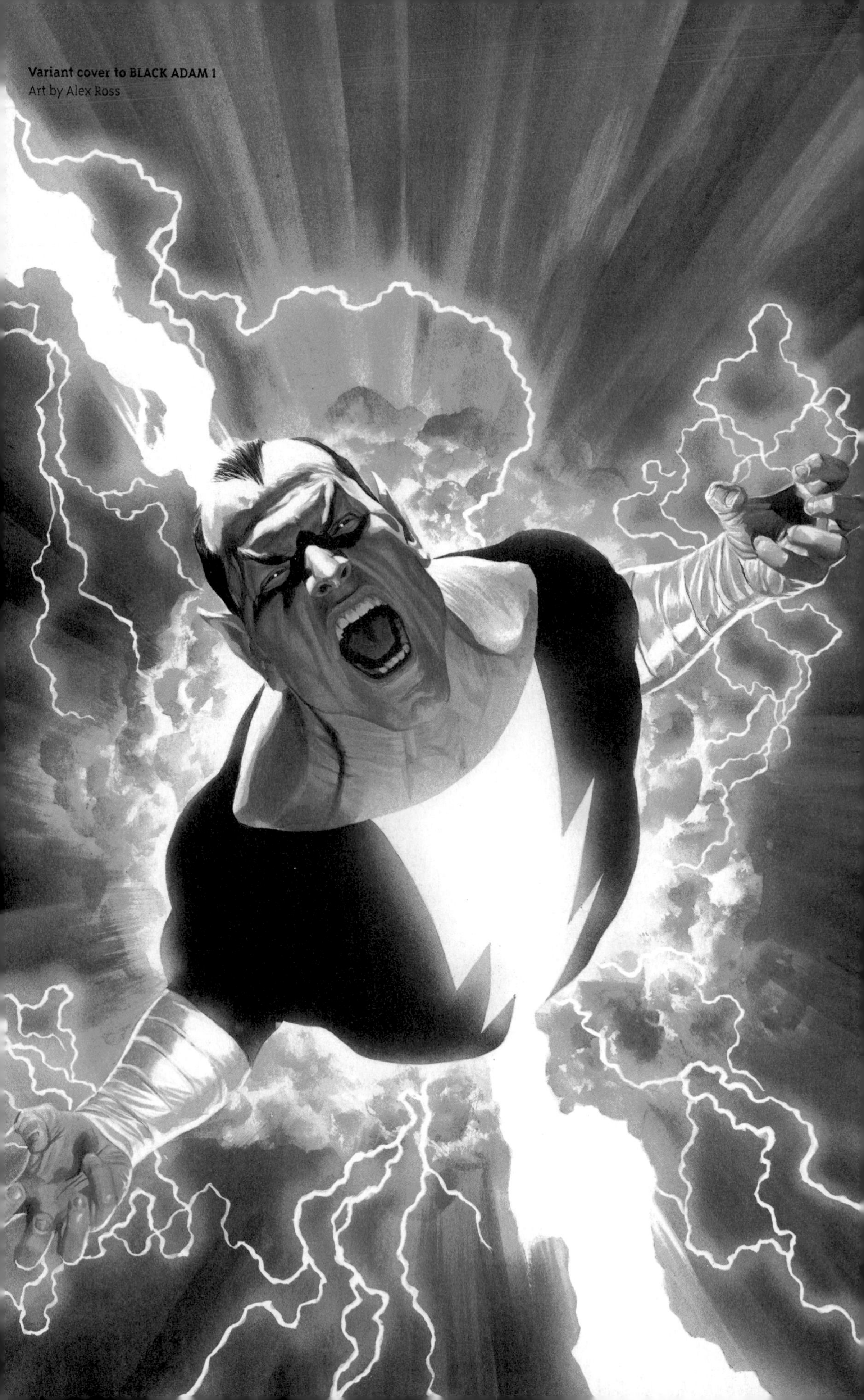

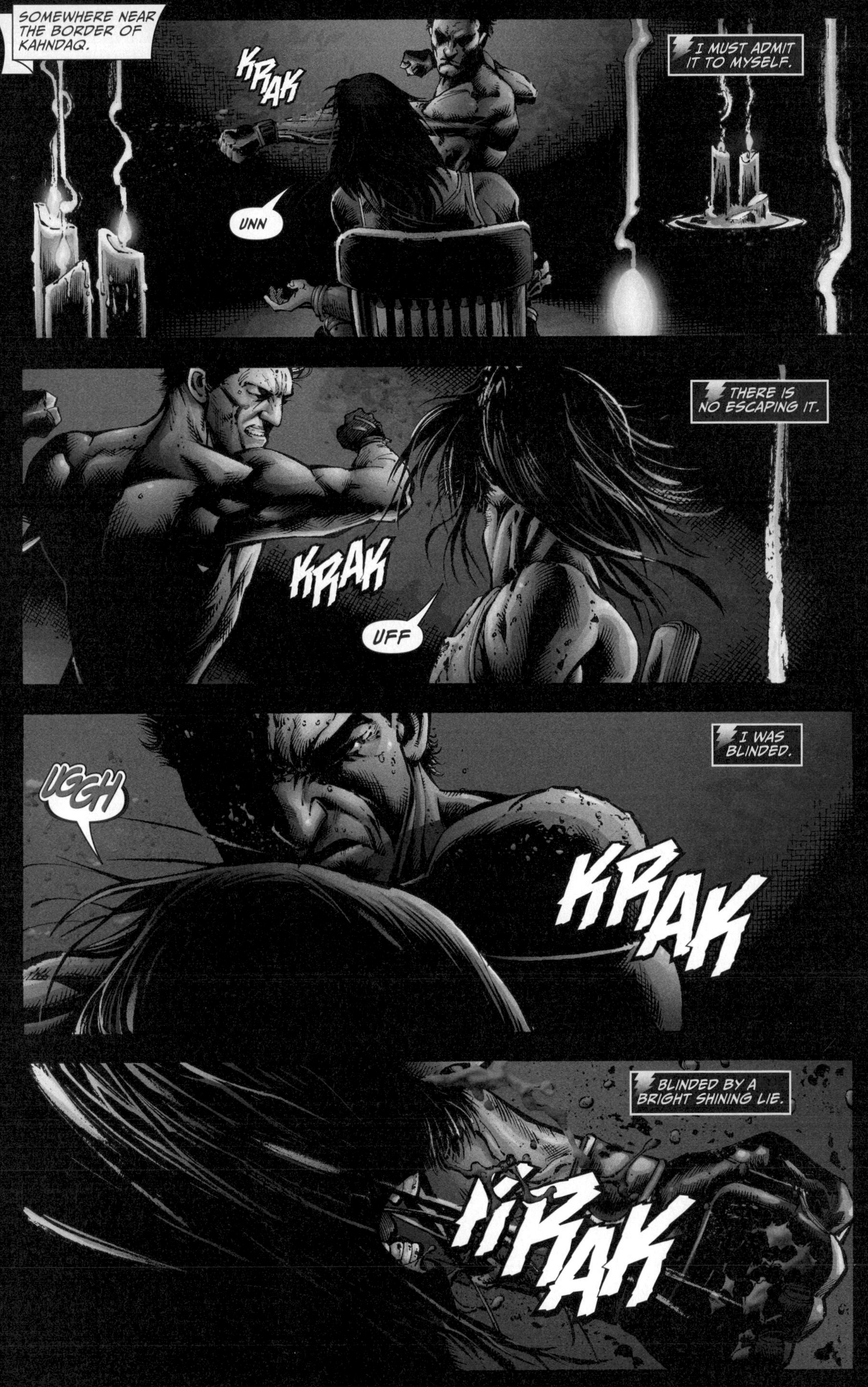
SOMEWHERE NEAR THE BORDER OF KAHNDAQ.
KRAK
I MUST ADMIT IT TO MYSELF.
UNN
THERE IS NO ESCAPING IT.
KRAK
UFF
I WAS BLINDED.
UGGH
KRAK
BLINDED BY A BRIGHT SHINING LIE.
KRAK

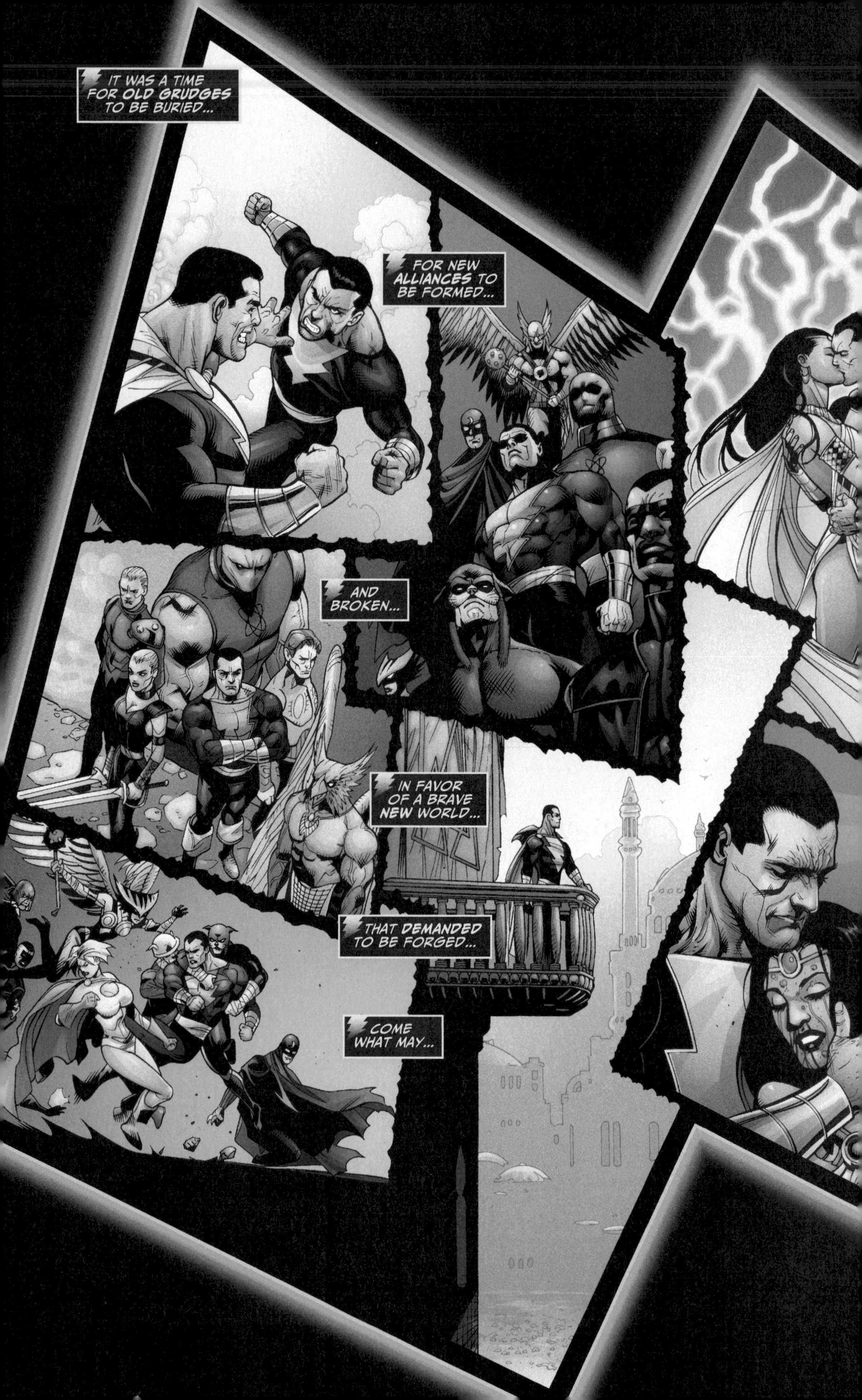
IT WAS A TIME FOR OLD GRUDGES TO BE BURIED...
FOR NEW ALLIANCES TO BE FORMED...
AND BROKEN...
IN FAVOR OF A BRAVE NEW WORLD...
THAT DEMANDED TO BE FORGED...
COME WHAT MAY...

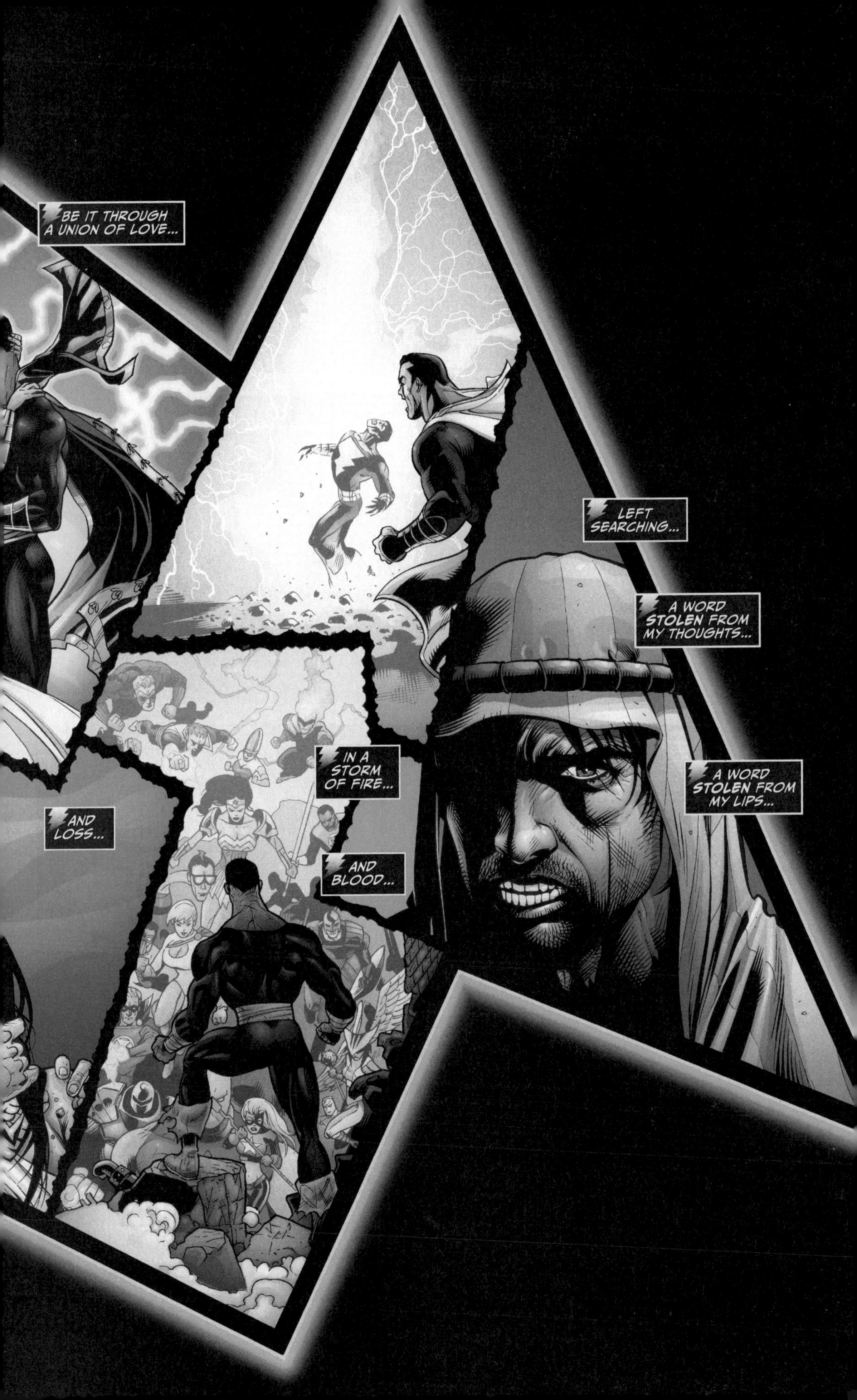
BE IT THROUGH A UNION OF LOVE...
LEFT SEARCHING...
A WORD STOLEN FROM MY THOUGHTS...
IN A STORM OF FIRE...
A WORD STOLEN FROM MY LIPS...
AND LOSS...
AND BLOOD...

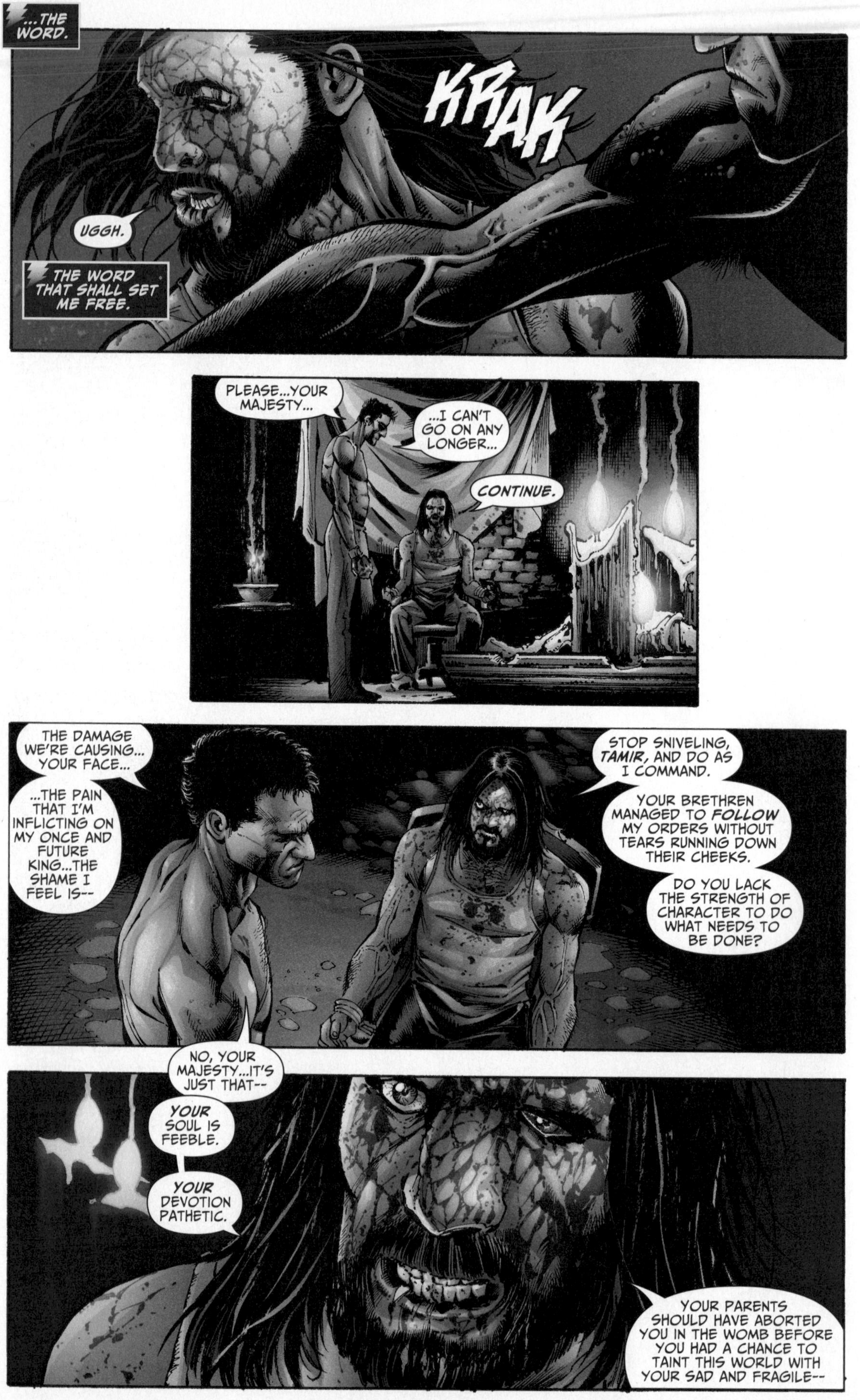
...THE WORD.
KRAK
UGGH.
THE WORD THAT SHALL SET ME FREE.
PLEASE...YOUR MAJESTY...
...I CAN'T GO ON ANY LONGER...
CONTINUE.
THE DAMAGE WE'RE CAUSING... YOUR FACE...
...THE PAIN THAT I'M INFLICTING ON MY ONCE AND FUTURE KING...THE SHAME I FEEL IS--
STOP SNIVELING, TAMIR, AND DO AS I COMMAND.
YOUR BRETHREN MANAGED TO FOLLOW MY ORDERS WITHOUT TEARS RUNNING DOWN THEIR CHEEKS.
DO YOU LACK THE STRENGTH OF CHARACTER TO DO WHAT NEEDS TO BE DONE?
NO, YOUR MAJESTY...IT'S JUST THAT--
YOUR SOUL IS FEEBLE.
YOUR DEVOTION PATHETIC.
YOUR PARENTS SHOULD HAVE ABORTED YOU IN THE WOMB BEFORE YOU HAD A CHANCE TO TAINT THIS WORLD WITH YOUR SAD AND FRAGILE--

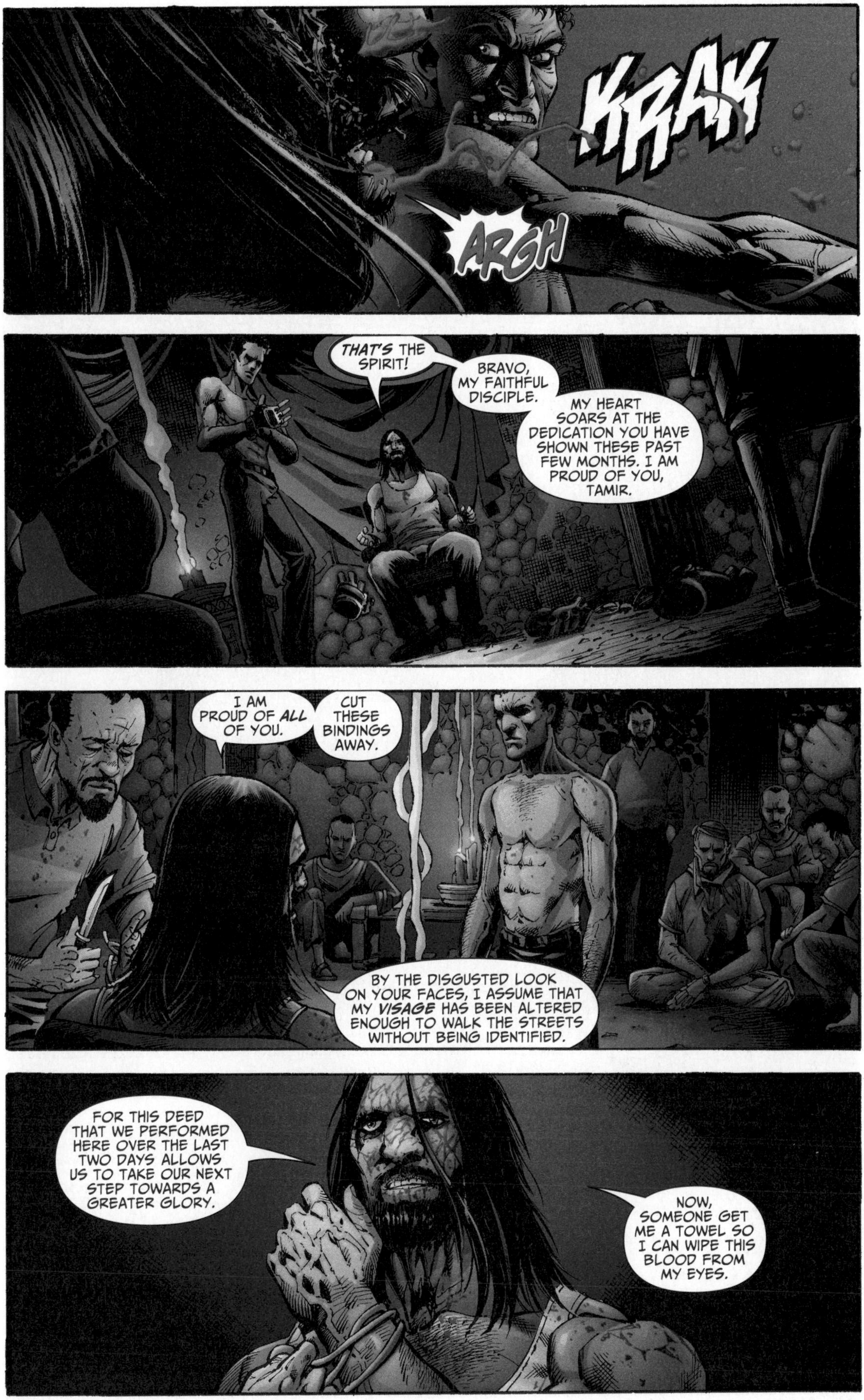
KRAK
ARGH
THAT'S THE SPIRIT!
BRAVO, MY FAITHFUL DISCIPLE.
MY HEART SOARS AT THE DEDICATION YOU HAVE SHOWN THESE PAST FEW MONTHS. I AM PROUD OF YOU, TAMIR.
I AM PROUD OF ALL OF YOU.
CUT THESE BINDINGS AWAY.
BY THE DISGUSTED LOOK ON YOUR FACES, I ASSUME THAT MY VISAGE HAS BEEN ALTERED ENOUGH TO WALK THE STREETS WITHOUT BEING IDENTIFIED.
FOR THIS DEED THAT WE PERFORMED HERE OVER THE LAST TWO DAYS ALLOWS US TO TAKE OUR NEXT STEP TOWARDS A GREATER GLORY.
NOW, SOMEONE GET ME A TOWEL SO I CAN WIPE THIS BLOOD FROM MY EYES.

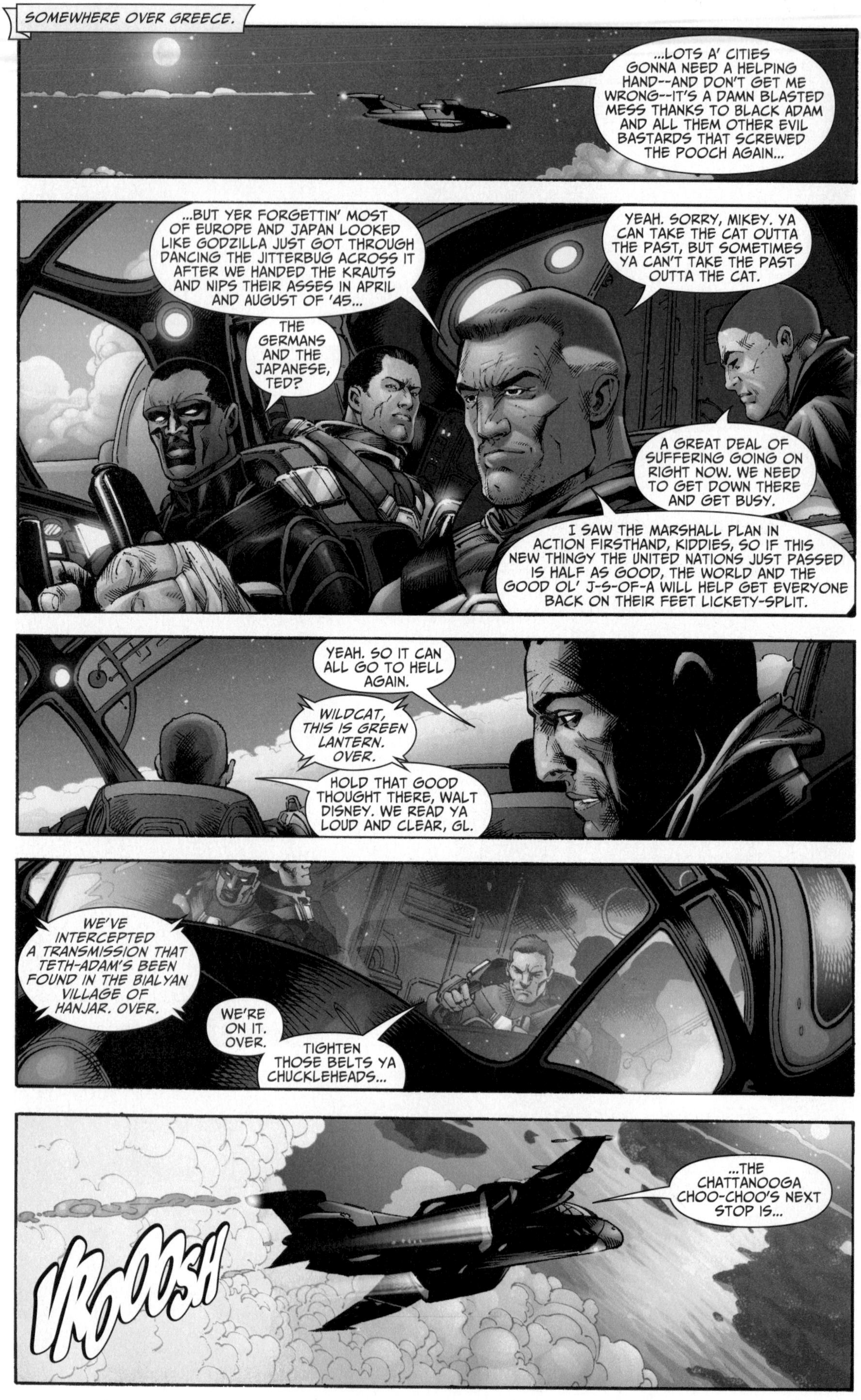
SOMEWHERE OVER GREECE.
...LOTS A' CITIES GONNA NEED A HELPING HAND--AND DON'T GET ME WRONG--IT'S A DAMN BLASTED MESS THANKS TO BLACK ADAM AND ALL THEM OTHER EVIL BASTARDS THAT SCREWED THE POOCH AGAIN...
...BUT YER FORGETTIN' MOST OF EUROPE AND JAPAN LOOKED LIKE GODZILLA JUST GOT THROUGH DANCING THE JITTERBUG ACROSS IT AFTER WE HANDED THE KRAUTS AND NIPS THEIR ASSES IN APRIL AND AUGUST OF '45...
THE GERMANS AND THE JAPANESE, TED?
YEAH. SORRY, MIKEY. YA CAN TAKE THE CAT OUTTA THE PAST, BUT SOMETIMES YA CAN'T TAKE THE PAST OUTTA THE CAT.
A GREAT DEAL OF SUFFERING GOING ON RIGHT NOW. WE NEED TO GET DOWN THERE AND GET BUSY.
I SAW THE MARSHALL PLAN IN ACTION FIRSTHAND, KIDDIES, SO IF THIS NEW THINGY THE UNITED NATIONS JUST PASSED IS HALF AS GOOD, THE WORLD AND THE GOOD OL' J-S-OF-A WILL HELP GET EVERYONE BACK ON THEIR FEET LICKETY-SPLIT.
YEAH. SO IT CAN ALL GO TO HELL AGAIN.
WILDCAT, THIS IS GREEN LANTERN. OVER.
HOLD THAT GOOD THOUGHT THERE, WALT DISNEY. WE READ YA LOUD AND CLEAR, GL.
WE'VE INTERCEPTED A TRANSMISSION THAT TETH-ADAM'S BEEN FOUND IN THE BIALYAN VILLAGE OF HANJAR. OVER.
WE'RE ON IT. OVER.
TIGHTEN THOSE BELTS YA CHUCKLEHEADS...
...THE CHATTANOOGA CHOO-CHOO'S NEXT STOP IS...
VROOOSH

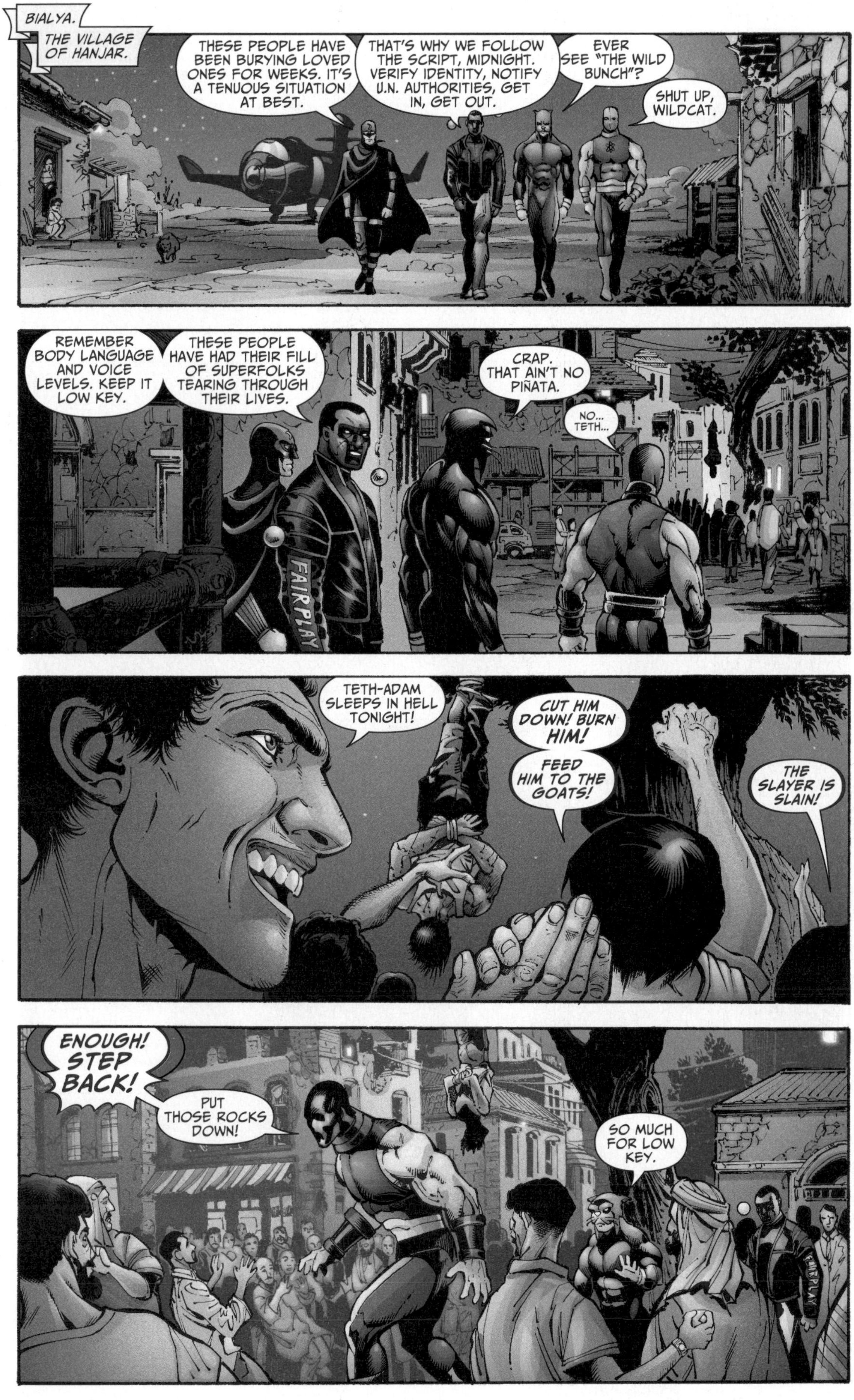
BIALYA.
THE VILLAGE OF HANJAR.
THESE PEOPLE HAVE BEEN BURYING LOVED ONES FOR WEEKS. IT'S A TENUOUS SITUATION AT BEST.
THAT'S WHY WE FOLLOW THE SCRIPT, MIDNIGHT. VERIFY IDENTITY, NOTIFY U.N. AUTHORITIES, GET IN, GET OUT.
EVER SEE "THE WILD BUNCH"?
SHUT UP, WILDCAT.
REMEMBER BODY LANGUAGE AND VOICE LEVELS. KEEP IT LOW KEY.
THESE PEOPLE HAVE HAD THEIR FILL OF SUPERFOLKS TEARING THROUGH THEIR LIVES.
FAIRPLAY
CRAP. THAT AIN'T NO PIÑATA.
NO... TETH...
TETH-ADAM SLEEPS IN HELL TONIGHT!
CUT HIM DOWN! BURN HIM!
FEED HIM TO THE GOATS!
THE SLAYER IS SLAIN!
ENOUGH! STEP BACK!
PUT THOSE ROCKS DOWN!
SO MUCH FOR LOW KEY.
FAIRPLAY

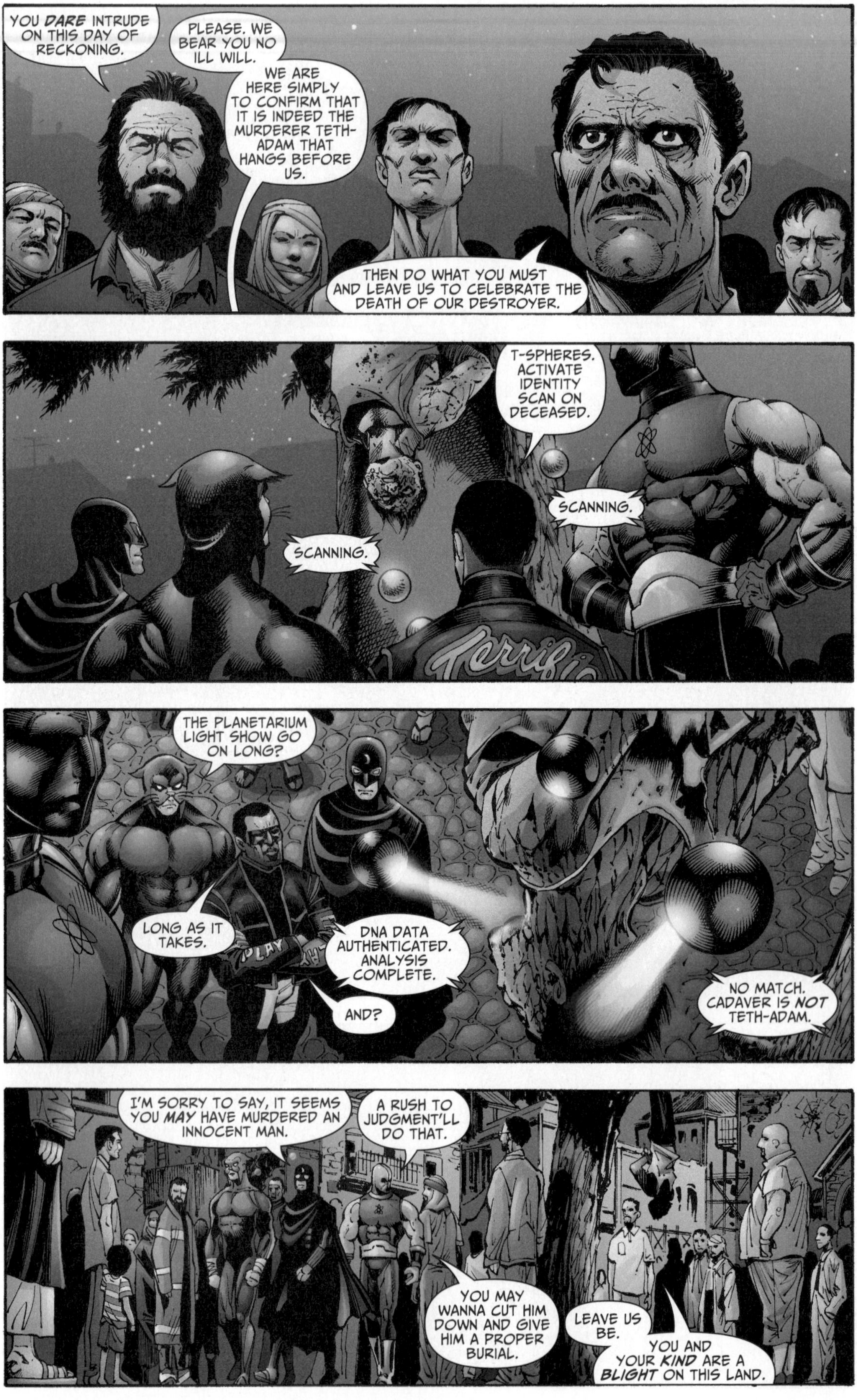

YOU DARE INTRUDE ON THIS DAY OF RECKONING.
PLEASE. WE BEAR YOU NO ILL WILL.
WE ARE HERE SIMPLY TO CONFIRM THAT IT IS INDEED THE MURDERER TETH-ADAM THAT HANGS BEFORE US.
THEN DO WHAT YOU MUST AND LEAVE US TO CELEBRATE THE DEATH OF OUR DESTROYER.
T-SPHERES. ACTIVATE IDENTITY SCAN ON DECEASED.
SCANNING.
SCANNING.
THE PLANETARIUM LIGHT SHOW GO ON LONG?
LONG AS IT TAKES.
DNA DATA AUTHENTICATED. ANALYSIS COMPLETE.
AND?
NO MATCH. CADAVER IS NOT TETH-ADAM.
I'M SORRY TO SAY, IT SEEMS YOU MAY HAVE MURDERED AN INNOCENT MAN.
A RUSH TO JUDGMENT'LL DO THAT.
YOU MAY WANNA CUT HIM DOWN AND GIVE HIM A PROPER BURIAL.
LEAVE US BE.
YOU AND YOUR KIND ARE A BLIGHT ON THIS LAND.

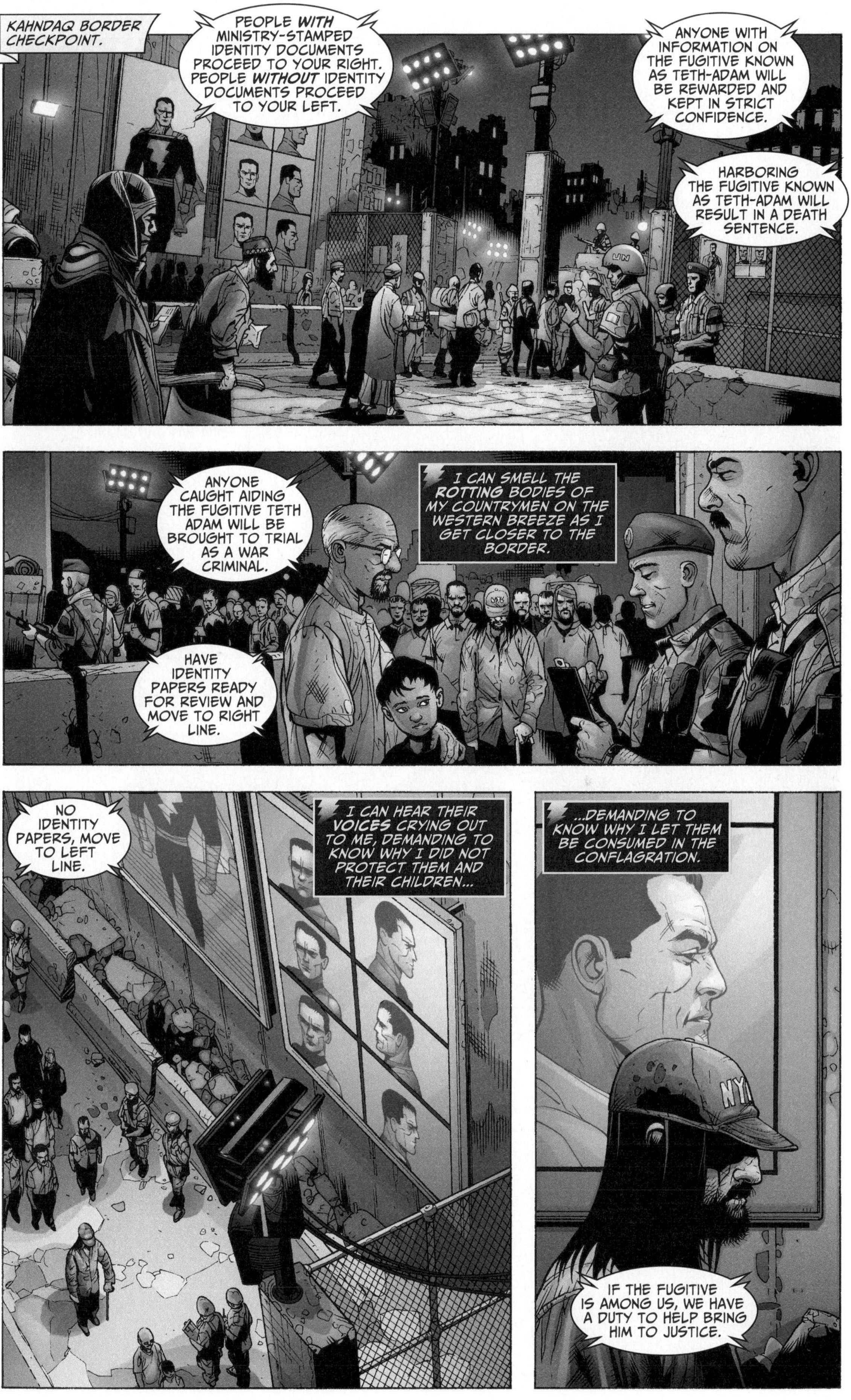

KAHNDAQ BORDER CHECKPOINT.
PEOPLE WITH MINISTRY-STAMPED IDENTITY DOCUMENTS PROCEED TO YOUR RIGHT. PEOPLE WITHOUT IDENTITY DOCUMENTS PROCEED TO YOUR LEFT.
ANYONE WITH INFORMATION ON THE FUGITIVE KNOWN AS TETH-ADAM WILL BE REWARDED AND KEPT IN STRICT CONFIDENCE.
HARBORING THE FUGITIVE KNOWN AS TETH-ADAM WILL RESULT IN A DEATH SENTENCE.
UN
ANYONE CAUGHT AIDING THE FUGITIVE TETH ADAM WILL BE BROUGHT TO TRIAL AS A WAR CRIMINAL.
I CAN SMELL THE ROTTING BODIES OF MY COUNTRYMEN ON THE WESTERN BREEZE AS I GET CLOSER TO THE BORDER.
HAVE IDENTITY PAPERS READY FOR REVIEW AND MOVE TO RIGHT LINE.
NO IDENTITY PAPERS, MOVE TO LEFT LINE.
I CAN HEAR THEIR VOICES CRYING OUT TO ME, DEMANDING TO KNOW WHY I DID NOT PROTECT THEM AND THEIR CHILDREN...
...DEMANDING TO KNOW WHY I LET THEM BE CONSUMED IN THE CONFLAGRATION.
IF THE FUGITIVE IS AMONG US, WE HAVE A DUTY TO HELP BRING HIM TO JUSTICE.

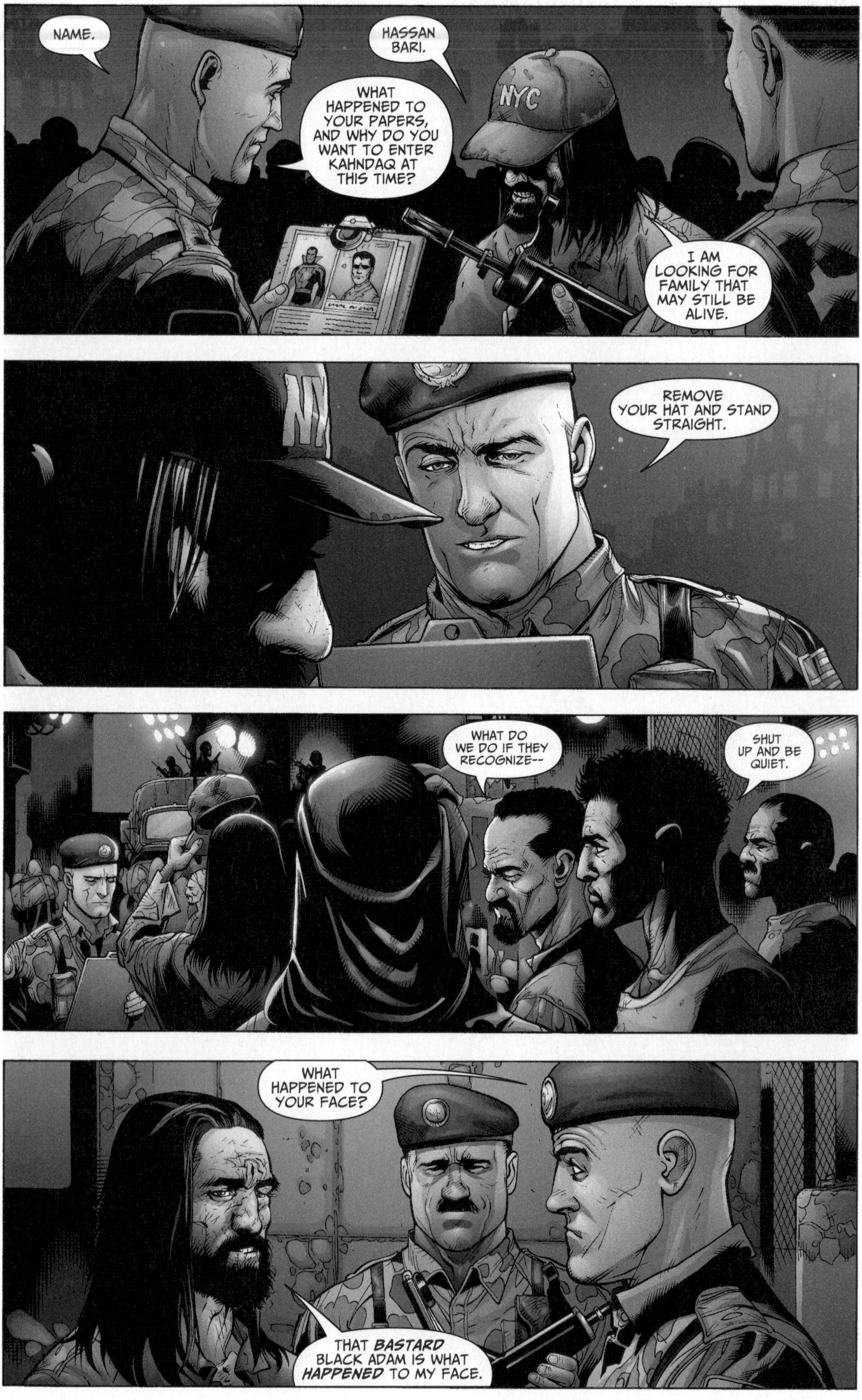
NAME.
HASSAN BARI.
WHAT HAPPENED TO YOUR PAPERS, AND WHY DO YOU WANT TO ENTER KAHNDAQ AT THIS TIME?
I AM LOOKING FOR FAMILY THAT MAY STILL BE ALIVE.
REMOVE YOUR HAT AND STAND STRAIGHT.
WHAT DO WE DO IF THEY RECOGNIZE--
SHUT UP AND BE QUIET.
WHAT HAPPENED TO YOUR FACE?
THAT *BASTARD* BLACK ADAM IS WHAT *HAPPENED* TO MY FACE.

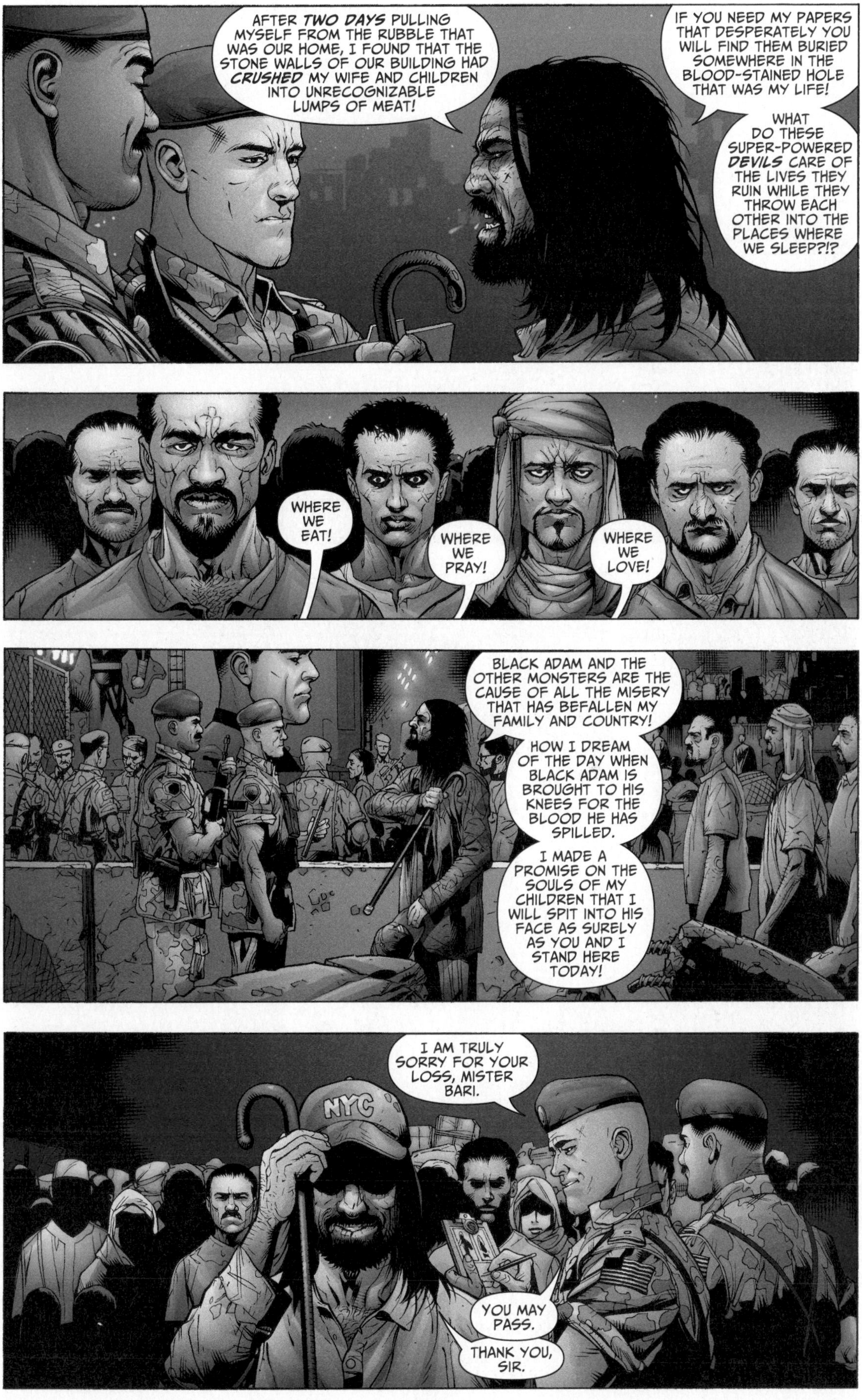
AFTER TWO DAYS PULLING MYSELF FROM THE RUBBLE THAT WAS OUR HOME, I FOUND THAT THE STONE WALLS OF OUR BUILDING HAD CRUSHED MY WIFE AND CHILDREN INTO UNRECOGNIZABLE LUMPS OF MEAT!
IF YOU NEED MY PAPERS THAT DESPERATELY YOU WILL FIND THEM BURIED SOMEWHERE IN THE BLOOD-STAINED HOLE THAT WAS MY LIFE!
WHAT DO THESE SUPER-POWERED DEVILS CARE OF THE LIVES THEY RUIN WHILE THEY THROW EACH OTHER INTO THE PLACES WHERE WE SLEEP?!?
WHERE WE EAT!
WHERE WE PRAY!
WHERE WE LOVE!
BLACK ADAM AND THE OTHER MONSTERS ARE THE CAUSE OF ALL THE MISERY THAT HAS BEFALLEN MY FAMILY AND COUNTRY!
HOW I DREAM OF THE DAY WHEN BLACK ADAM IS BROUGHT TO HIS KNEES FOR THE BLOOD HE HAS SPILLED.
I MADE A PROMISE ON THE SOULS OF MY CHILDREN THAT I WILL SPIT INTO HIS FACE AS SURELY AS YOU AND I STAND HERE TODAY!
I AM TRULY SORRY FOR YOUR LOSS, MISTER BARI.
NYC
YOU MAY PASS.
THANK YOU, SIR.

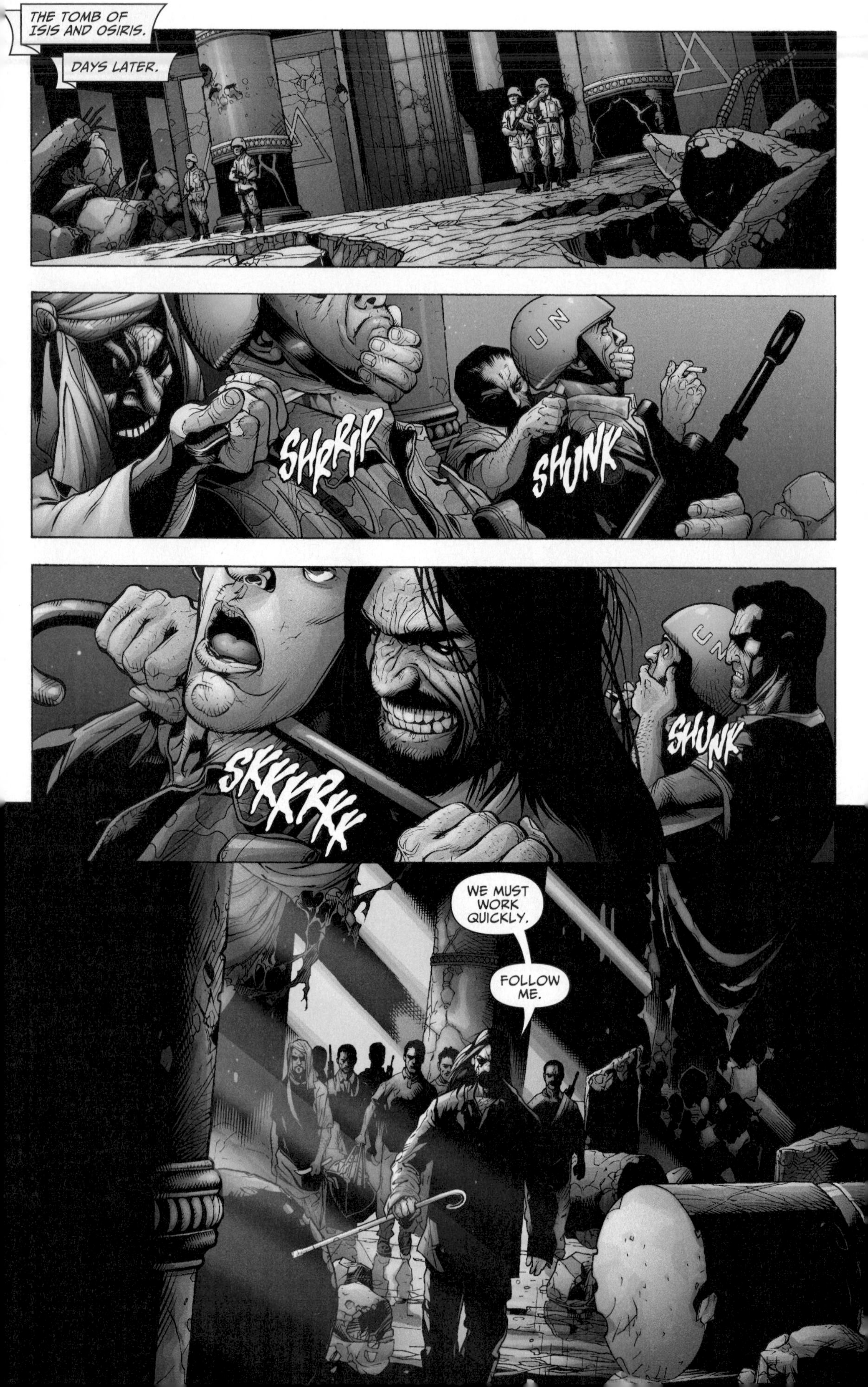
THE TOMB OF ISIS AND OSIRIS.
DAYS LATER.
UN
SHRRIP
SHUNK
UN
SKKKRKK
SHUNK
WE MUST WORK QUICKLY.
FOLLOW ME.

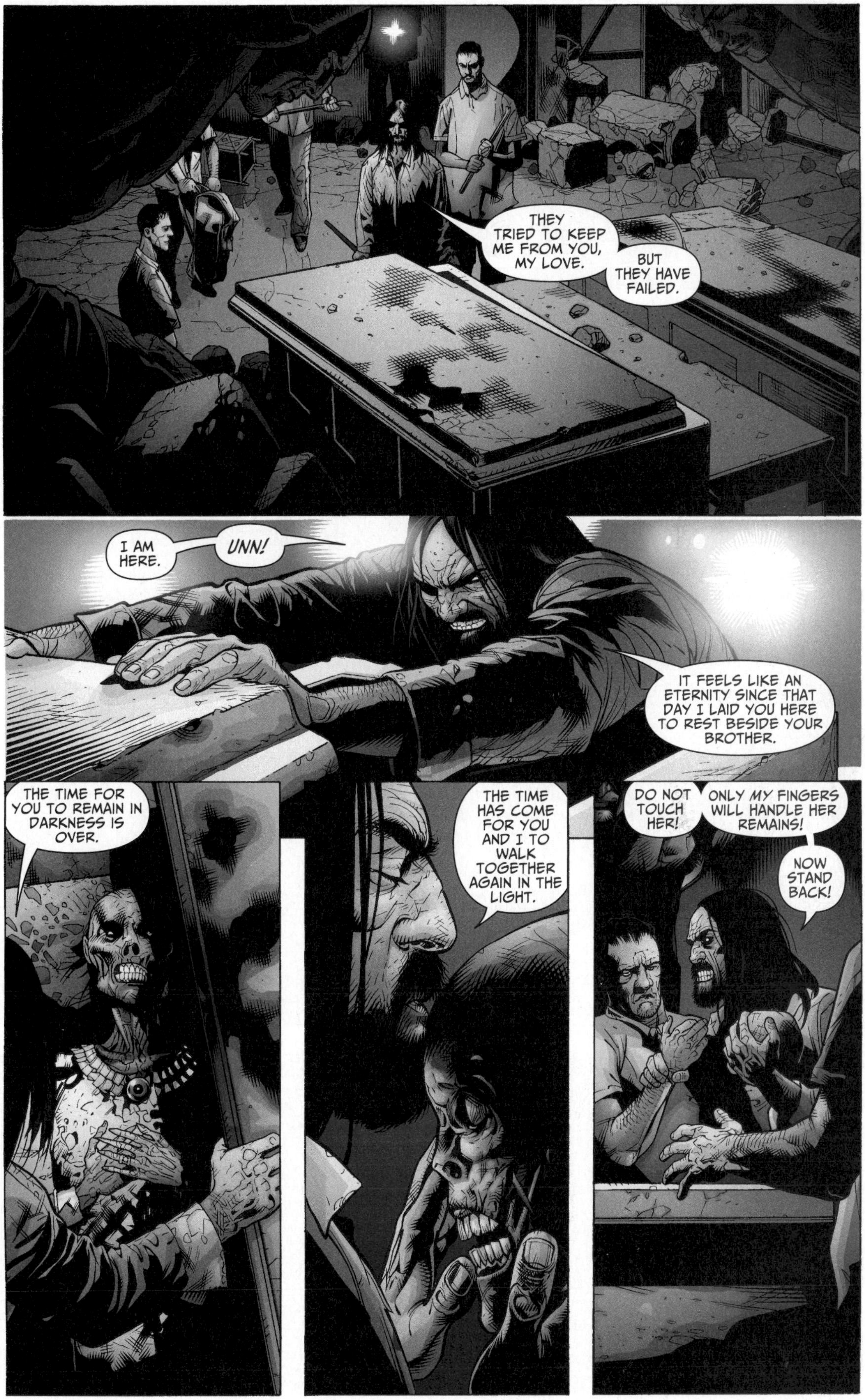
THEY TRIED TO KEEP ME FROM YOU, MY LOVE.
BUT THEY HAVE FAILED.
I AM HERE.
UNN!
IT FEELS LIKE AN ETERNITY SINCE THAT DAY I LAID YOU HERE TO REST BESIDE YOUR BROTHER.
THE TIME FOR YOU TO REMAIN IN DARKNESS IS OVER.
THE TIME HAS COME FOR YOU AND I TO WALK TOGETHER AGAIN IN THE LIGHT.
DO NOT TOUCH HER!
ONLY *MY* FINGERS WILL HANDLE HER REMAINS!
NOW STAND BACK!

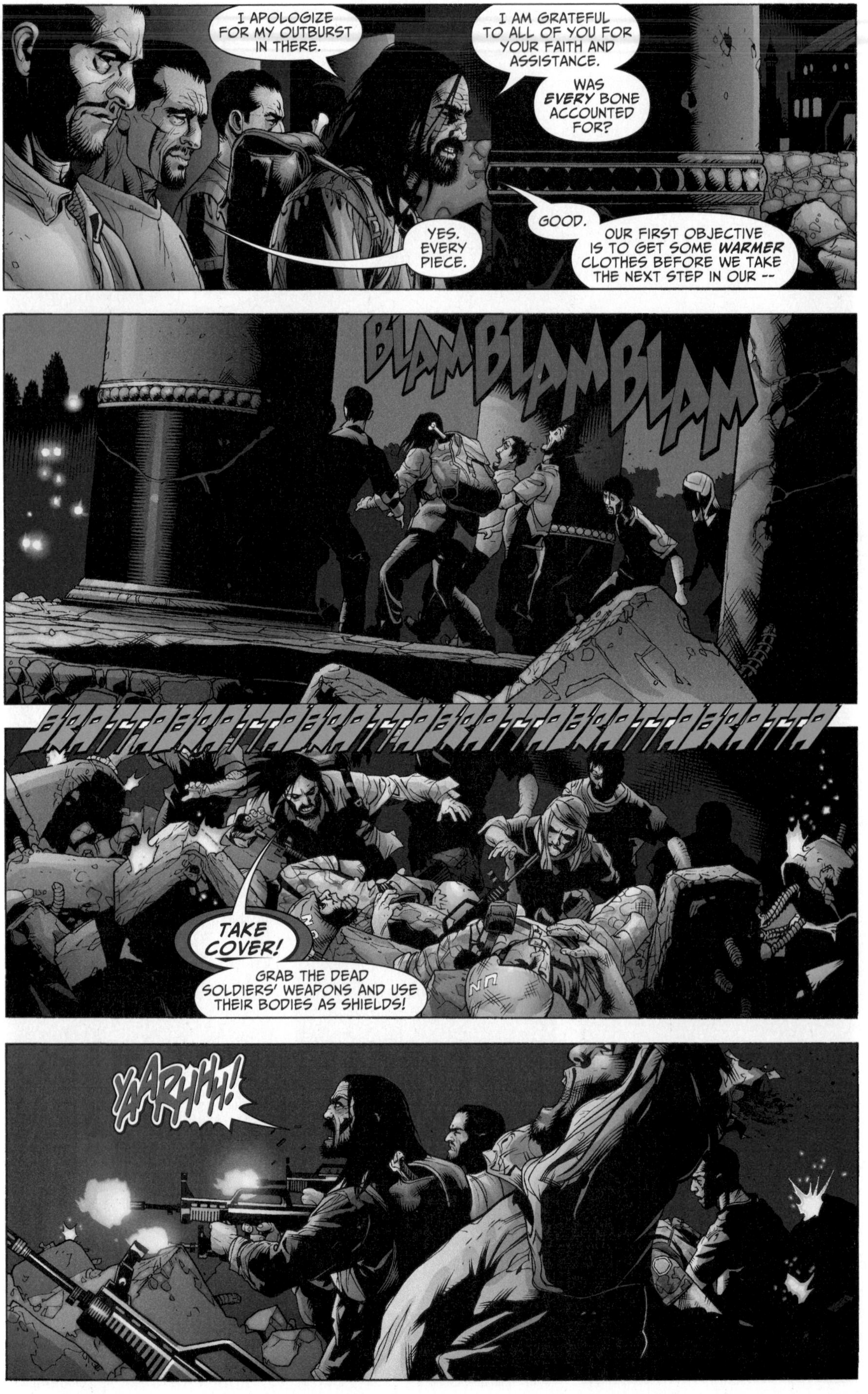
I APOLOGIZE FOR MY OUTBURST IN THERE.
I AM GRATEFUL TO ALL OF YOU FOR YOUR FAITH AND ASSISTANCE.
WAS *EVERY* BONE ACCOUNTED FOR?
YES. EVERY PIECE.
GOOD.
OUR FIRST OBJECTIVE IS TO GET SOME *WARMER* CLOTHES BEFORE WE TAKE THE NEXT STEP IN OUR --
BLAM BLAM BLAM
BRATTABRATTABRATTABRATTABRATTABRATTABRATTA
TAKE COVER!
GRAB THE DEAD SOLDIERS' WEAPONS AND USE THEIR BODIES AS SHIELDS!
YAARHHH!

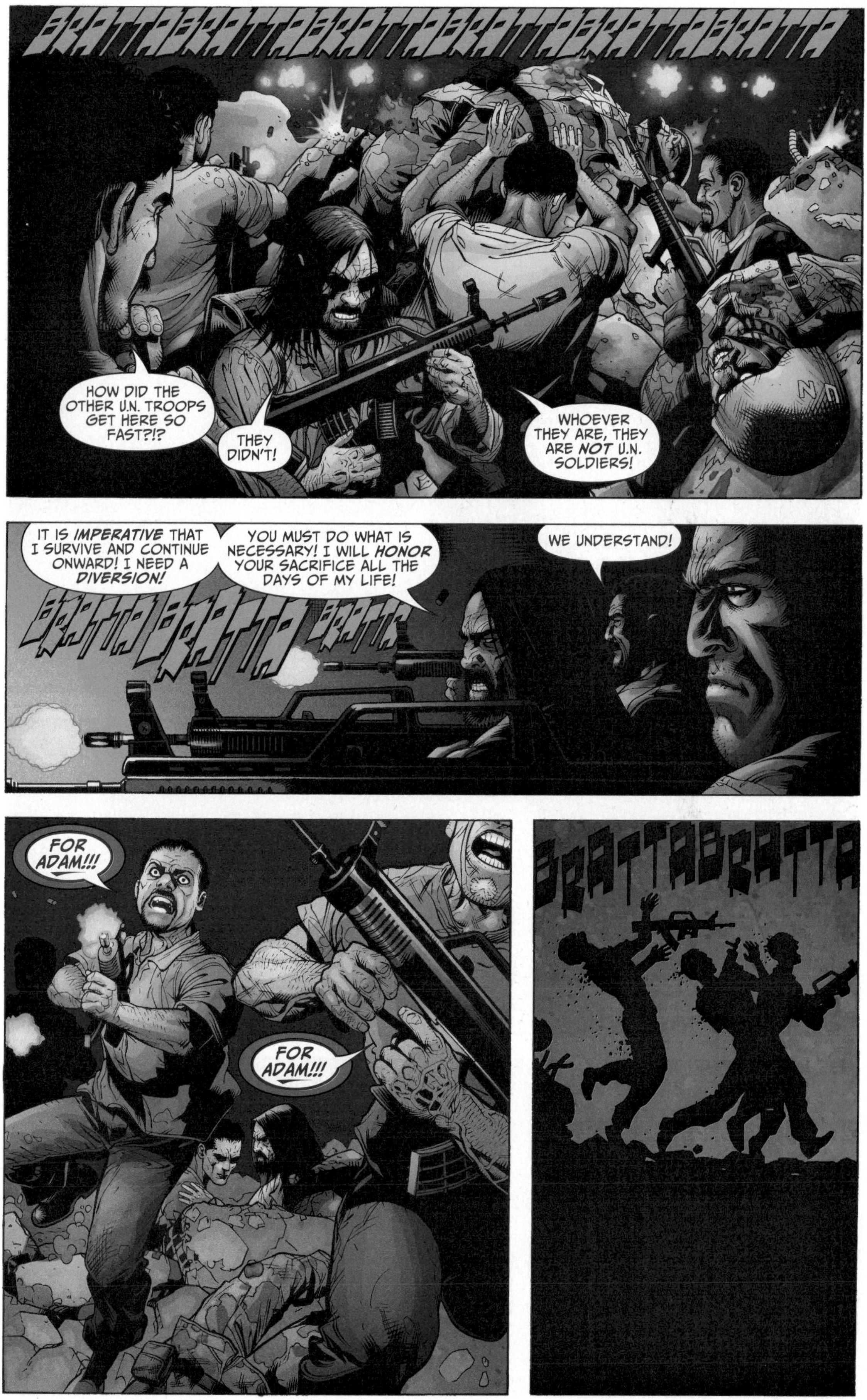

BRATTABRATTABRATTABRATTABRATTABRATTA
HOW DID THE OTHER U.N. TROOPS GET HERE SO FAST?!?
THEY DIDN'T!
WHOEVER THEY ARE, THEY ARE *NOT* U.N. SOLDIERS!
IT IS *IMPERATIVE* THAT I SURVIVE AND CONTINUE ONWARD! I NEED A *DIVERSION!*
YOU MUST DO WHAT IS NECESSARY! I WILL *HONOR* YOUR SACRIFICE ALL THE DAYS OF MY LIFE!
WE UNDERSTAND!
BRATTA BRATTA BRATTA
FOR ADAM!!!
FOR ADAM!!!
BRATTABRATTA

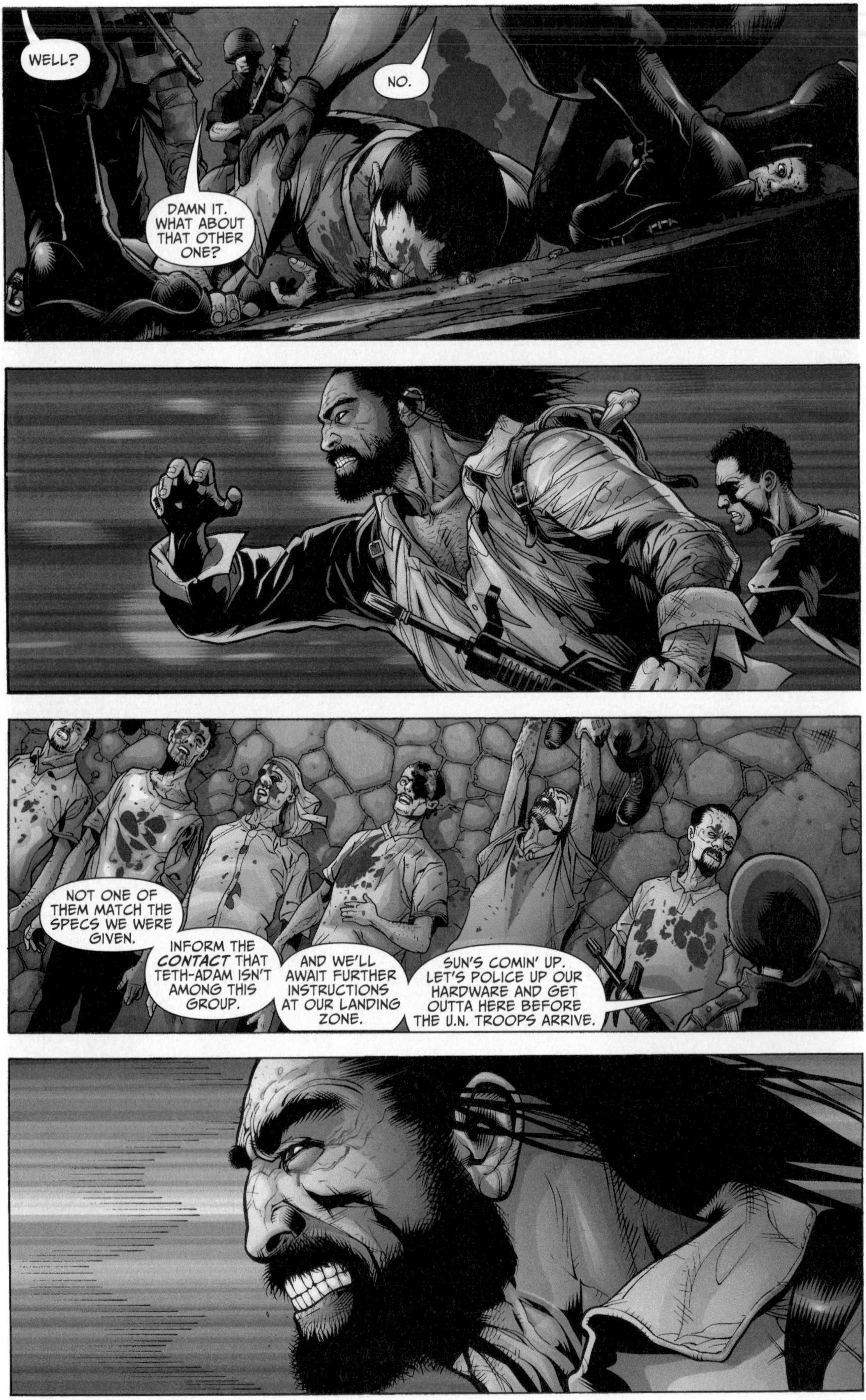
WELL?
NO.
DAMN IT. WHAT ABOUT THAT OTHER ONE?
NOT ONE OF THEM MATCH THE SPECS WE WERE GIVEN.
INFORM THE *CONTACT* THAT TETH-ADAM ISN'T AMONG THIS GROUP.
AND WE'LL AWAIT FURTHER INSTRUCTIONS AT OUR LANDING ZONE.
SUN'S COMIN' UP. LET'S POLICE UP OUR HARDWARE AND GET OUTTA HERE BEFORE THE U.N. TROOPS ARRIVE.

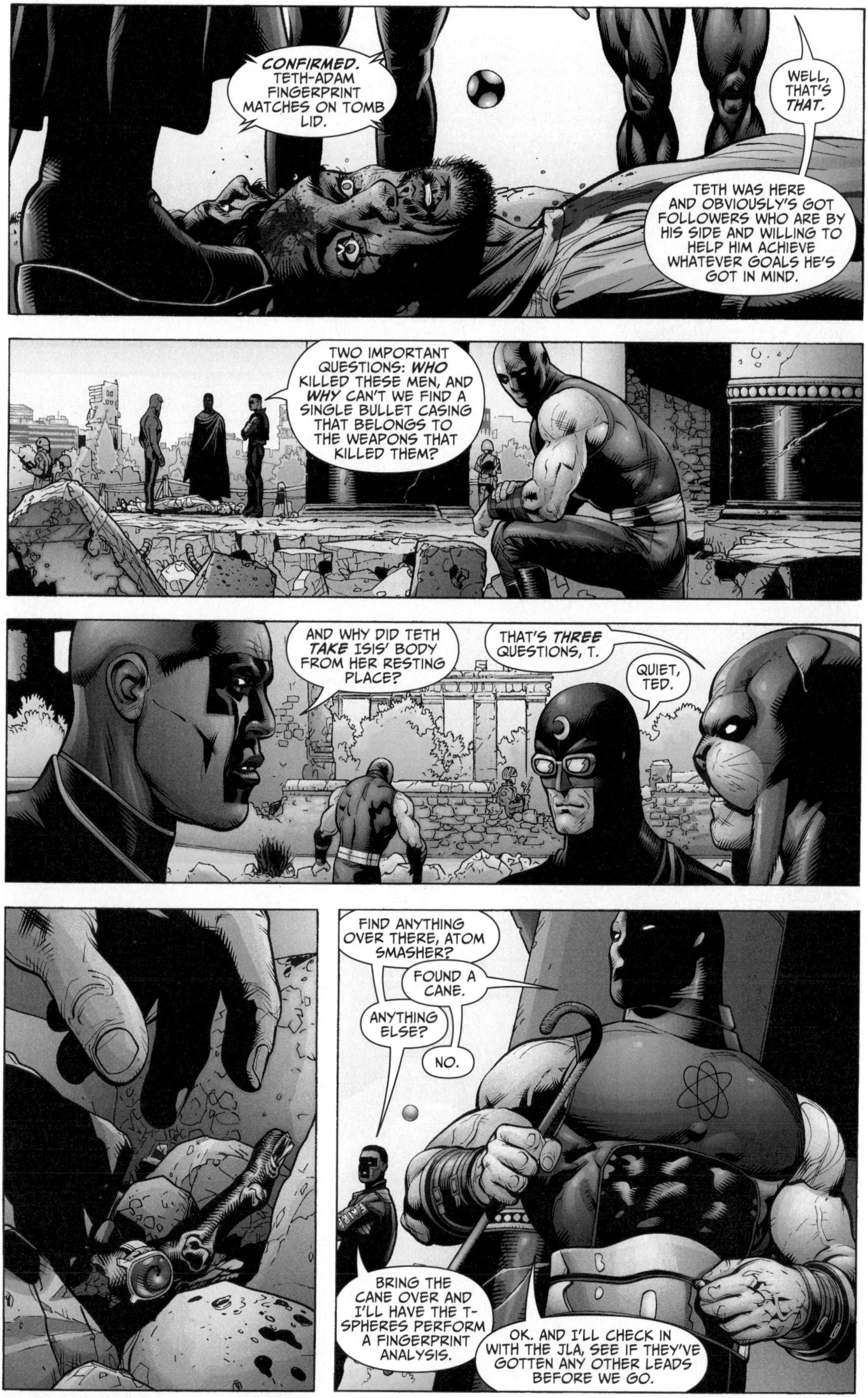
CONFIRMED. TETH-ADAM FINGERPRINT MATCHES ON TOMB LID.
WELL, THAT'S THAT.
TETH WAS HERE AND OBVIOUSLY'S GOT FOLLOWERS WHO ARE BY HIS SIDE AND WILLING TO HELP HIM ACHIEVE WHATEVER GOALS HE'S GOT IN MIND.
TWO IMPORTANT QUESTIONS: WHO KILLED THESE MEN, AND WHY CAN'T WE FIND A SINGLE BULLET CASING THAT BELONGS TO THE WEAPONS THAT KILLED THEM?
AND WHY DID TETH TAKE ISIS' BODY FROM HER RESTING PLACE?
THAT'S THREE QUESTIONS, T.
QUIET, TED.
FIND ANYTHING OVER THERE, ATOM SMASHER?
FOUND A CANE.
ANYTHING ELSE?
NO.
BRING THE CANE OVER AND I'LL HAVE THE T-SPHERES PERFORM A FINGERPRINT ANALYSIS.
OK. AND I'LL CHECK IN WITH THE JLA, SEE IF THEY'VE GOTTEN ANY OTHER LEADS BEFORE WE GO.

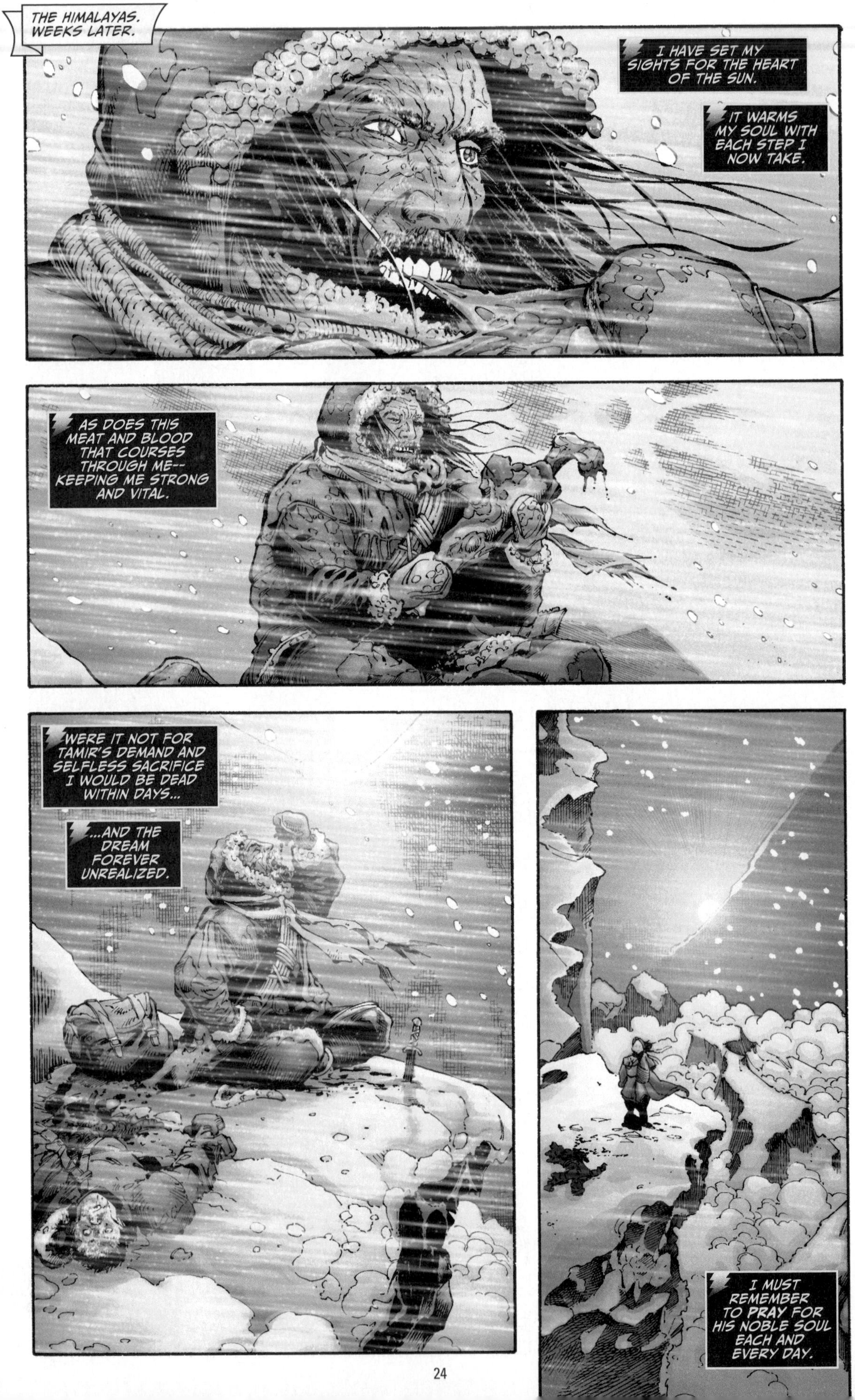
THE HIMALAYAS. WEEKS LATER.
I HAVE SET MY SIGHTS FOR THE HEART OF THE SUN.
IT WARMS MY SOUL WITH EACH STEP I NOW TAKE.
AS DOES THIS MEAT AND BLOOD THAT COURSES THROUGH ME-- KEEPING ME STRONG AND VITAL.
WERE IT NOT FOR TAMIR'S DEMAND AND SELFLESS SACRIFICE I WOULD BE DEAD WITHIN DAYS...
...AND THE DREAM FOREVER UNREALIZED.
I MUST REMEMBER TO PRAY FOR HIS NOBLE SOUL EACH AND EVERY DAY.

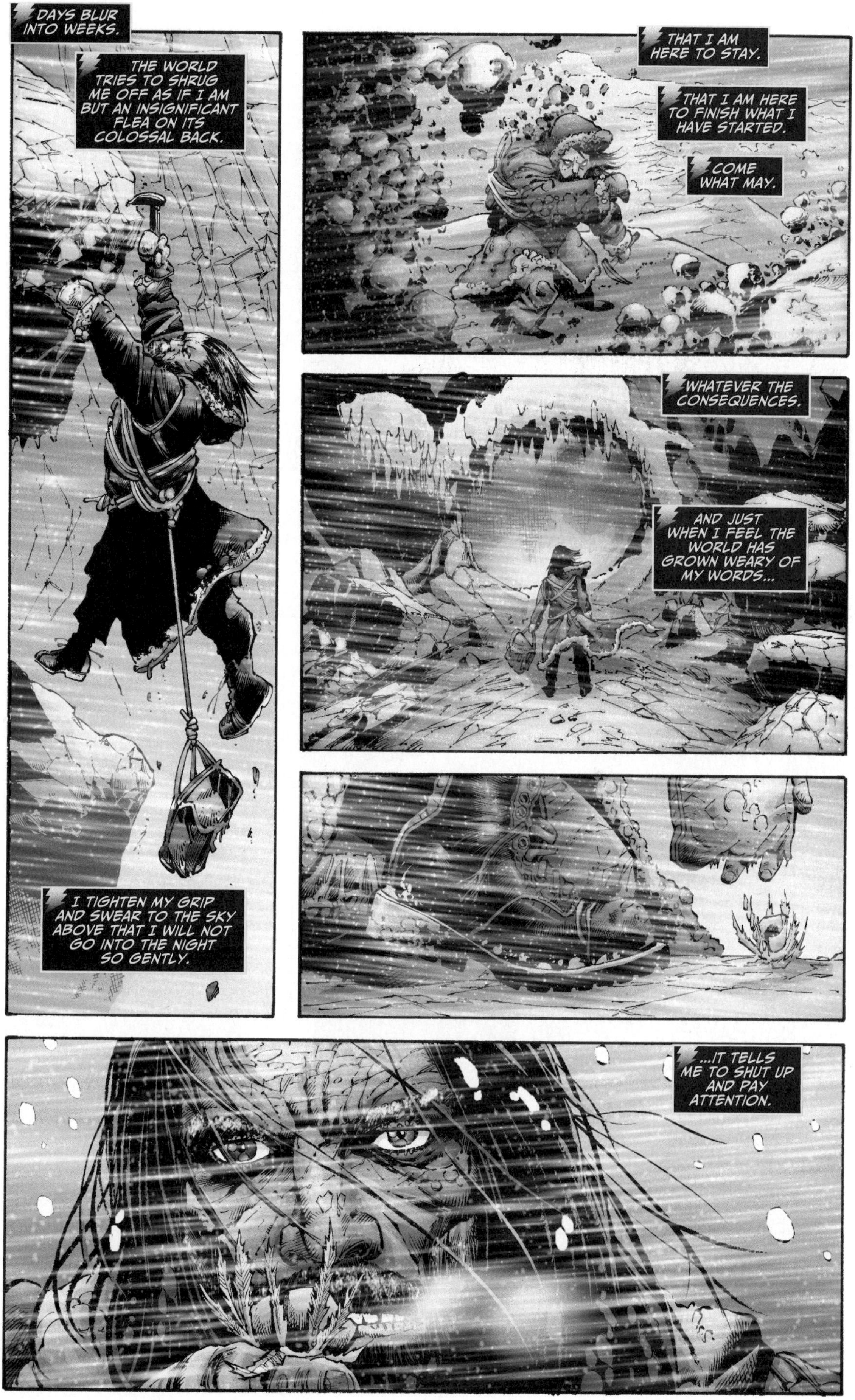
DAYS BLUR INTO WEEKS.
THE WORLD TRIES TO SHRUG ME OFF AS IF I AM BUT AN INSIGNIFICANT FLEA ON ITS COLOSSAL BACK.
I TIGHTEN MY GRIP AND SWEAR TO THE SKY ABOVE THAT I WILL NOT GO INTO THE NIGHT SO GENTLY.
THAT I AM HERE TO STAY.
THAT I AM HERE TO FINISH WHAT I HAVE STARTED.
COME WHAT MAY.
WHATEVER THE CONSEQUENCES.
AND JUST WHEN I FEEL THE WORLD HAS GROWN WEARY OF MY WORDS...
...IT TELLS ME TO SHUT UP AND PAY ATTENTION.

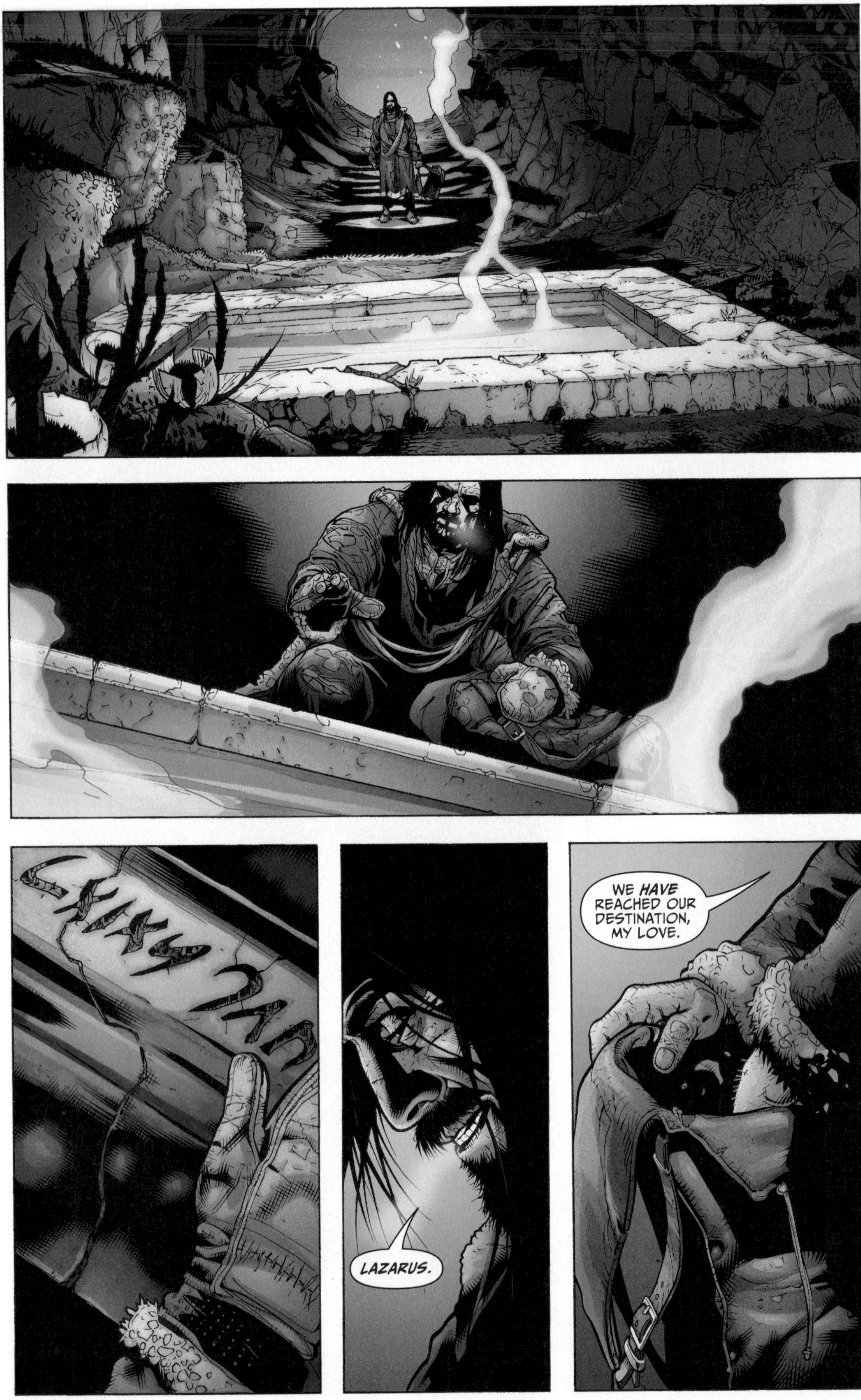
LAZARUS.
WE HAVE REACHED OUR DESTINATION, MY LOVE.

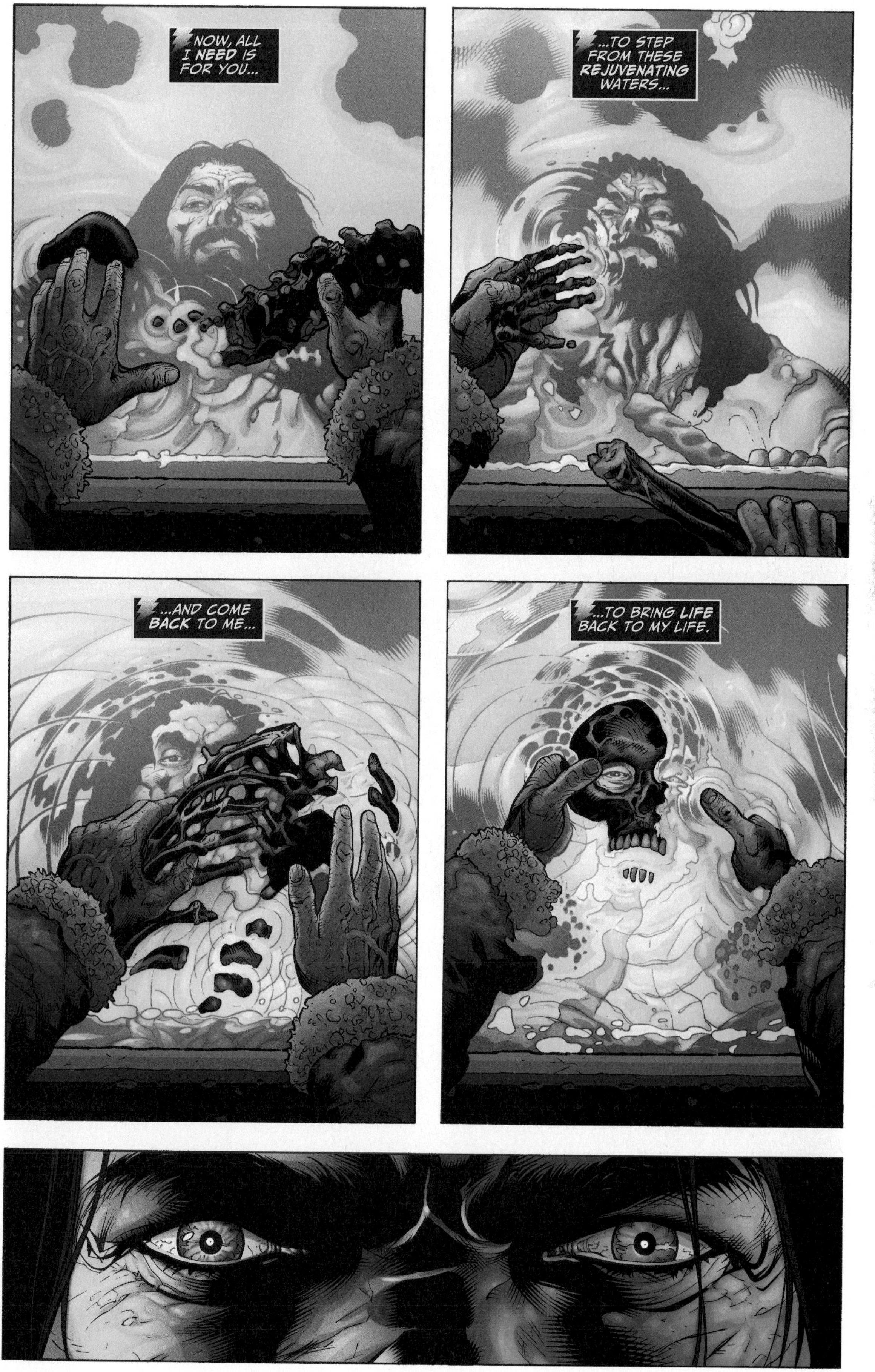
NOW, ALL I NEED IS FOR YOU...
...TO STEP FROM THESE REJUVENATING WATERS...
...AND COME BACK TO ME...
...TO BRING LIFE BACK TO MY LIFE.

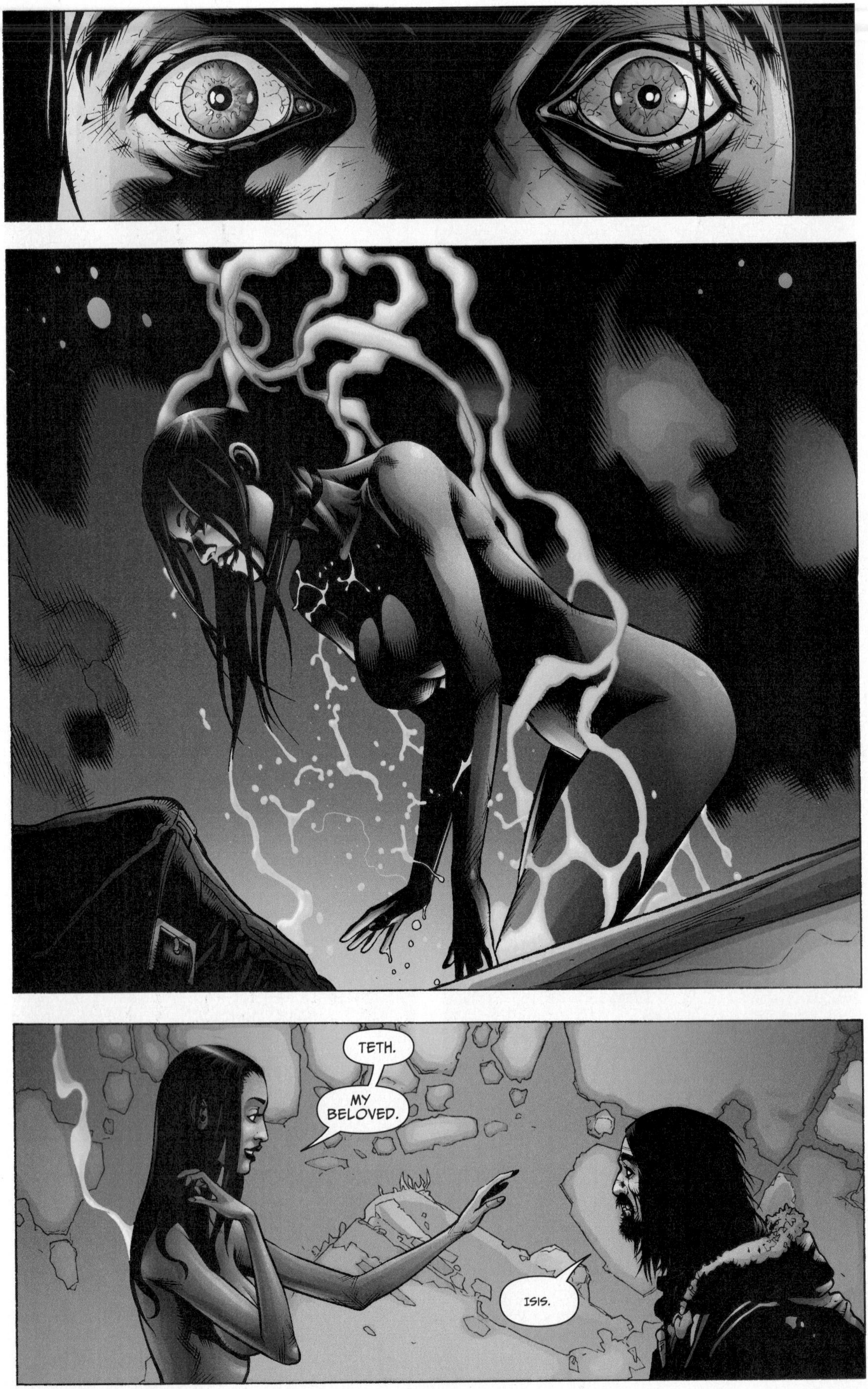
TETH.
MY BELOVED.
ISIS.

Chapter Two

This chapter inked by
Christian Alamy

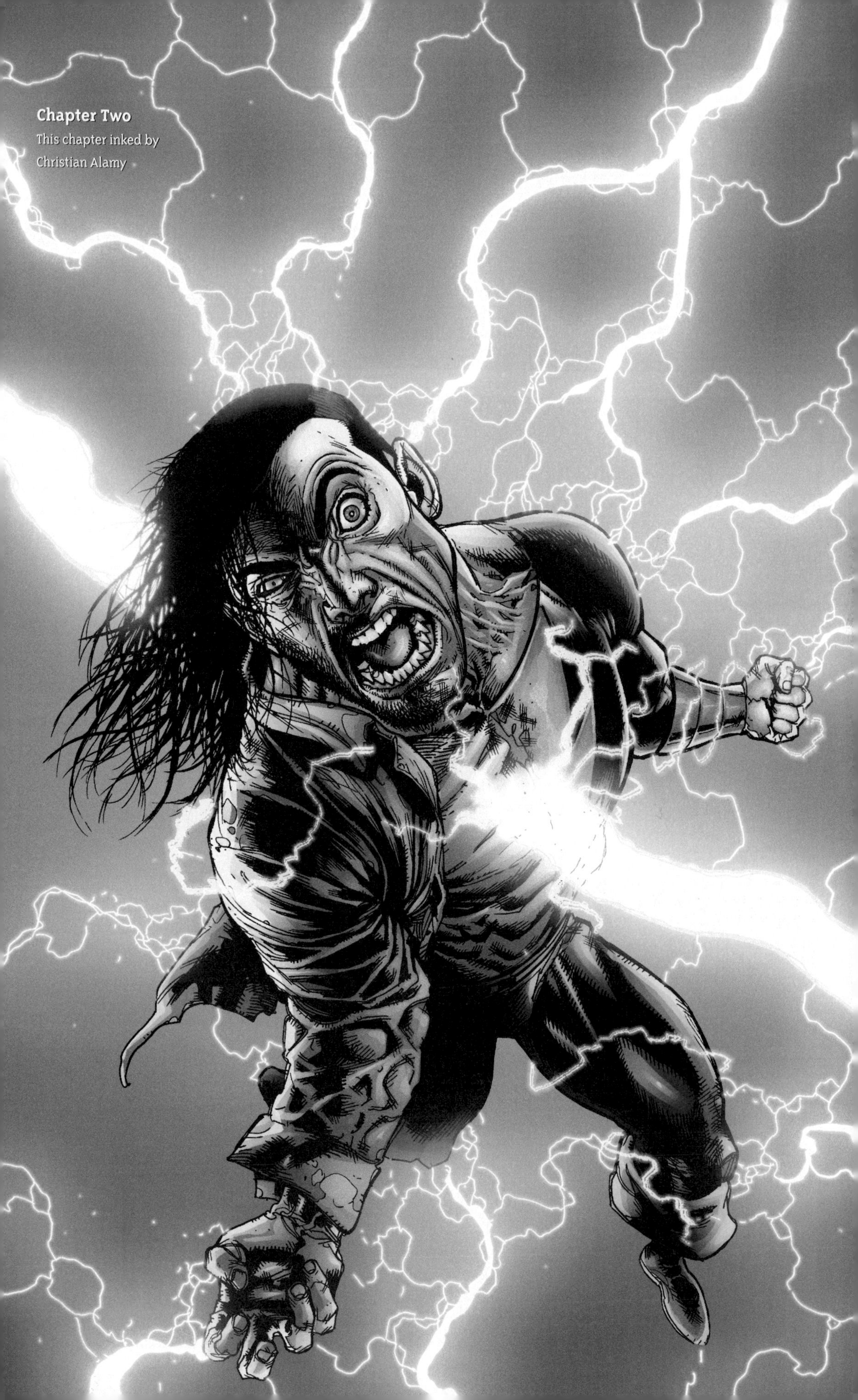

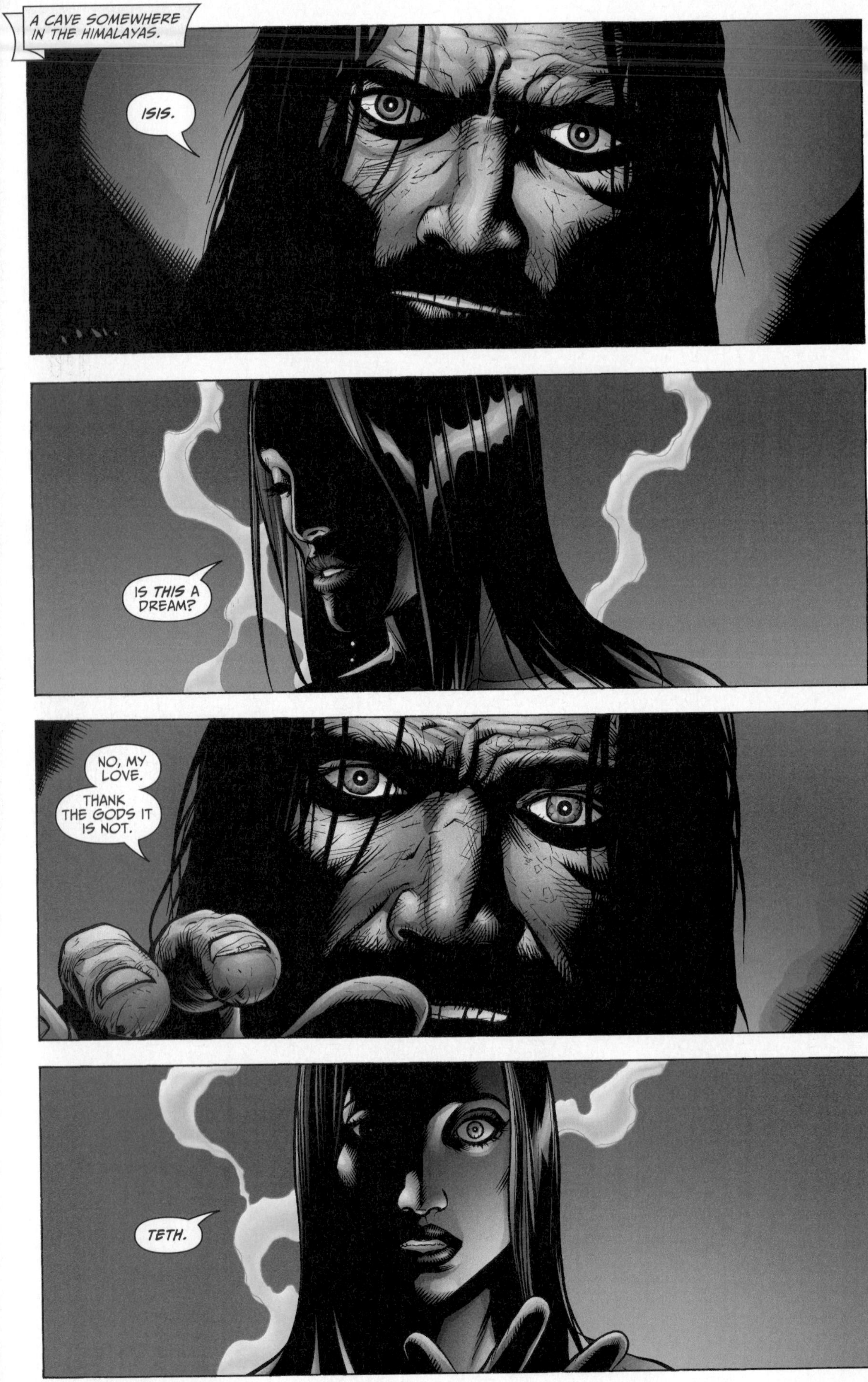
A CAVE SOMEWHERE IN THE HIMALAYAS.
ISIS.
IS *THIS* A DREAM?
NO, MY LOVE.
THANK THE GODS IT IS NOT.
TETH.

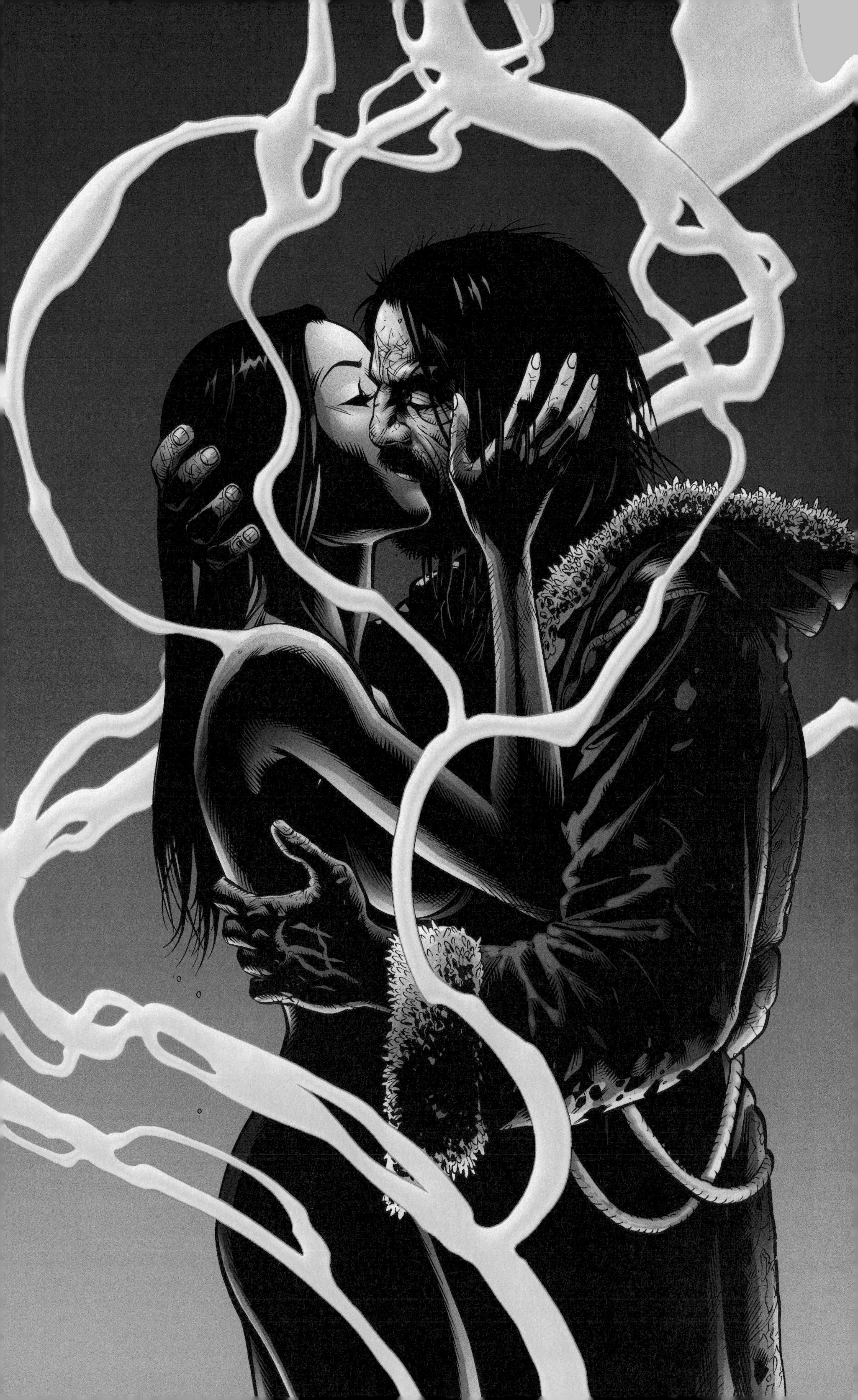

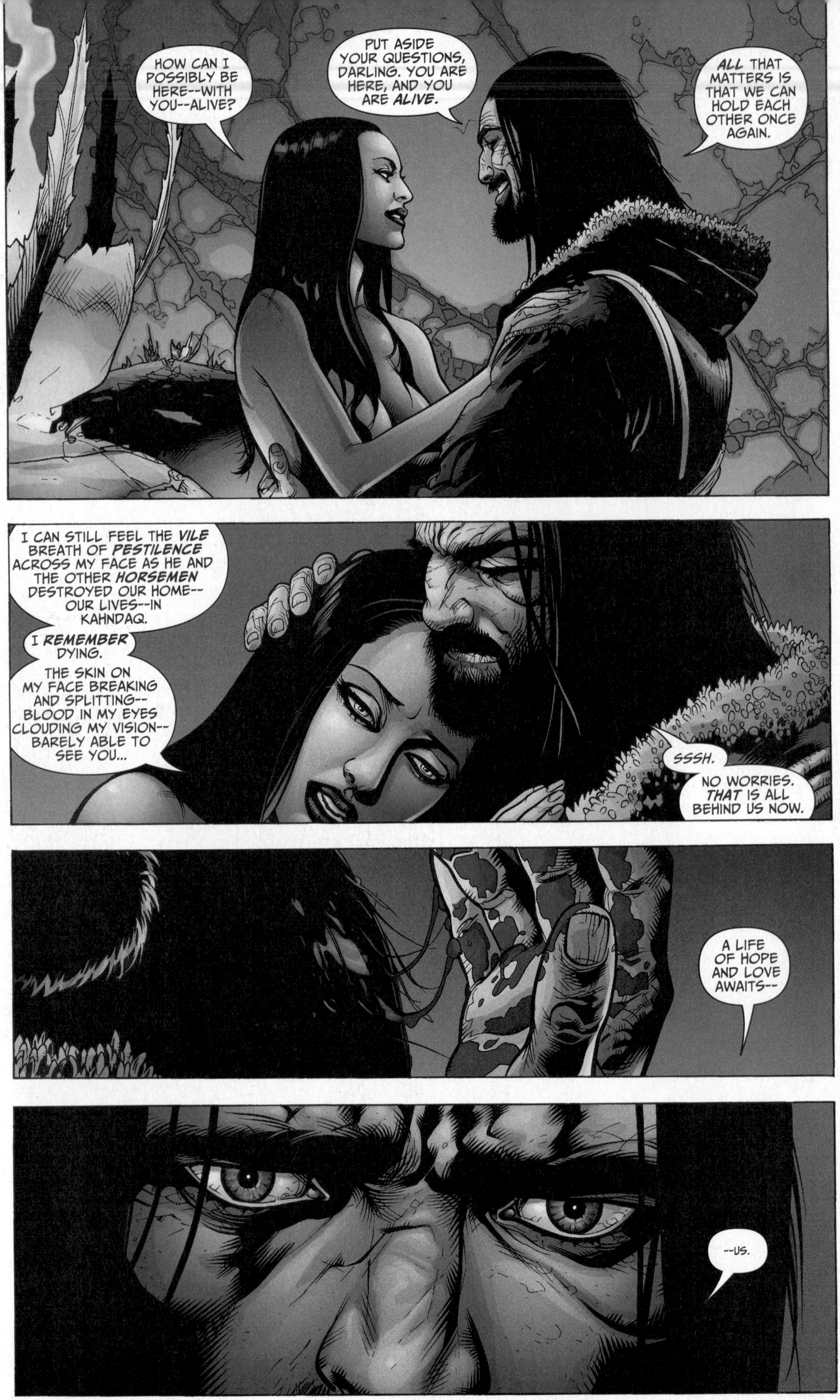
HOW CAN I POSSIBLY BE HERE--WITH YOU--ALIVE?
PUT ASIDE YOUR QUESTIONS, DARLING. YOU ARE HERE, AND YOU ARE ALIVE.
ALL THAT MATTERS IS THAT WE CAN HOLD EACH OTHER ONCE AGAIN.
I CAN STILL FEEL THE VILE BREATH OF PESTILENCE ACROSS MY FACE AS HE AND THE OTHER HORSEMEN DESTROYED OUR HOME--OUR LIVES--IN KAHNDAQ.
I REMEMBER DYING.
THE SKIN ON MY FACE BREAKING AND SPLITTING--BLOOD IN MY EYES CLOUDING MY VISION--BARELY ABLE TO SEE YOU...
SSSH.
NO WORRIES. THAT IS ALL BEHIND US NOW.
A LIFE OF HOPE AND LOVE AWAITS--
--US.

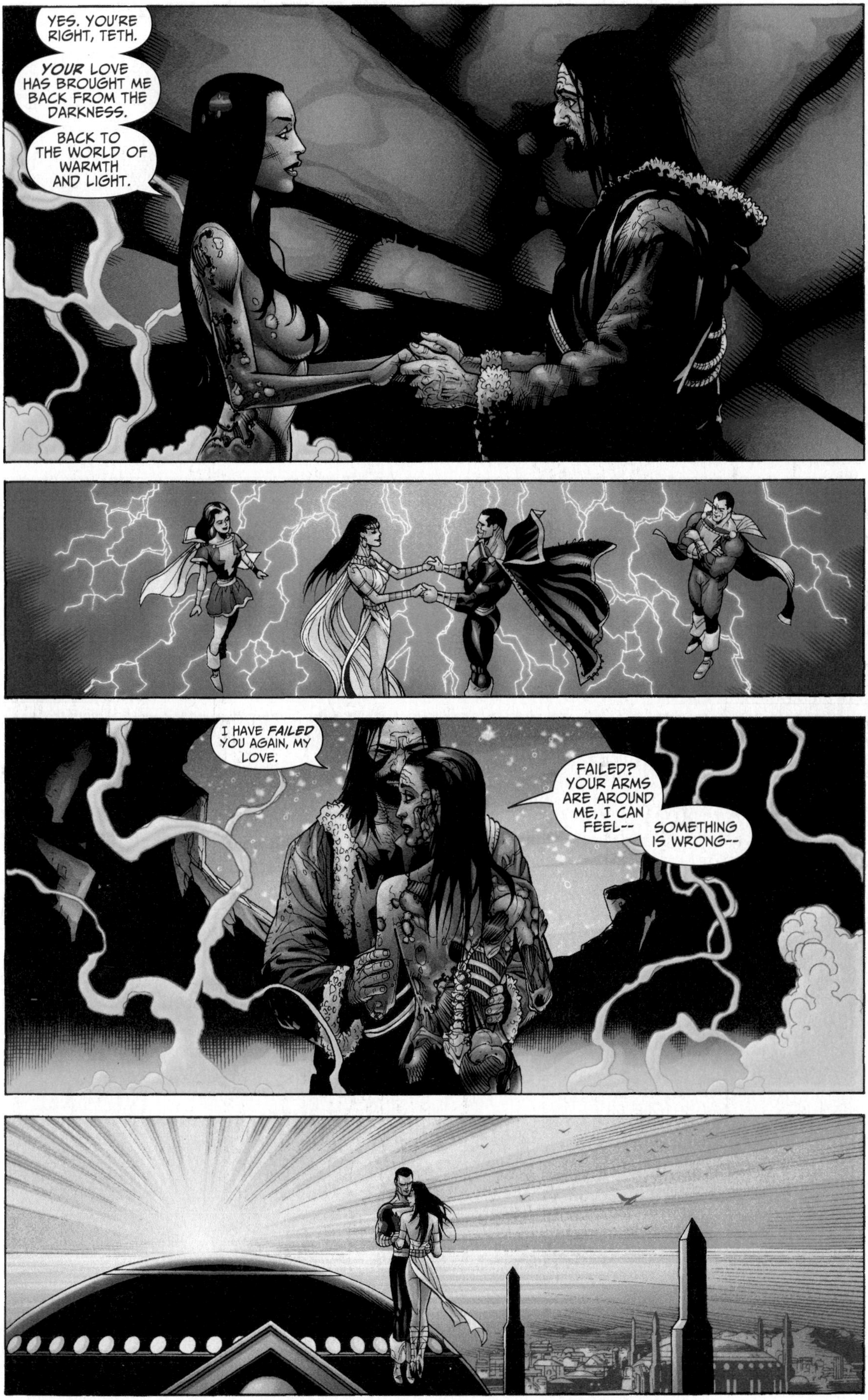
YES. YOU'RE RIGHT, TETH.
YOUR LOVE HAS BROUGHT ME BACK FROM THE DARKNESS.
BACK TO THE WORLD OF WARMTH AND LIGHT.
I HAVE FAILED YOU AGAIN, MY LOVE.
FAILED? YOUR ARMS ARE AROUND ME, I CAN FEEL--
SOMETHING IS WRONG--

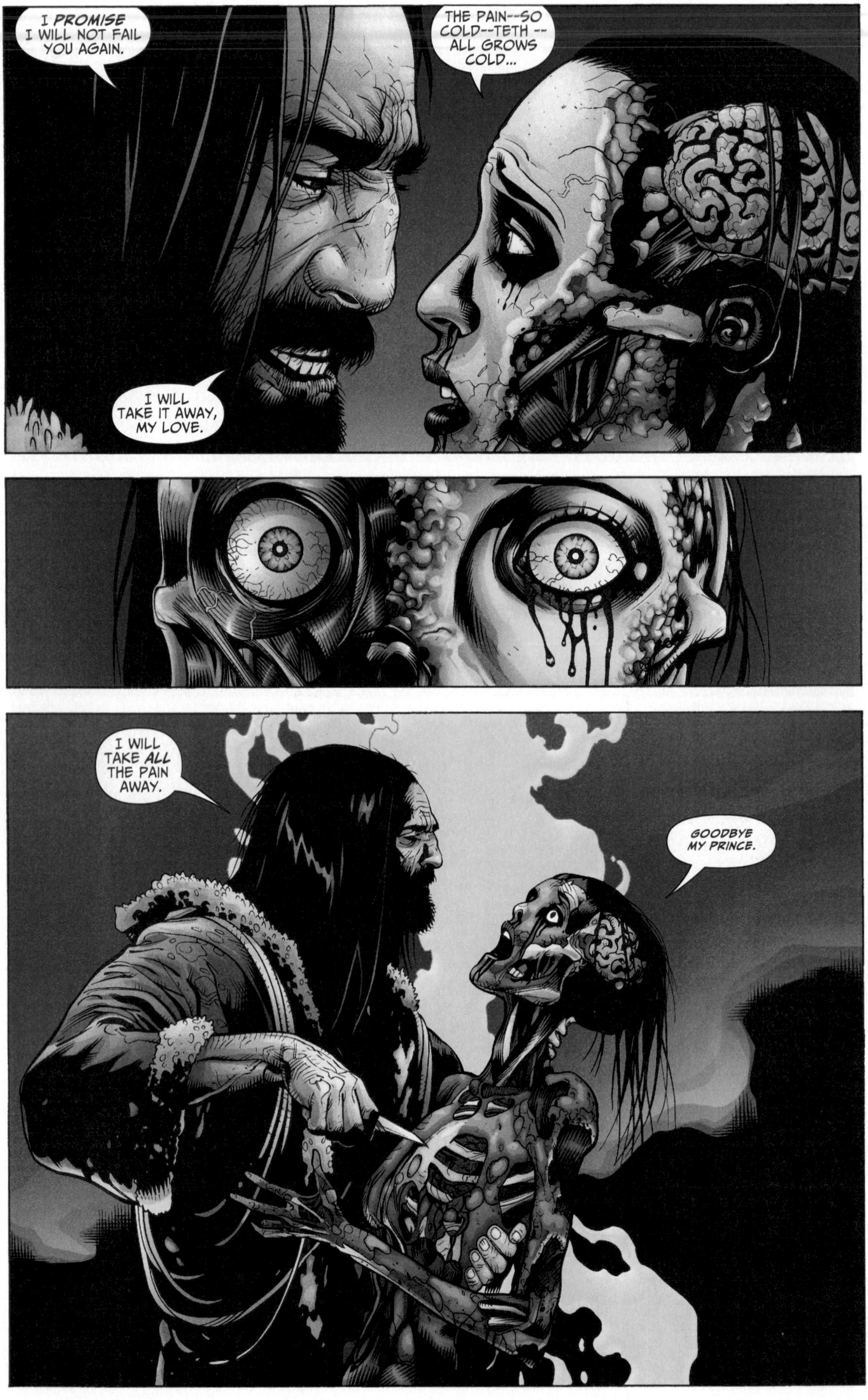
I PROMISE I WILL NOT FAIL YOU AGAIN.
THE PAIN--SO COLD--TETH --ALL GROWS COLD...
I WILL TAKE IT AWAY, MY LOVE.
I WILL TAKE ALL THE PAIN AWAY.
GOODBYE MY PRINCE.

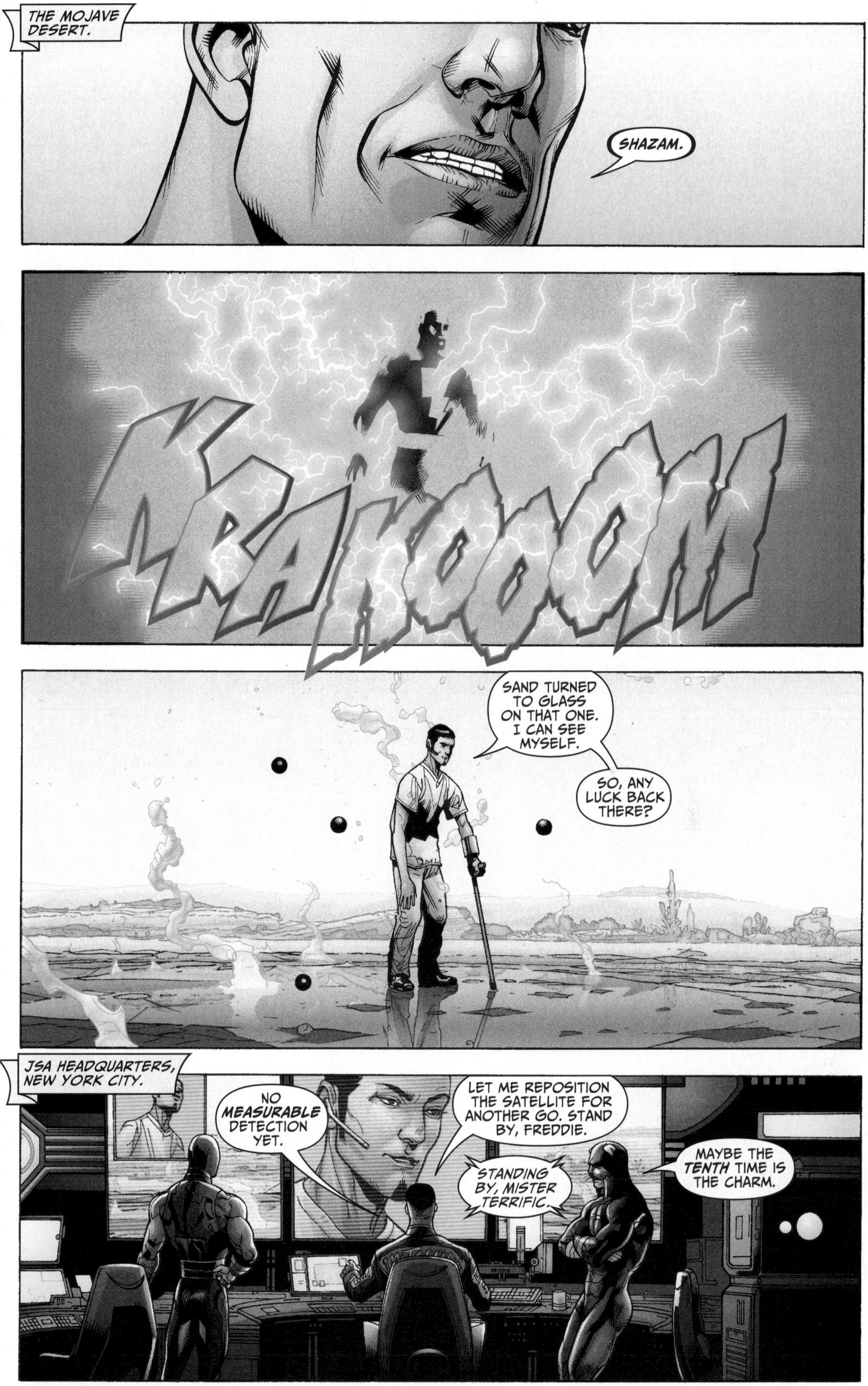
THE MOJAVE DESERT.
SHAZAM.
KRAKOOOM
SAND TURNED TO GLASS ON THAT ONE. I CAN SEE MYSELF.
SO, ANY LUCK BACK THERE?
JSA HEADQUARTERS, NEW YORK CITY.
NO MEASURABLE DETECTION YET.
LET ME REPOSITION THE SATELLITE FOR ANOTHER GO. STAND BY, FREDDIE.
STANDING BY, MISTER TERRIFIC.
MAYBE THE TENTH TIME IS THE CHARM.

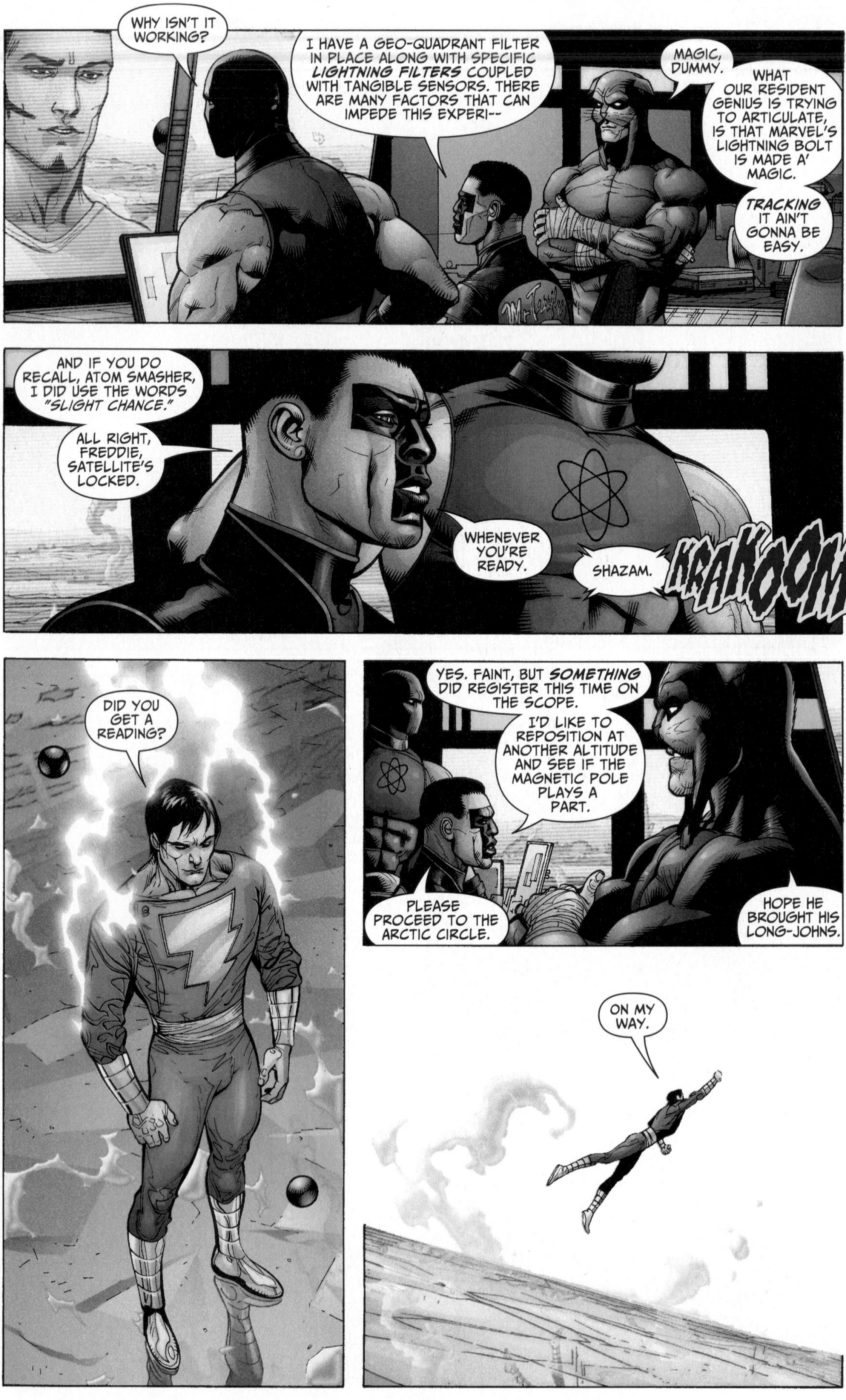
WHY ISN'T IT WORKING?
I HAVE A GEO-QUADRANT FILTER IN PLACE ALONG WITH SPECIFIC LIGHTNING FILTERS COUPLED WITH TANGIBLE SENSORS. THERE ARE MANY FACTORS THAT CAN IMPEDE THIS EXPERI--
MAGIC, DUMMY.
WHAT OUR RESIDENT GENIUS IS TRYING TO ARTICULATE, IS THAT MARVEL'S LIGHTNING BOLT IS MADE A' MAGIC.
TRACKING IT AIN'T GONNA BE EASY.
AND IF YOU DO RECALL, ATOM SMASHER, I DID USE THE WORDS "SLIGHT CHANCE."
ALL RIGHT, FREDDIE, SATELLITE'S LOCKED.
WHENEVER YOU'RE READY.
SHAZAM.
KRAKOOM
DID YOU GET A READING?
YES. FAINT, BUT SOMETHING DID REGISTER THIS TIME ON THE SCOPE.
I'D LIKE TO REPOSITION AT ANOTHER ALTITUDE AND SEE IF THE MAGNETIC POLE PLAYS A PART.
PLEASE PROCEED TO THE ARCTIC CIRCLE.
HOPE HE BROUGHT HIS LONG-JOHNS.
ON MY WAY.

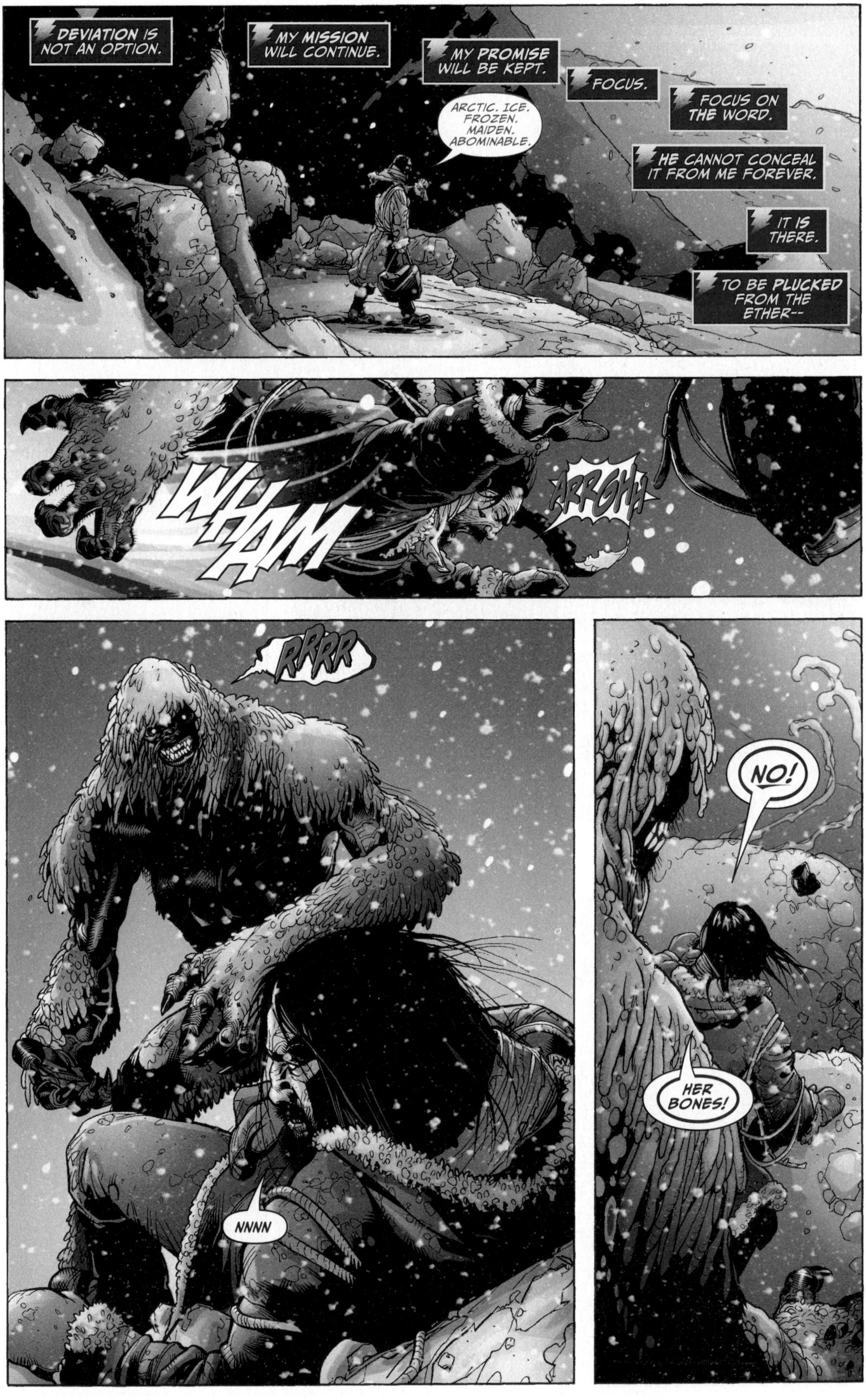
DEVIATION IS NOT AN OPTION.
MY MISSION WILL CONTINUE.
MY PROMISE WILL BE KEPT.
ARCTIC. ICE. FROZEN. MAIDEN. ABOMINABLE.
FOCUS.
FOCUS ON THE WORD.
HE CANNOT CONCEAL IT FROM ME FOREVER.
IT IS THERE.
TO BE PLUCKED FROM THE ETHER--
WHAM
ARRGHH
RRRR
NNNN
NO!
HER BONES!

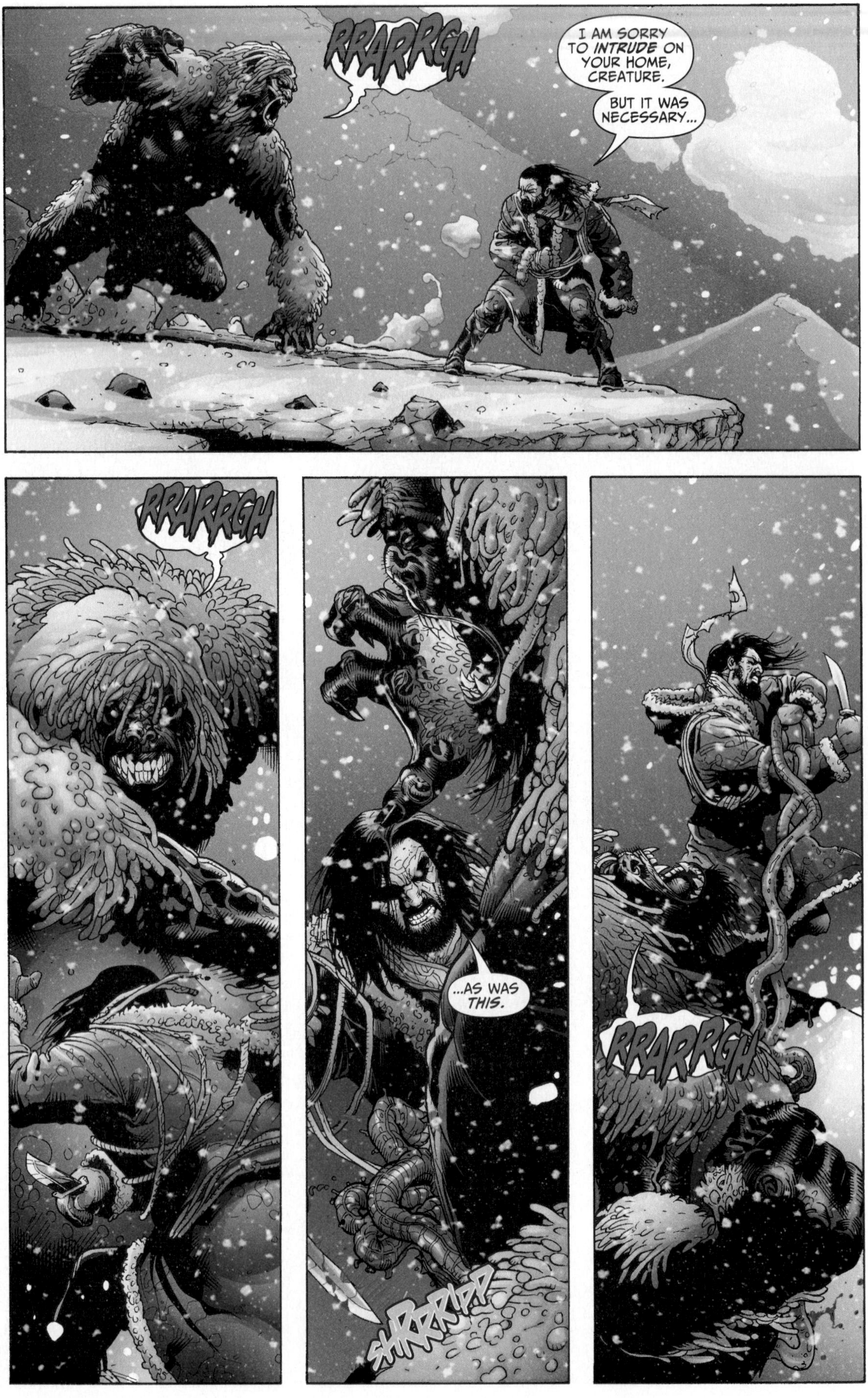
RRARRGH
I AM SORRY TO INTRUDE ON YOUR HOME, CREATURE.
BUT IT WAS NECESSARY...
RRARRGH
...AS WAS THIS.
SHRRRIPP
RRARRGH

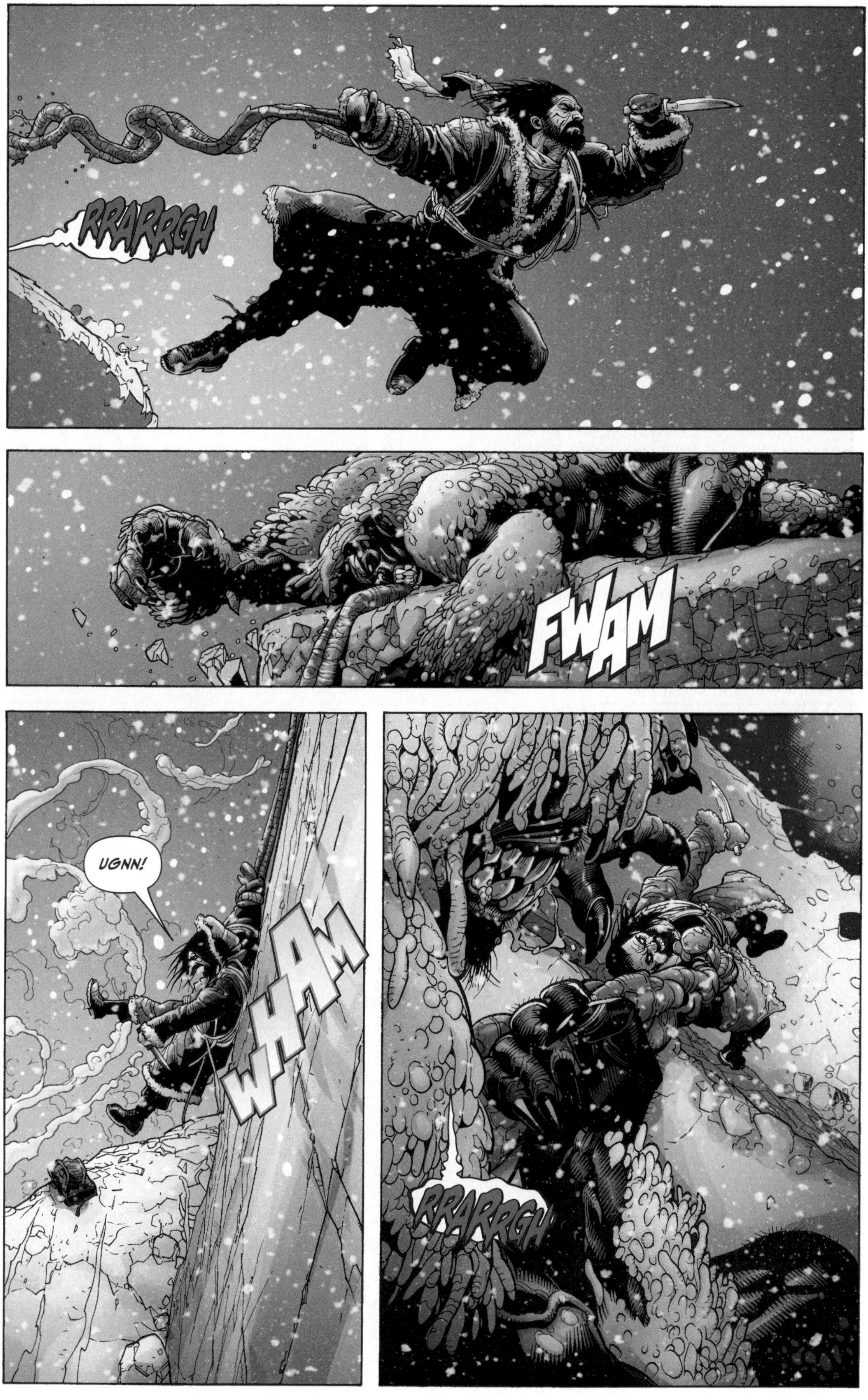
RRARRGH
FWAM
UGNN!
WHAM
RRARRGH

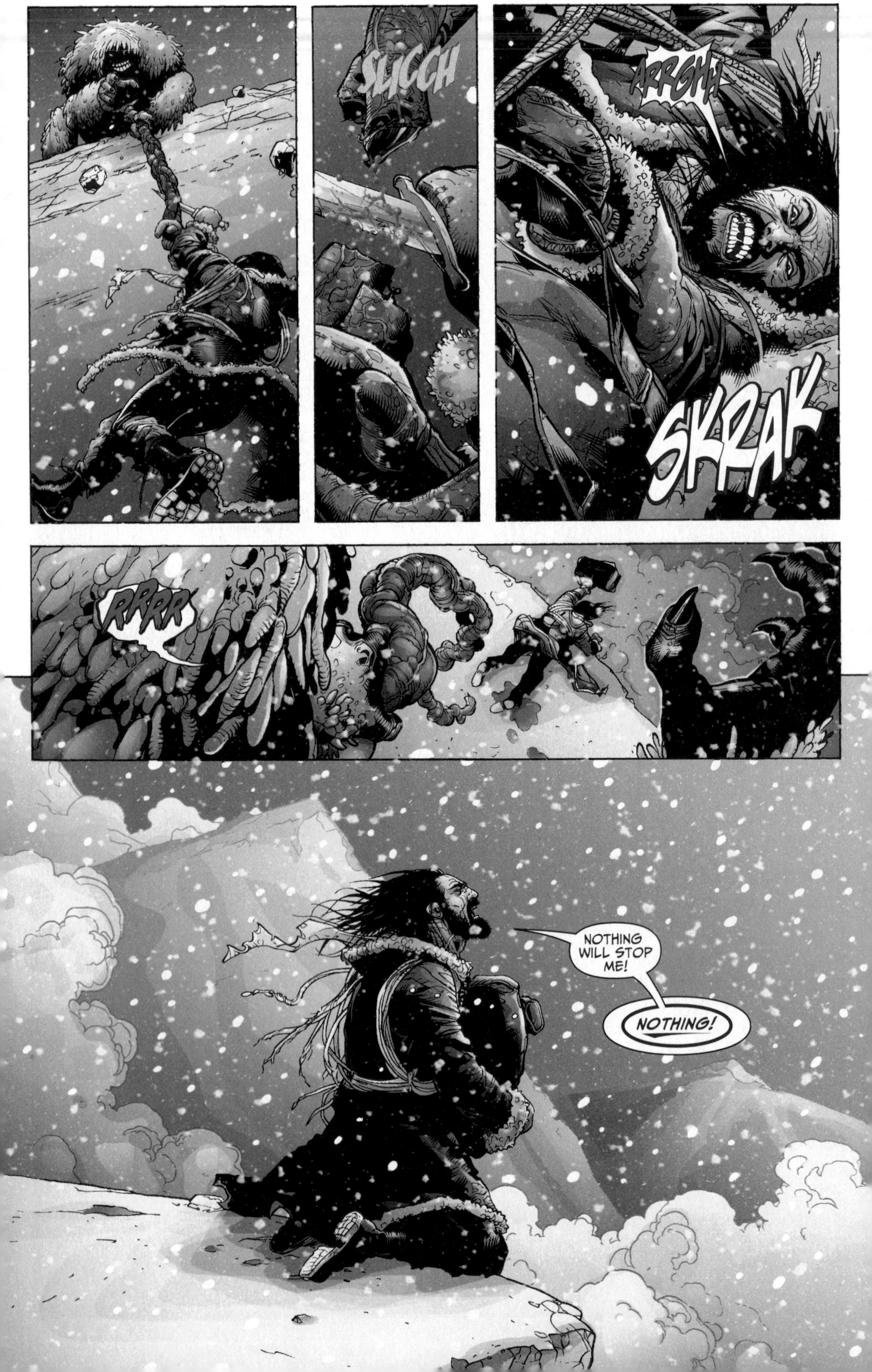
SLICCH
ARRGHH
SKRAK
RRRR
NOTHING WILL STOP ME!
NOTHING!

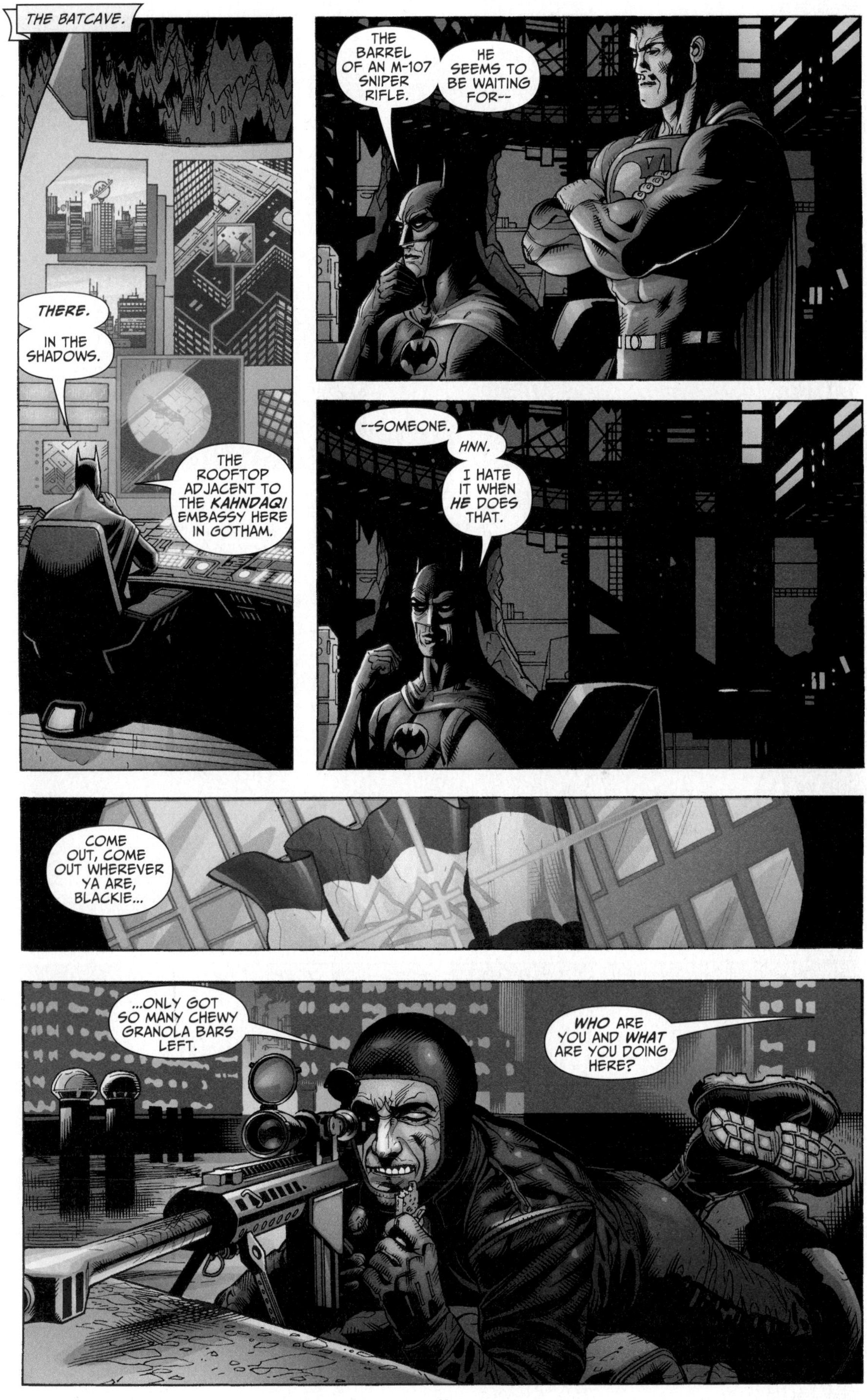
THE BATCAVE.
THERE.
IN THE SHADOWS.
THE ROOFTOP ADJACENT TO THE KAHNDAQI EMBASSY HERE IN GOTHAM.
THE BARREL OF AN M-107 SNIPER RIFLE.
HE SEEMS TO BE WAITING FOR--
--SOMEONE.
HNN.
I HATE IT WHEN HE DOES THAT.
COME OUT, COME OUT WHEREVER YA ARE, BLACKIE...
...ONLY GOT SO MANY CHEWY GRANOLA BARS LEFT.
WHO ARE YOU AND WHAT ARE YOU DOING HERE?

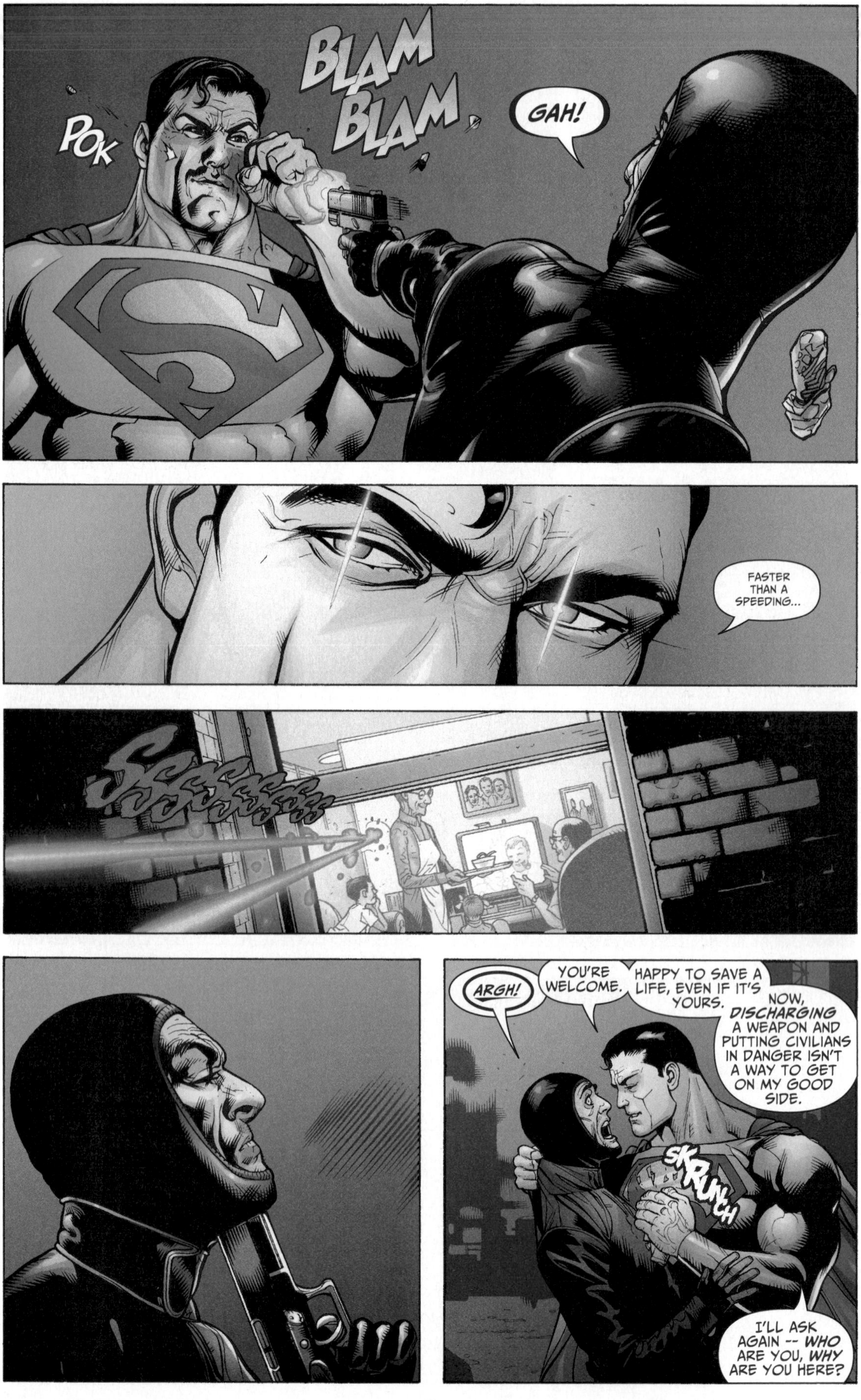
BLAM
BLAM
POK
GAH!
FASTER THAN A SPEEDING...
SSSSSSSSS
ARGH!
YOU'RE WELCOME.
HAPPY TO SAVE A LIFE, EVEN IF IT'S YOURS.
NOW, DISCHARGING A WEAPON AND PUTTING CIVILIANS IN DANGER ISN'T A WAY TO GET ON MY GOOD SIDE.
SKRUNCH
I'LL ASK AGAIN -- WHO ARE YOU, WHY ARE YOU HERE?

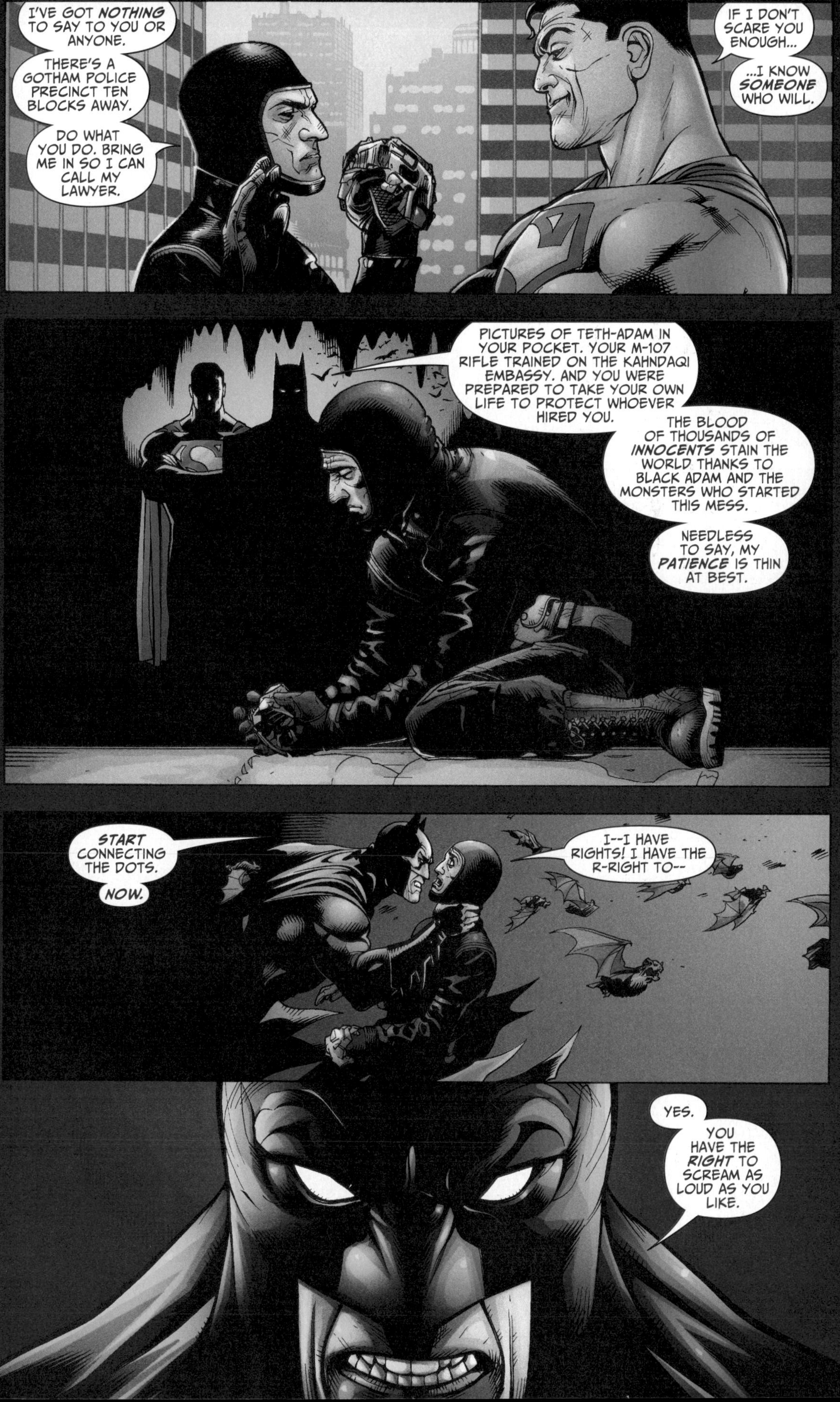
I'VE GOT NOTHING TO SAY TO YOU OR ANYONE.
THERE'S A GOTHAM POLICE PRECINCT TEN BLOCKS AWAY.
DO WHAT YOU DO. BRING ME IN SO I CAN CALL MY LAWYER.
IF I DON'T SCARE YOU ENOUGH...
...I KNOW SOMEONE WHO WILL.
PICTURES OF TETH-ADAM IN YOUR POCKET. YOUR M-107 RIFLE TRAINED ON THE KAHNDAQI EMBASSY. AND YOU WERE PREPARED TO TAKE YOUR OWN LIFE TO PROTECT WHOEVER HIRED YOU.
THE BLOOD OF THOUSANDS OF INNOCENTS STAIN THE WORLD THANKS TO BLACK ADAM AND THE MONSTERS WHO STARTED THIS MESS.
NEEDLESS TO SAY, MY PATIENCE IS THIN AT BEST.
START CONNECTING THE DOTS.
NOW.
I--I HAVE RIGHTS! I HAVE THE R-RIGHT TO--
YES.
YOU HAVE THE RIGHT TO SCREAM AS LOUD AS YOU LIKE.

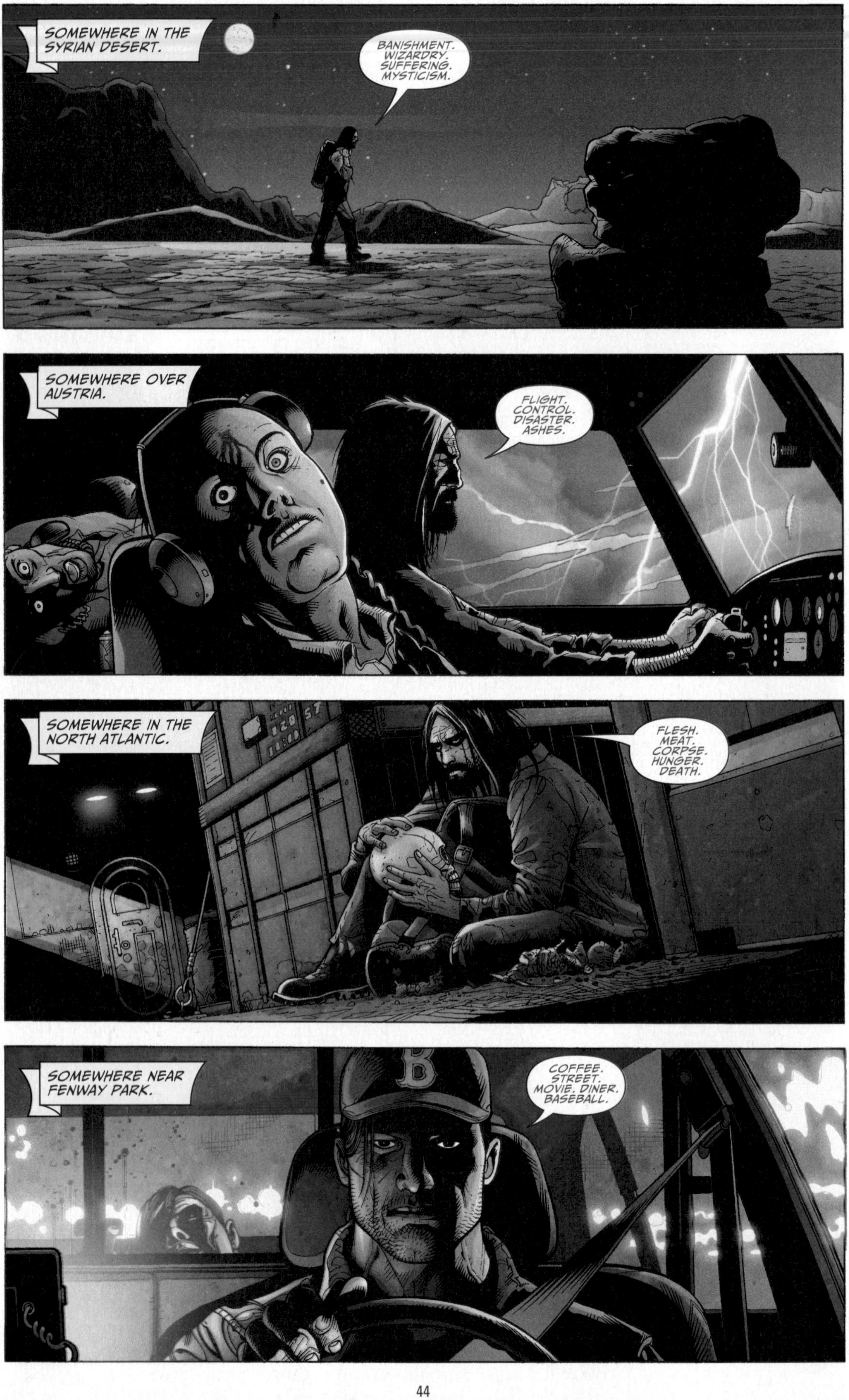
SOMEWHERE IN THE SYRIAN DESERT.
BANISHMENT. WIZARDRY. SUFFERING. MYSTICISM.
SOMEWHERE OVER AUSTRIA.
FLIGHT. CONTROL. DISASTER. ASHES.
SOMEWHERE IN THE NORTH ATLANTIC.
FLESH. MEAT. CORPSE. HUNGER. DEATH.
SOMEWHERE NEAR FENWAY PARK.
COFFEE. STREET. MOVIE. DINER. BASEBALL.

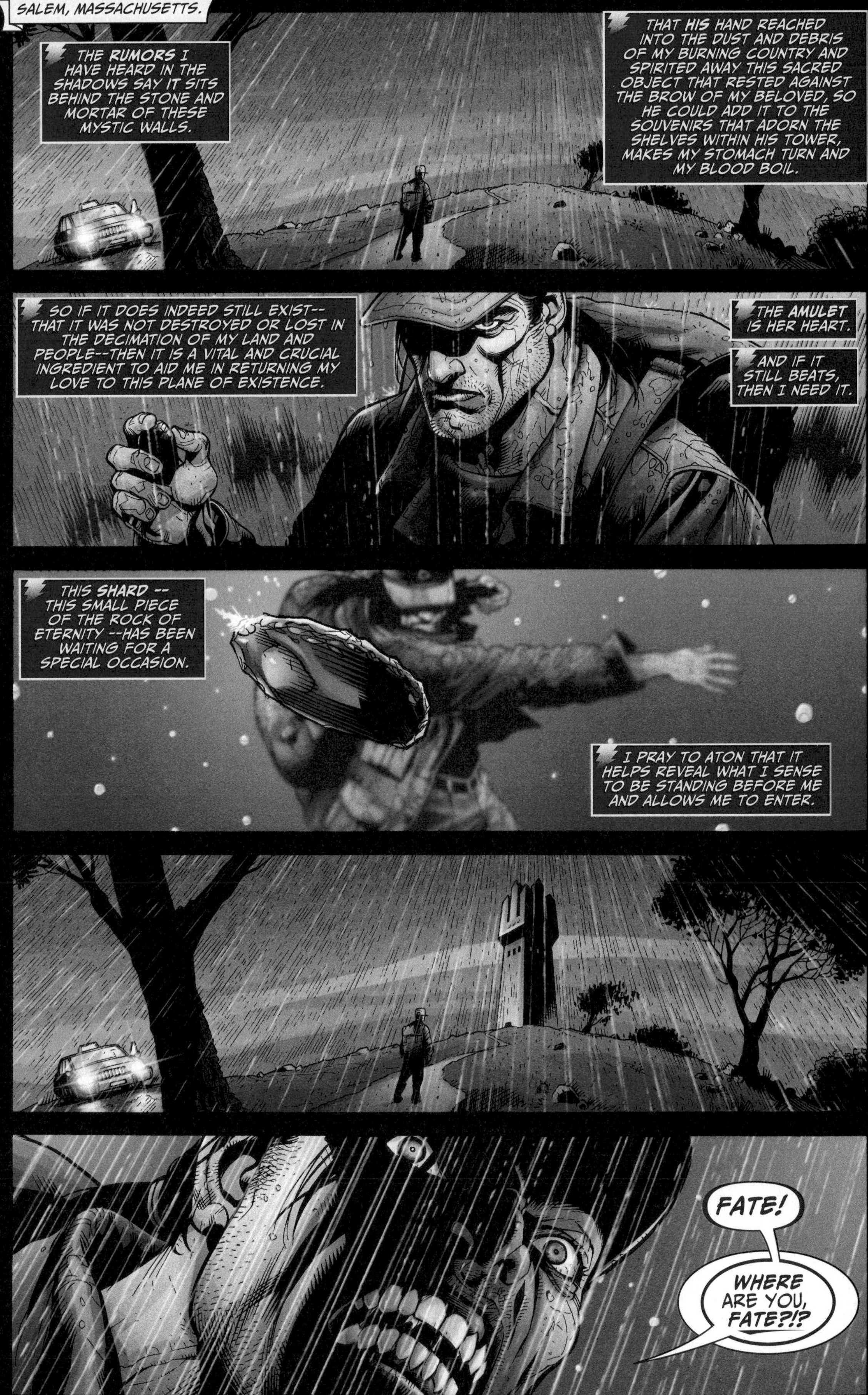
SALEM, MASSACHUSETTS.
THE RUMORS I HAVE HEARD IN THE SHADOWS SAY IT SITS BEHIND THE STONE AND MORTAR OF THESE MYSTIC WALLS.
THAT HIS HAND REACHED INTO THE DUST AND DEBRIS OF MY BURNING COUNTRY AND SPIRITED AWAY THIS SACRED OBJECT THAT RESTED AGAINST THE BROW OF MY BELOVED, SO HE COULD ADD IT TO THE SOUVENIRS THAT ADORN THE SHELVES WITHIN HIS TOWER, MAKES MY STOMACH TURN AND MY BLOOD BOIL.
SO IF IT DOES INDEED STILL EXIST--THAT IT WAS NOT DESTROYED OR LOST IN THE DECIMATION OF MY LAND AND PEOPLE--THEN IT IS A VITAL AND CRUCIAL INGREDIENT TO AID ME IN RETURNING MY LOVE TO THIS PLANE OF EXISTENCE.
THE AMULET IS HER HEART.
AND IF IT STILL BEATS, THEN I NEED IT.
THIS SHARD -- THIS SMALL PIECE OF THE ROCK OF ETERNITY --HAS BEEN WAITING FOR A SPECIAL OCCASION.
I PRAY TO ATON THAT IT HELPS REVEAL WHAT I SENSE TO BE STANDING BEFORE ME AND ALLOWS ME TO ENTER.
FATE!
WHERE ARE YOU, FATE?!?

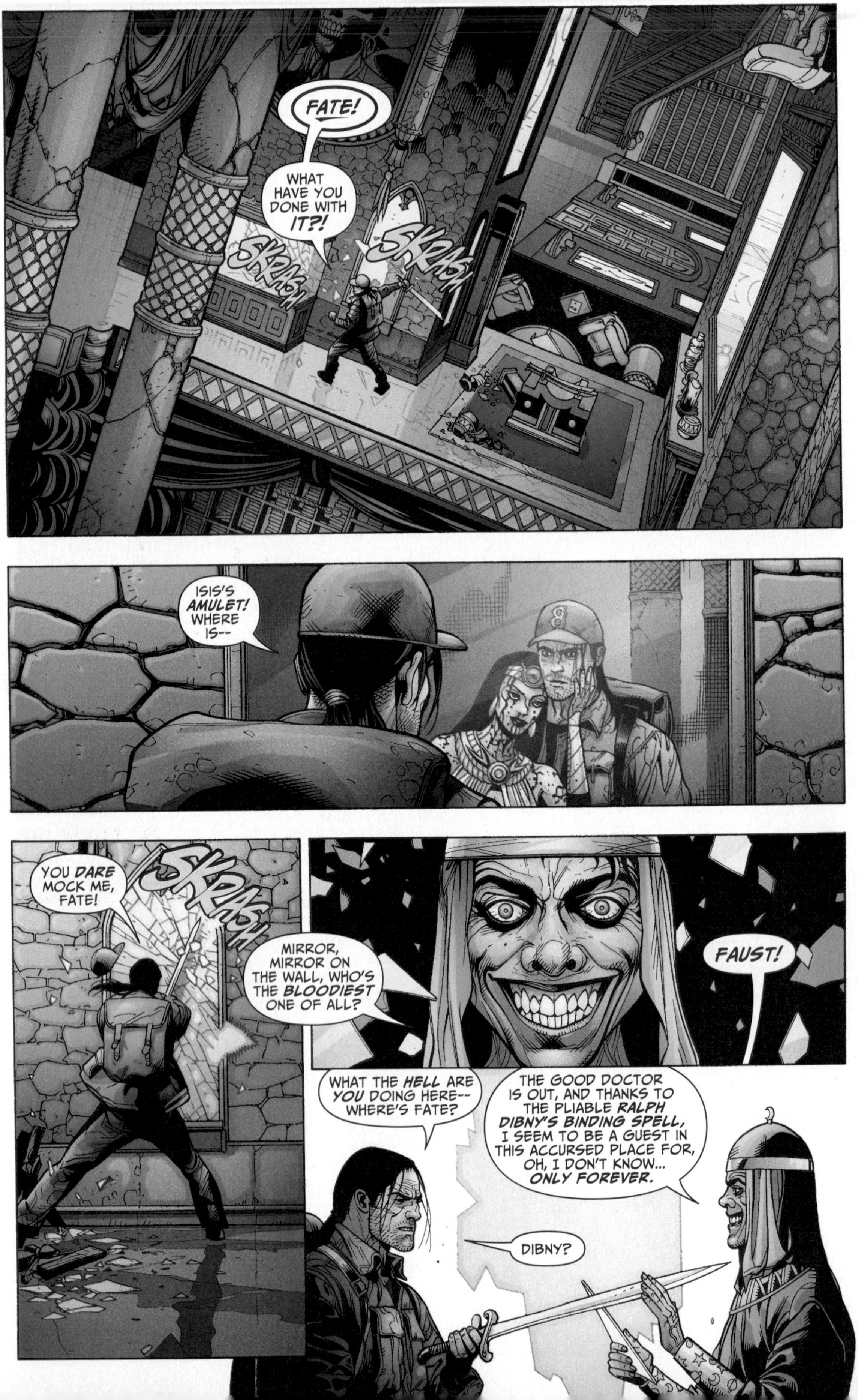
FATE!
WHAT HAVE YOU DONE WITH IT?!
SKRASH
SKRASH
ISIS'S AMULET! WHERE IS--
YOU DARE MOCK ME, FATE!
SKRASH
MIRROR, MIRROR ON THE WALL, WHO'S THE BLOODIEST ONE OF ALL?
FAUST!
WHAT THE HELL ARE YOU DOING HERE-- WHERE'S FATE?
THE GOOD DOCTOR IS OUT, AND THANKS TO THE PLIABLE RALPH DIBNY'S BINDING SPELL, I SEEM TO BE A GUEST IN THIS ACCURSED PLACE FOR, OH, I DON'T KNOW... ONLY FOREVER.
DIBNY?

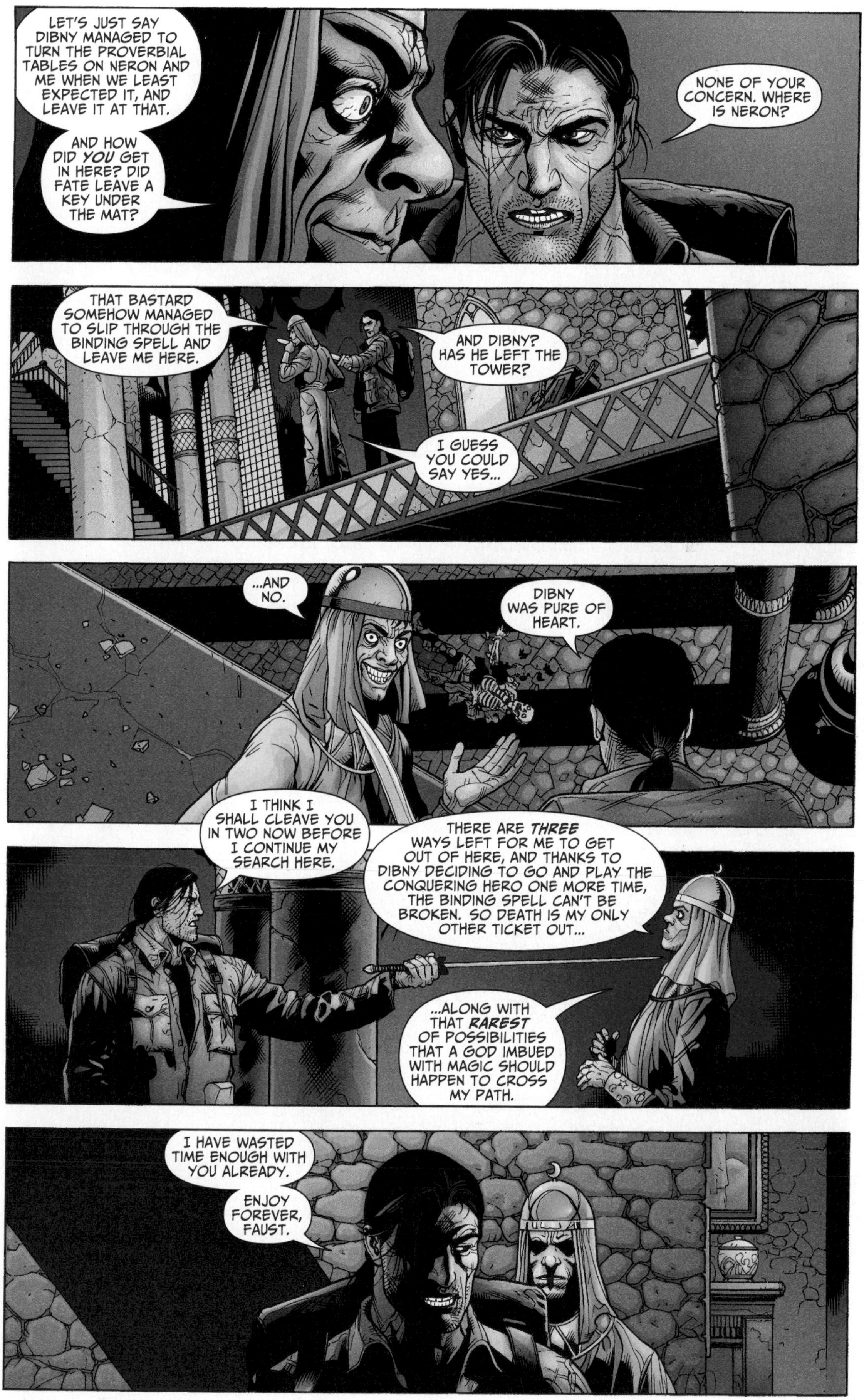
LET'S JUST SAY DIBNY MANAGED TO TURN THE PROVERBIAL TABLES ON NERON AND ME WHEN WE LEAST EXPECTED IT, AND LEAVE IT AT THAT.
AND HOW DID *YOU* GET IN HERE? DID FATE LEAVE A KEY UNDER THE MAT?
NONE OF YOUR CONCERN. WHERE IS NERON?
THAT BASTARD SOMEHOW MANAGED TO SLIP THROUGH THE BINDING SPELL AND LEAVE ME HERE.
AND DIBNY? HAS HE LEFT THE TOWER?
I GUESS YOU COULD SAY YES...
...AND NO.
DIBNY WAS PURE OF HEART.
I THINK I SHALL CLEAVE YOU IN TWO NOW BEFORE I CONTINUE MY SEARCH HERE.
THERE ARE *THREE* WAYS LEFT FOR ME TO GET OUT OF HERE, AND THANKS TO DIBNY DECIDING TO GO AND PLAY THE CONQUERING HERO ONE MORE TIME, THE BINDING SPELL CAN'T BE BROKEN. SO DEATH IS MY ONLY OTHER TICKET OUT...
...ALONG WITH THAT *RAREST* OF POSSIBILITIES THAT A GOD IMBUED WITH MAGIC SHOULD HAPPEN TO CROSS MY PATH.
I HAVE WASTED TIME ENOUGH WITH YOU ALREADY.
ENJOY FOREVER, FAUST.

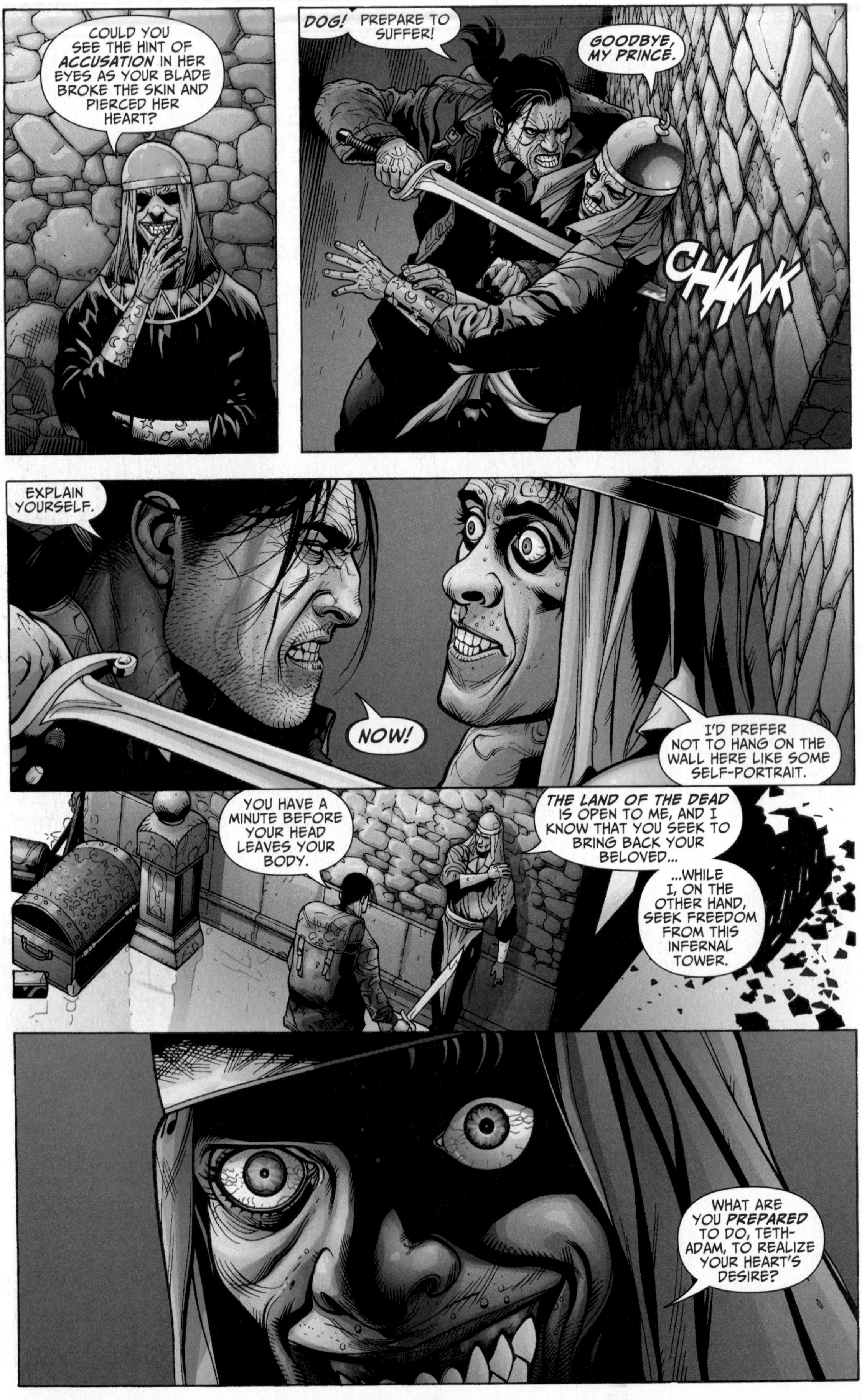
COULD YOU SEE THE HINT OF ACCUSATION IN HER EYES AS YOUR BLADE BROKE THE SKIN AND PIERCED HER HEART?
DOG!
PREPARE TO SUFFER!
GOODBYE, MY PRINCE.
CHANK
EXPLAIN YOURSELF.
NOW!
I'D PREFER NOT TO HANG ON THE WALL HERE LIKE SOME SELF-PORTRAIT.
YOU HAVE A MINUTE BEFORE YOUR HEAD LEAVES YOUR BODY.
THE LAND OF THE DEAD IS OPEN TO ME, AND I KNOW THAT YOU SEEK TO BRING BACK YOUR BELOVED...
...WHILE I, ON THE OTHER HAND, SEEK FREEDOM FROM THIS INFERNAL TOWER.
WHAT ARE YOU PREPARED TO DO, TETH-ADAM, TO REALIZE YOUR HEART'S DESIRE?

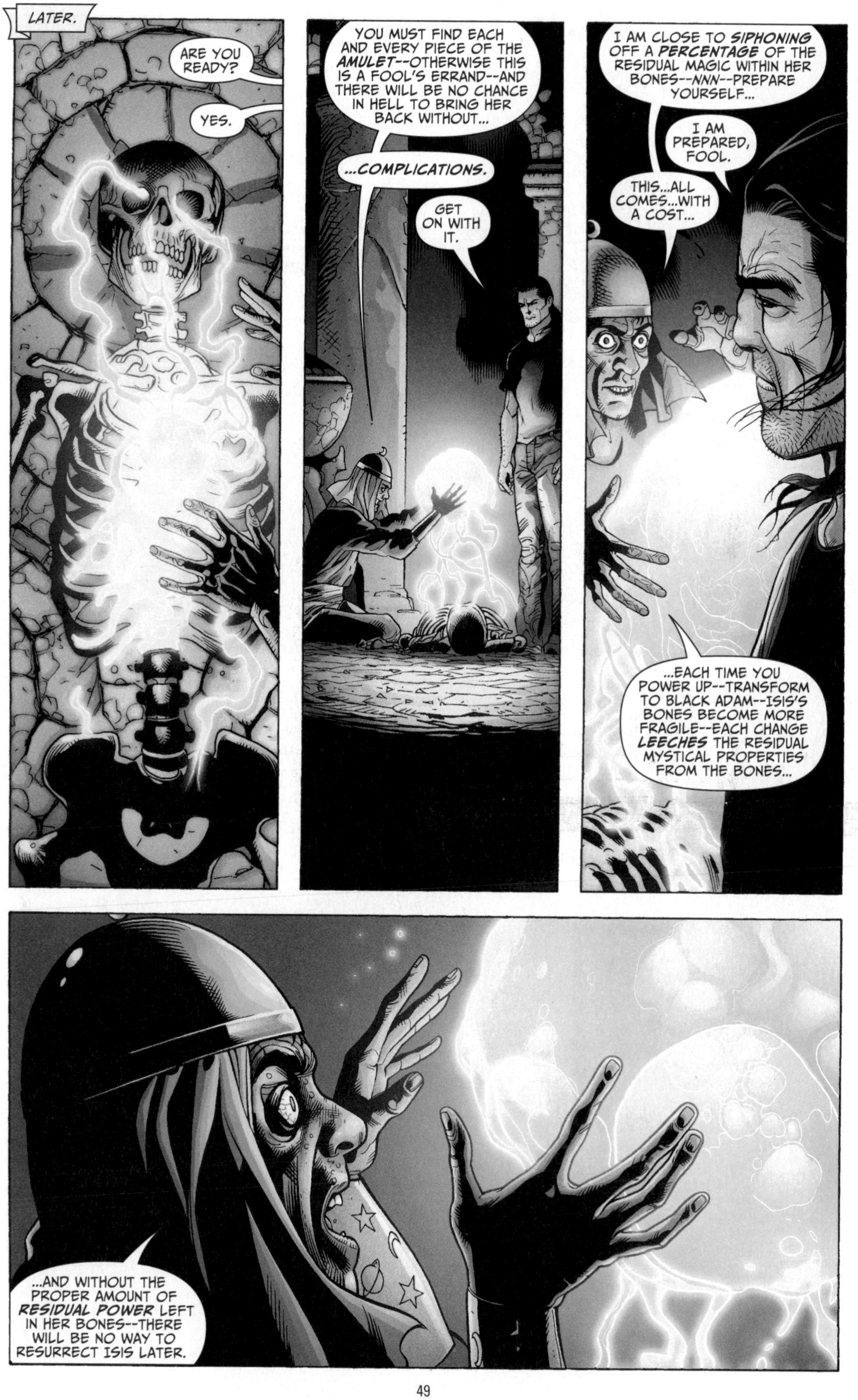
LATER.
ARE YOU READY?
YES.
YOU MUST FIND EACH AND EVERY PIECE OF THE AMULET--OTHERWISE THIS IS A FOOL'S ERRAND--AND THERE WILL BE NO CHANCE IN HELL TO BRING HER BACK WITHOUT...
...COMPLICATIONS.
GET ON WITH IT.
I AM CLOSE TO SIPHONING OFF A PERCENTAGE OF THE RESIDUAL MAGIC WITHIN HER BONES--NNN--PREPARE YOURSELF...
I AM PREPARED, FOOL.
THIS...ALL COMES...WITH A COST...
...EACH TIME YOU POWER UP--TRANSFORM TO BLACK ADAM--ISIS'S BONES BECOME MORE FRAGILE--EACH CHANGE LEECHES THE RESIDUAL MYSTICAL PROPERTIES FROM THE BONES...
...AND WITHOUT THE PROPER AMOUNT OF RESIDUAL POWER LEFT IN HER BONES--THERE WILL BE NO WAY TO RESURRECT ISIS LATER.

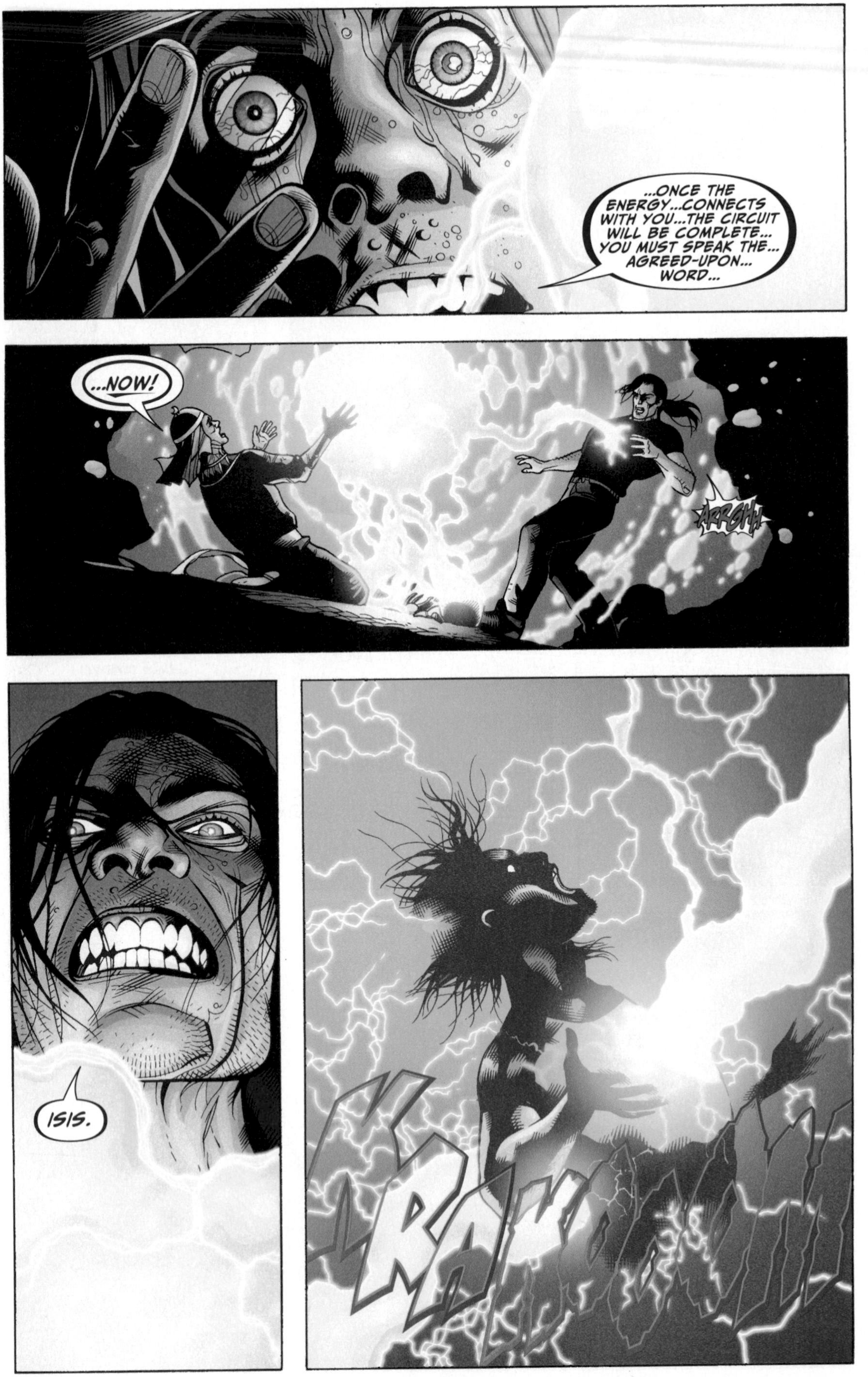
...ONCE THE ENERGY...CONNECTS WITH YOU...THE CIRCUIT WILL BE COMPLETE... YOU MUST SPEAK THE... AGREED-UPON... WORD...
...NOW!
ARRGHH
ISIS.

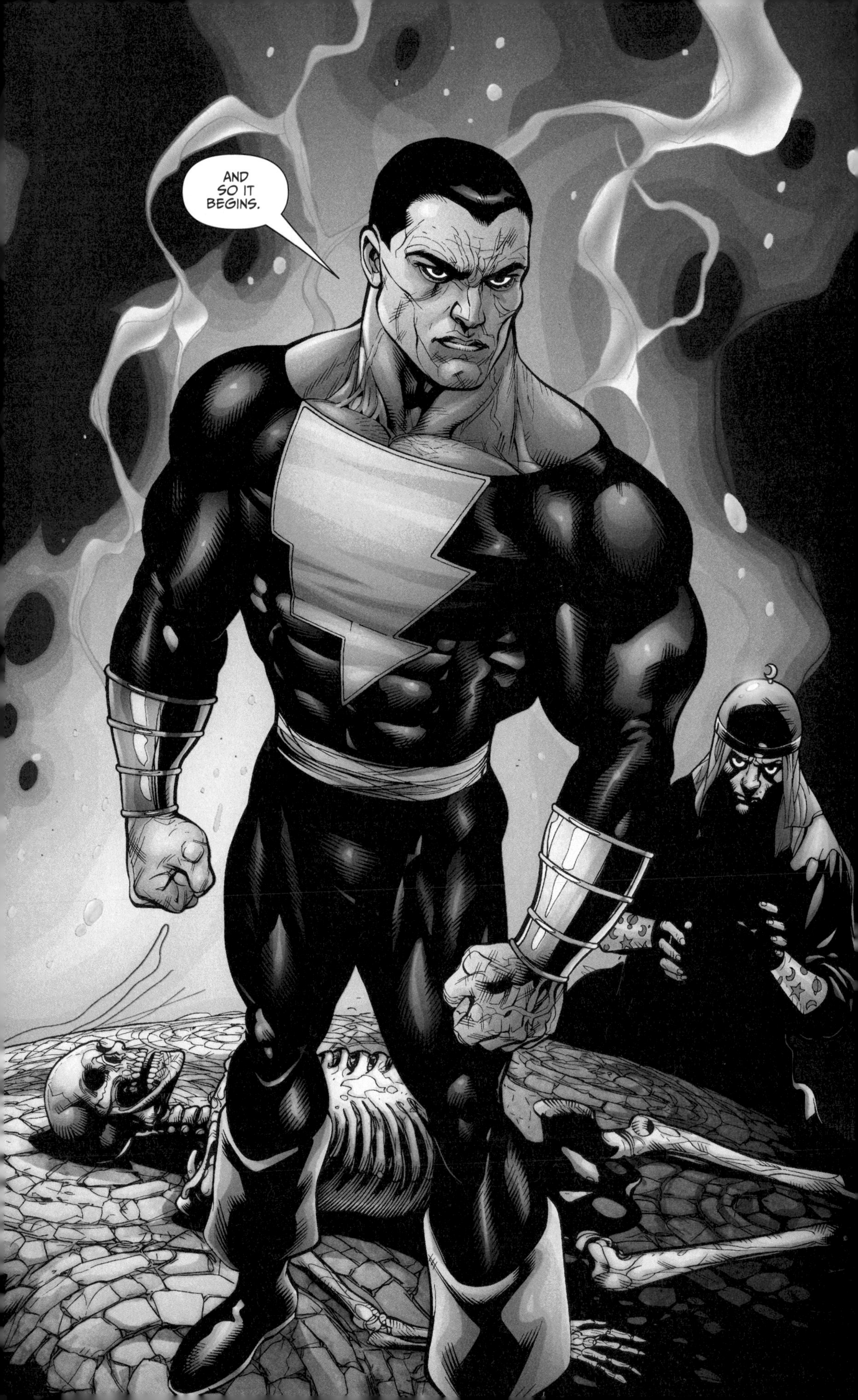
AND SO IT BEGINS.

Chapter Three

This chapter inked by Christian Alamy and Rodney Ramos

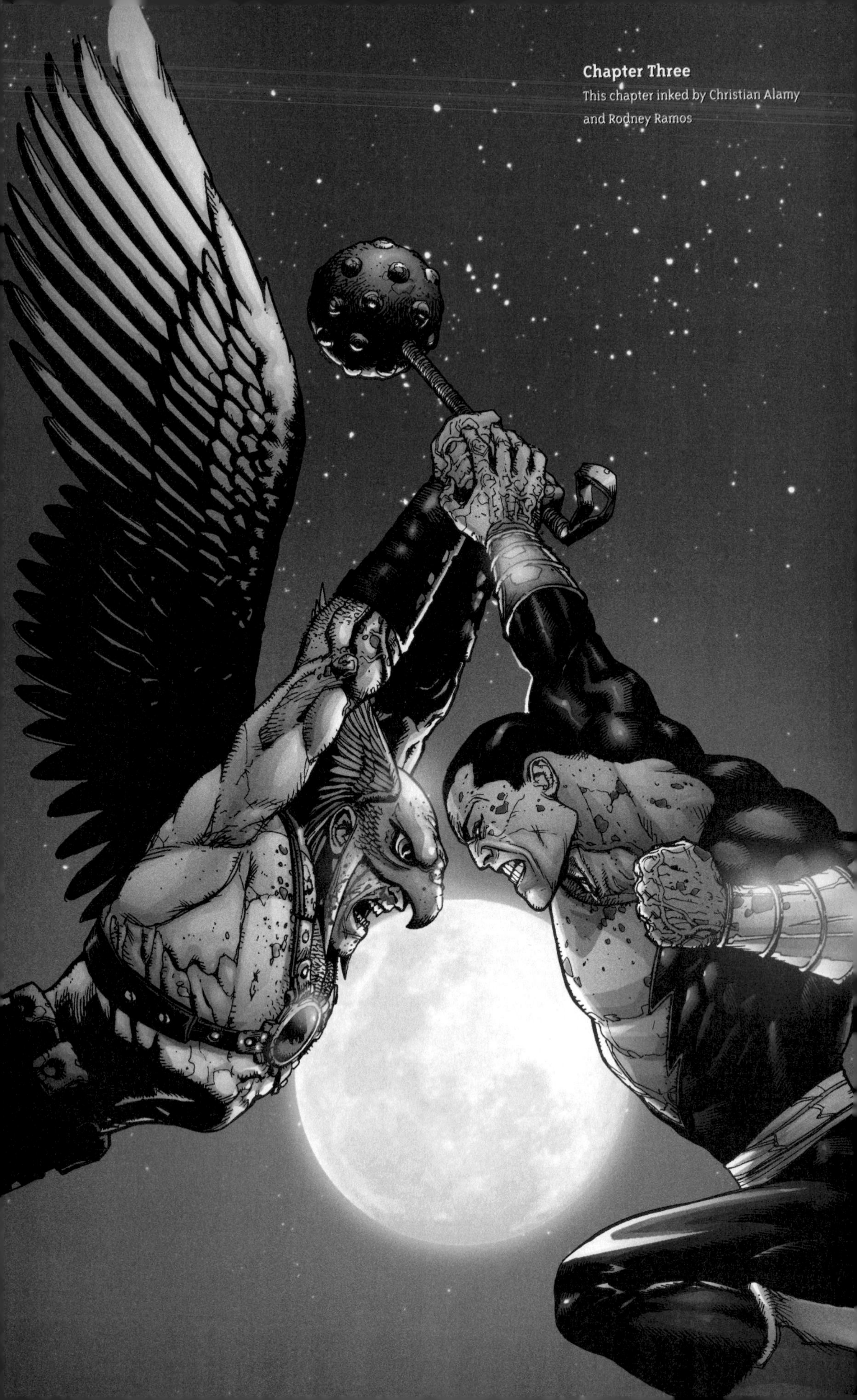

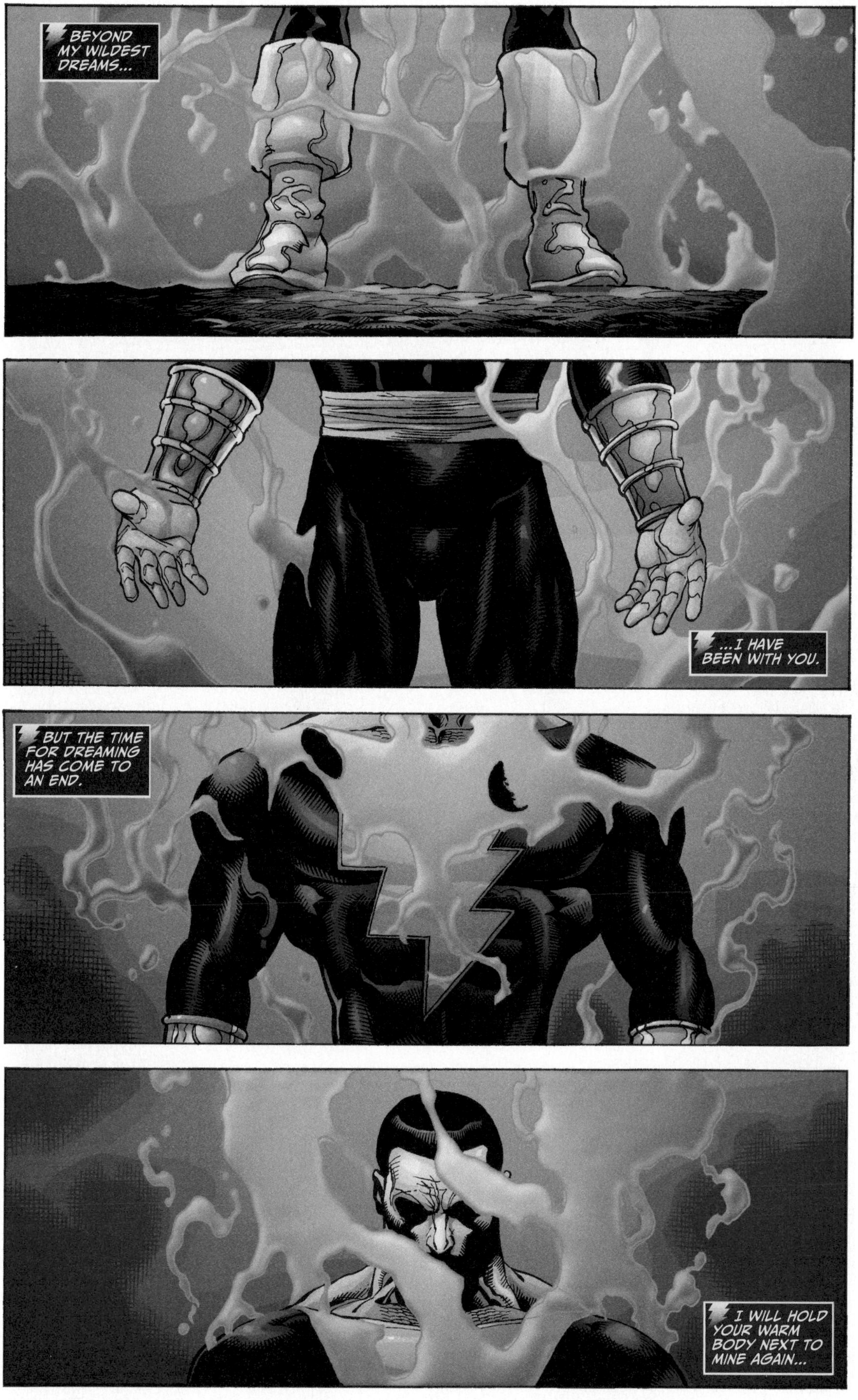

BEYOND MY WILDEST DREAMS...
...I HAVE BEEN WITH YOU.
BUT THE TIME FOR DREAMING HAS COME TO AN END.
I WILL HOLD YOUR WARM BODY NEXT TO MINE AGAIN...

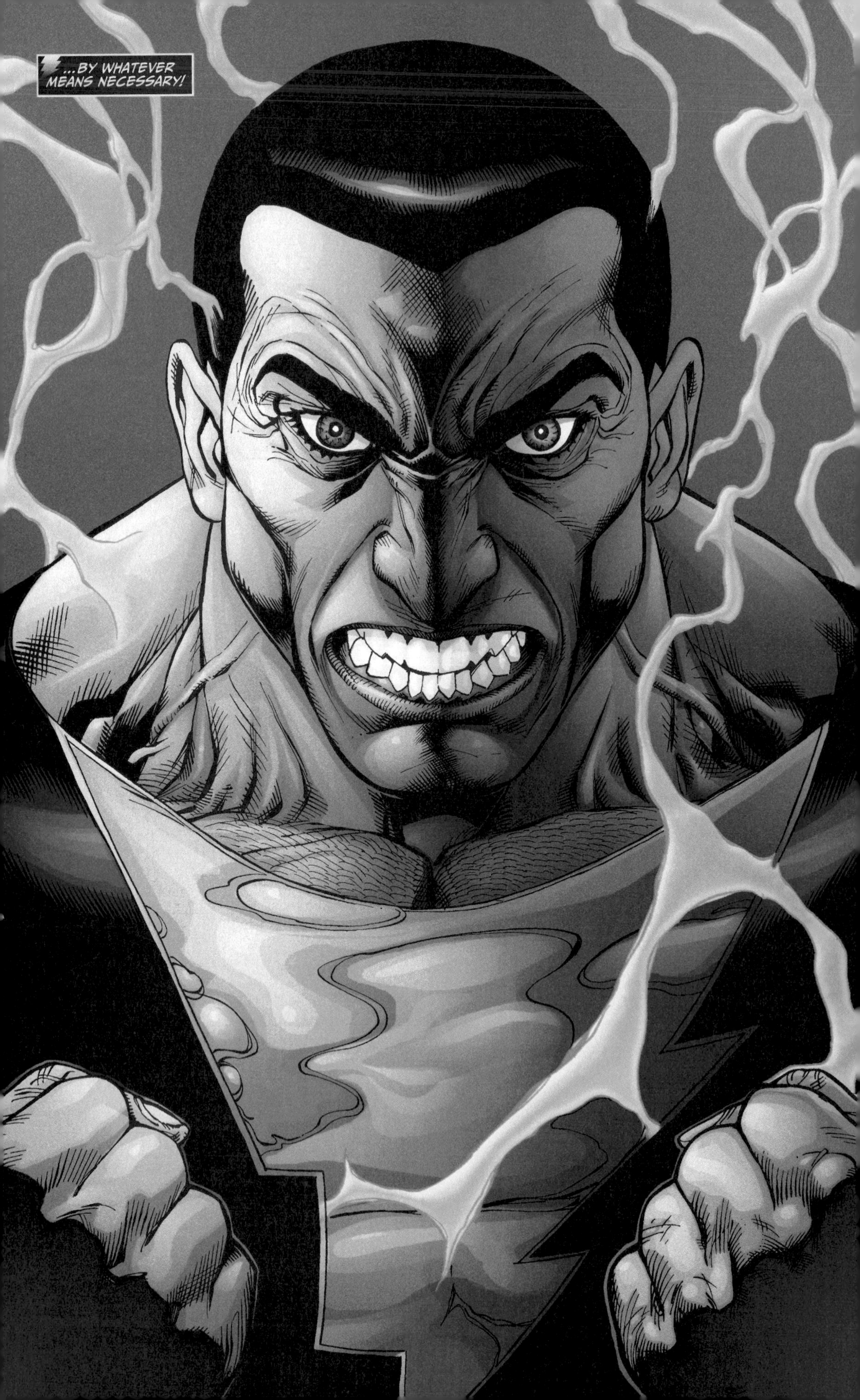
...BY WHATEVER MEANS NECESSARY!

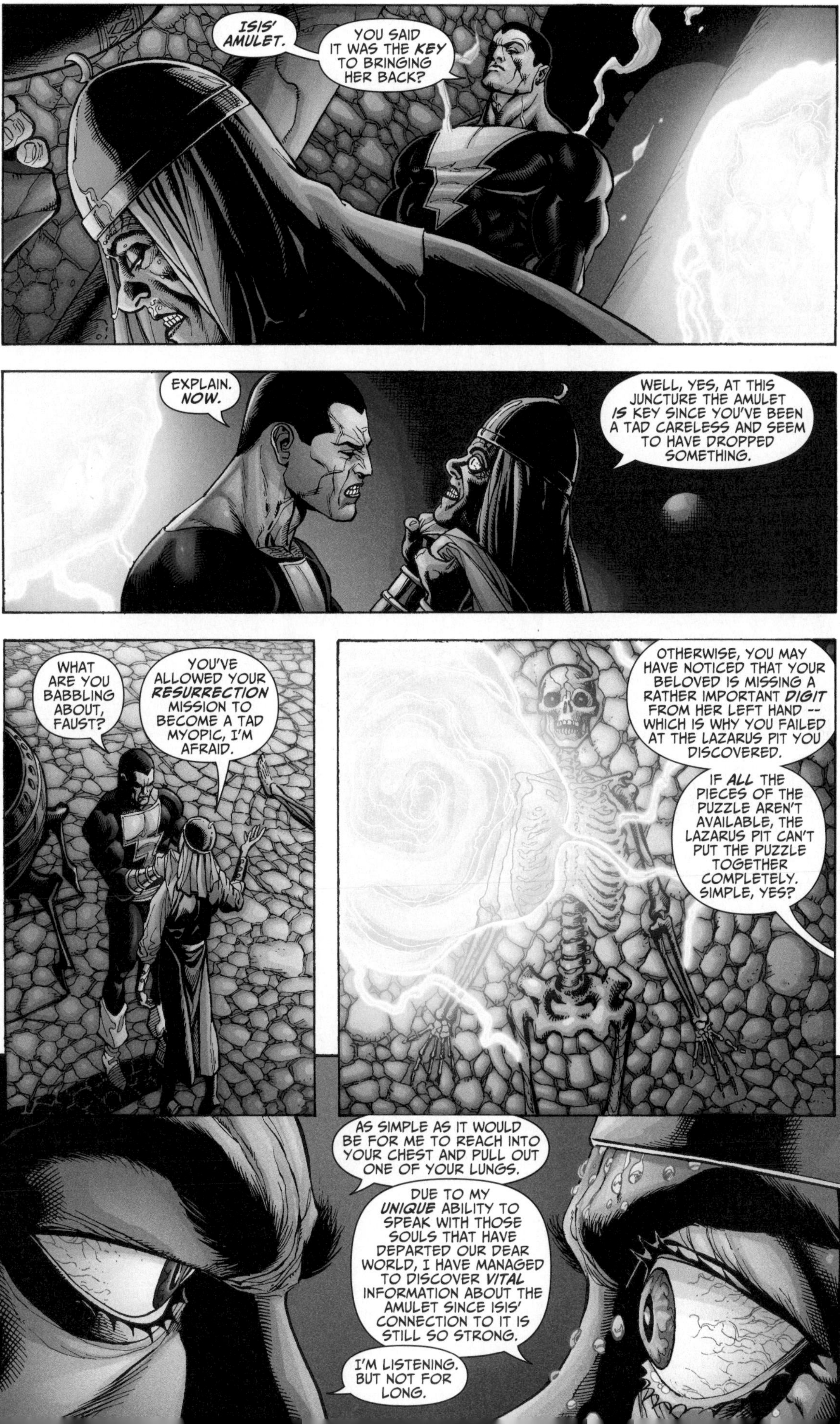
ISIS' AMULET.
YOU SAID IT WAS THE KEY TO BRINGING HER BACK?
EXPLAIN. NOW.
WELL, YES, AT THIS JUNCTURE THE AMULET IS KEY SINCE YOU'VE BEEN A TAD CARELESS AND SEEM TO HAVE DROPPED SOMETHING.
WHAT ARE YOU BABBLING ABOUT, FAUST?
YOU'VE ALLOWED YOUR RESURRECTION MISSION TO BECOME A TAD MYOPIC, I'M AFRAID.
OTHERWISE, YOU MAY HAVE NOTICED THAT YOUR BELOVED IS MISSING A RATHER IMPORTANT DIGIT FROM HER LEFT HAND -- WHICH IS WHY YOU FAILED AT THE LAZARUS PIT YOU DISCOVERED.
IF ALL THE PIECES OF THE PUZZLE AREN'T AVAILABLE, THE LAZARUS PIT CAN'T PUT THE PUZZLE TOGETHER COMPLETELY. SIMPLE, YES?
AS SIMPLE AS IT WOULD BE FOR ME TO REACH INTO YOUR CHEST AND PULL OUT ONE OF YOUR LUNGS.
DUE TO MY UNIQUE ABILITY TO SPEAK WITH THOSE SOULS THAT HAVE DEPARTED OUR DEAR WORLD, I HAVE MANAGED TO DISCOVER VITAL INFORMATION ABOUT THE AMULET SINCE ISIS' CONNECTION TO IT IS STILL SO STRONG.
I'M LISTENING. BUT NOT FOR LONG.

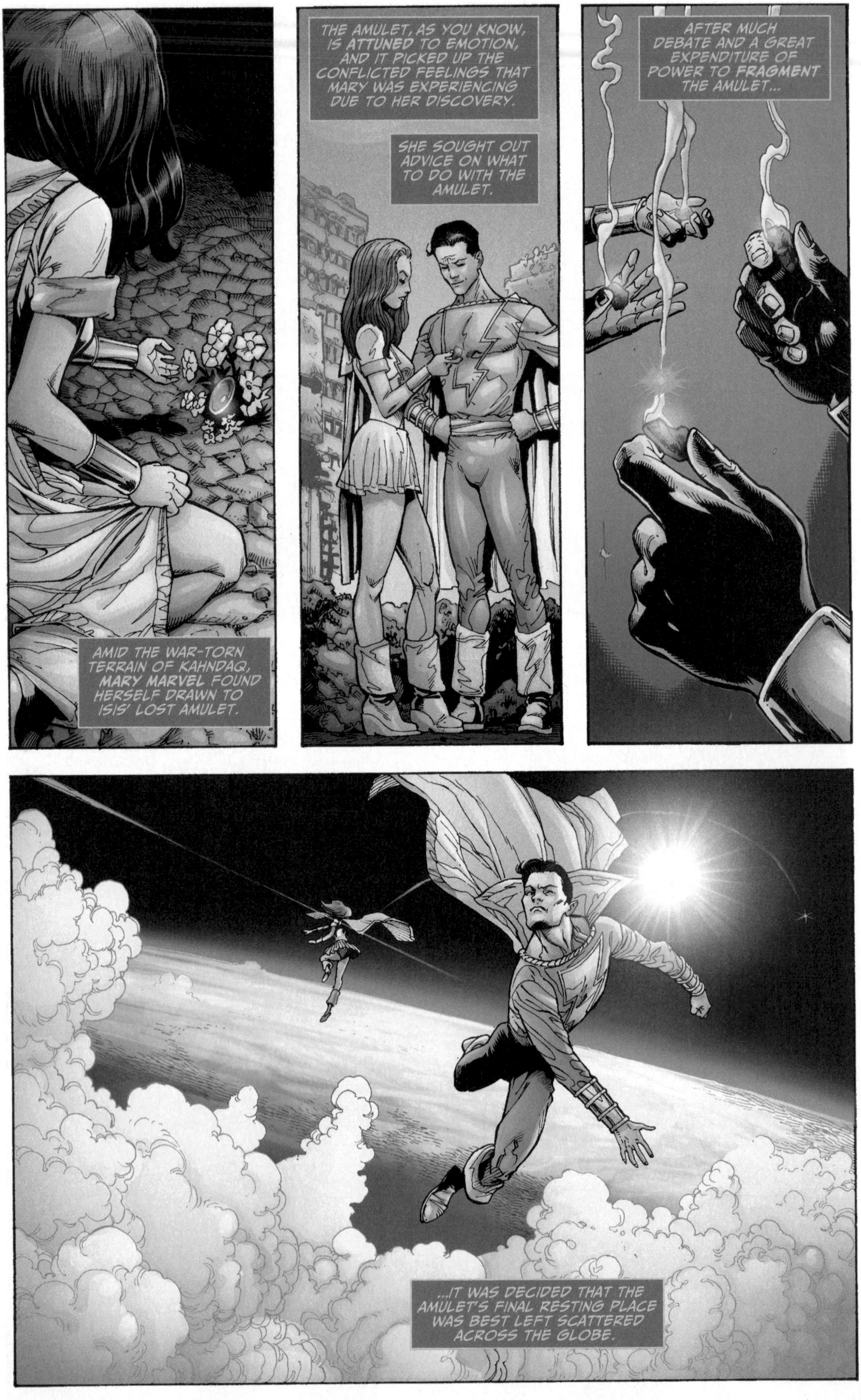
AMID THE WAR-TORN TERRAIN OF KAHNDAQ, MARY MARVEL FOUND HERSELF DRAWN TO ISIS' LOST AMULET.
THE AMULET, AS YOU KNOW, IS ATTUNED TO EMOTION, AND IT PICKED UP THE CONFLICTED FEELINGS THAT MARY WAS EXPERIENCING DUE TO HER DISCOVERY.
SHE SOUGHT OUT ADVICE ON WHAT TO DO WITH THE AMULET.
AFTER MUCH DEBATE AND A GREAT EXPENDITURE OF POWER TO FRAGMENT THE AMULET...
...IT WAS DECIDED THAT THE AMULET'S FINAL RESTING PLACE WAS BEST LEFT SCATTERED ACROSS THE GLOBE.

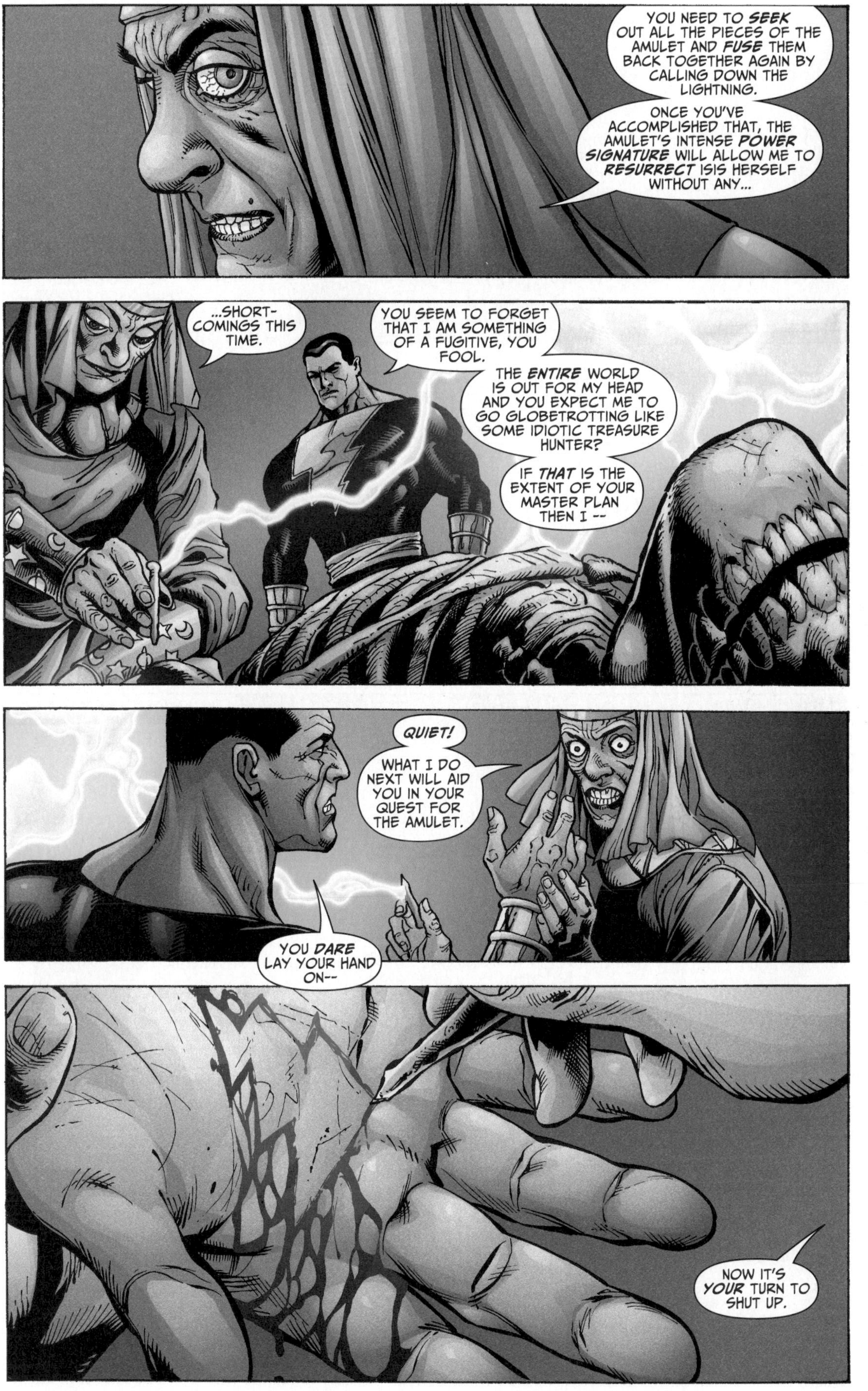
YOU NEED TO SEEK OUT ALL THE PIECES OF THE AMULET AND FUSE THEM BACK TOGETHER AGAIN BY CALLING DOWN THE LIGHTNING.
ONCE YOU'VE ACCOMPLISHED THAT, THE AMULET'S INTENSE POWER SIGNATURE WILL ALLOW ME TO RESURRECT ISIS HERSELF WITHOUT ANY...
...SHORT-COMINGS THIS TIME.
YOU SEEM TO FORGET THAT I AM SOMETHING OF A FUGITIVE, YOU FOOL.
THE ENTIRE WORLD IS OUT FOR MY HEAD AND YOU EXPECT ME TO GO GLOBETROTTING LIKE SOME IDIOTIC TREASURE HUNTER?
IF THAT IS THE EXTENT OF YOUR MASTER PLAN THEN I --
QUIET!
WHAT I DO NEXT WILL AID YOU IN YOUR QUEST FOR THE AMULET.
YOU DARE LAY YOUR HAND ON--
NOW IT'S YOUR TURN TO SHUT UP.

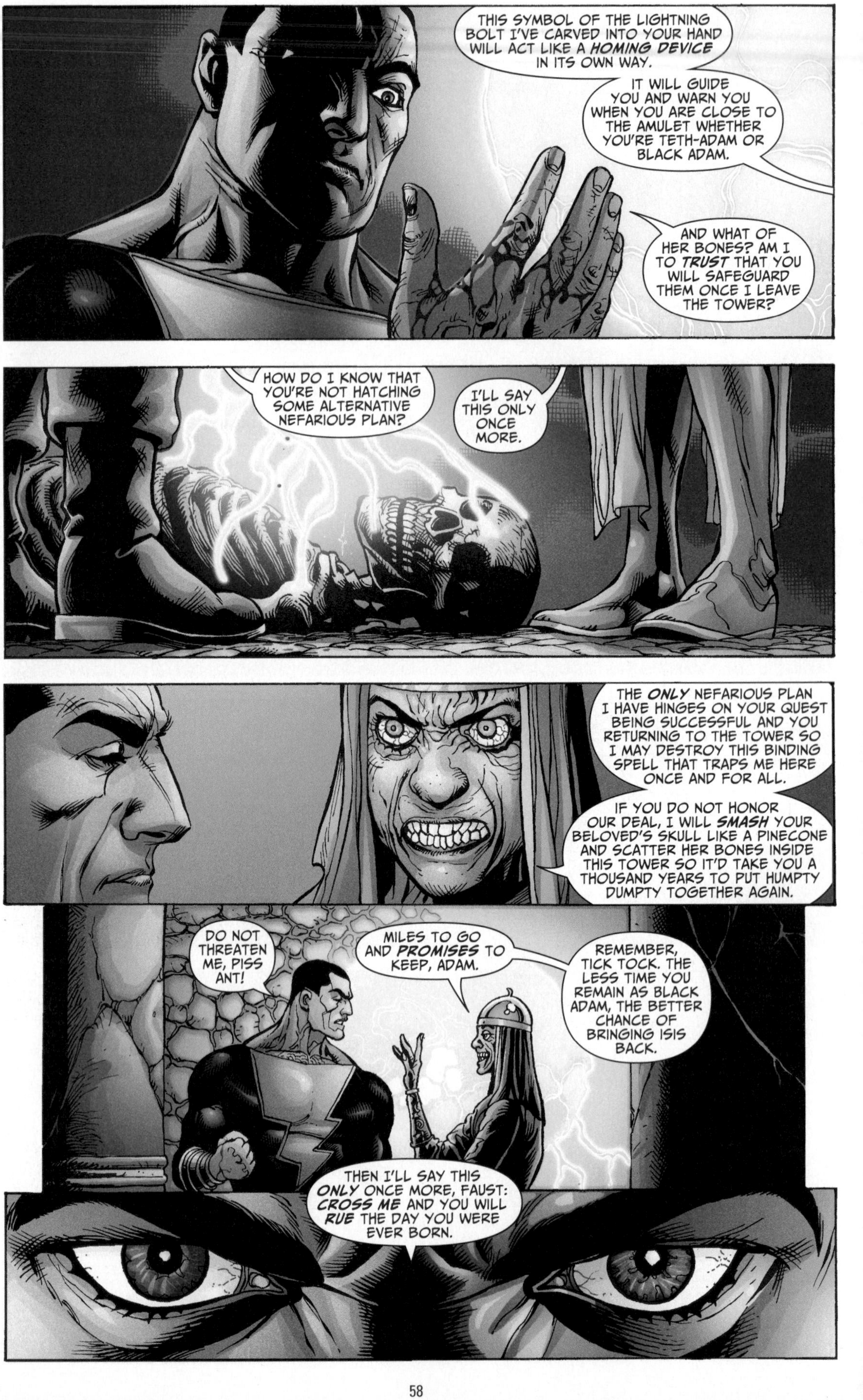

THIS SYMBOL OF THE LIGHTNING BOLT I'VE CARVED INTO YOUR HAND WILL ACT LIKE A HOMING DEVICE IN ITS OWN WAY.
IT WILL GUIDE YOU AND WARN YOU WHEN YOU ARE CLOSE TO THE AMULET WHETHER YOU'RE TETH-ADAM OR BLACK ADAM.
AND WHAT OF HER BONES? AM I TO TRUST THAT YOU WILL SAFEGUARD THEM ONCE I LEAVE THE TOWER?
HOW DO I KNOW THAT YOU'RE NOT HATCHING SOME ALTERNATIVE NEFARIOUS PLAN?
I'LL SAY THIS ONLY ONCE MORE.
THE ONLY NEFARIOUS PLAN I HAVE HINGES ON YOUR QUEST BEING SUCCESSFUL AND YOU RETURNING TO THE TOWER SO I MAY DESTROY THIS BINDING SPELL THAT TRAPS ME HERE ONCE AND FOR ALL.
IF YOU DO NOT HONOR OUR DEAL, I WILL SMASH YOUR BELOVED'S SKULL LIKE A PINECONE AND SCATTER HER BONES INSIDE THIS TOWER SO IT'D TAKE YOU A THOUSAND YEARS TO PUT HUMPTY DUMPTY TOGETHER AGAIN.
DO NOT THREATEN ME, PISS ANT!
MILES TO GO AND PROMISES TO KEEP, ADAM.
REMEMBER, TICK TOCK. THE LESS TIME YOU REMAIN AS BLACK ADAM, THE BETTER CHANCE OF BRINGING ISIS BACK.
THEN I'LL SAY THIS ONLY ONCE MORE, FAUST: CROSS ME AND YOU WILL RUE THE DAY YOU WERE EVER BORN.

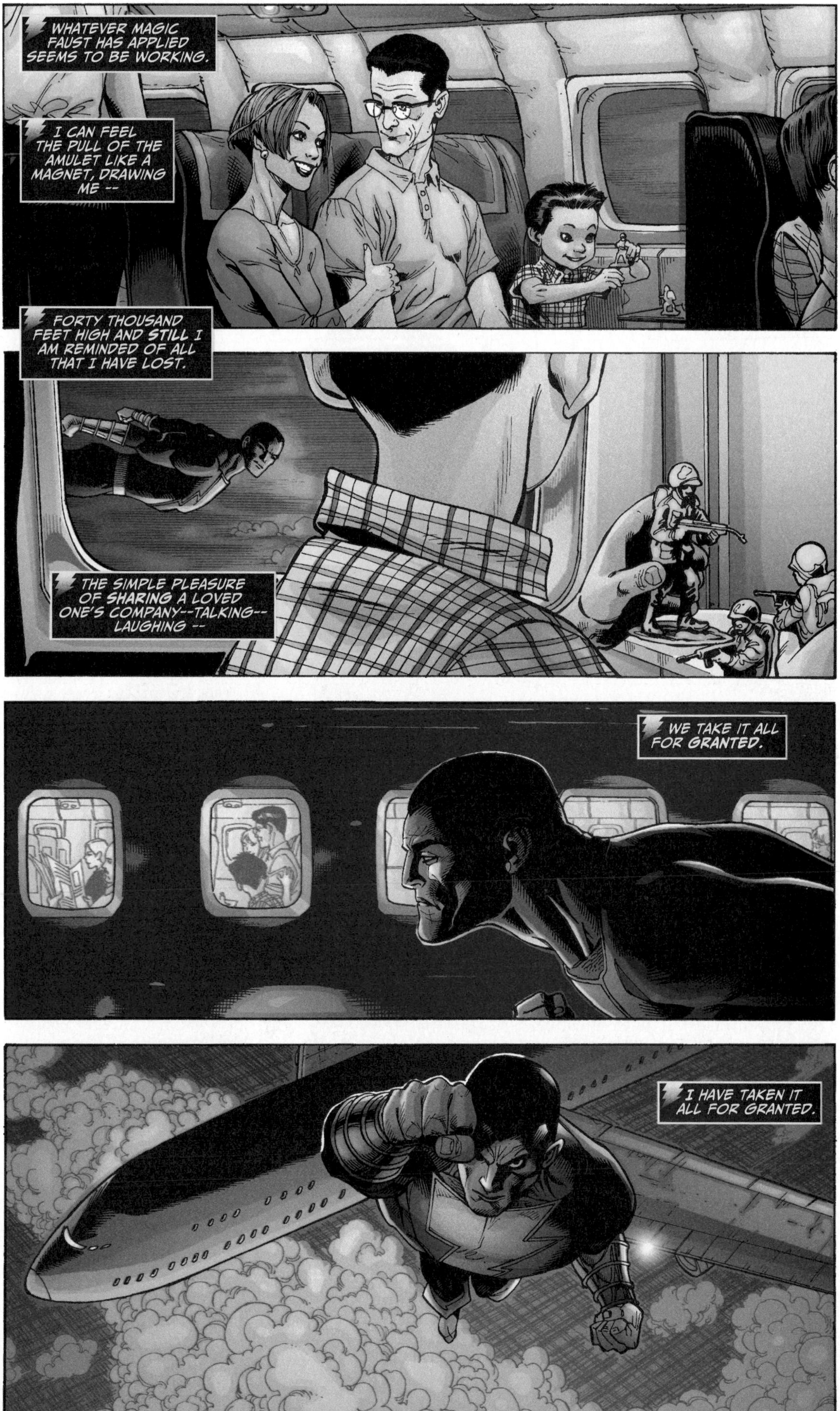
WHATEVER MAGIC FAUST HAS APPLIED SEEMS TO BE WORKING.
I CAN FEEL THE PULL OF THE AMULET LIKE A MAGNET, DRAWING ME --
FORTY THOUSAND FEET HIGH AND STILL I AM REMINDED OF ALL THAT I HAVE LOST.
THE SIMPLE PLEASURE OF SHARING A LOVED ONE'S COMPANY--TALKING--LAUGHING --
WE TAKE IT ALL FOR GRANTED.
I HAVE TAKEN IT ALL FOR GRANTED.

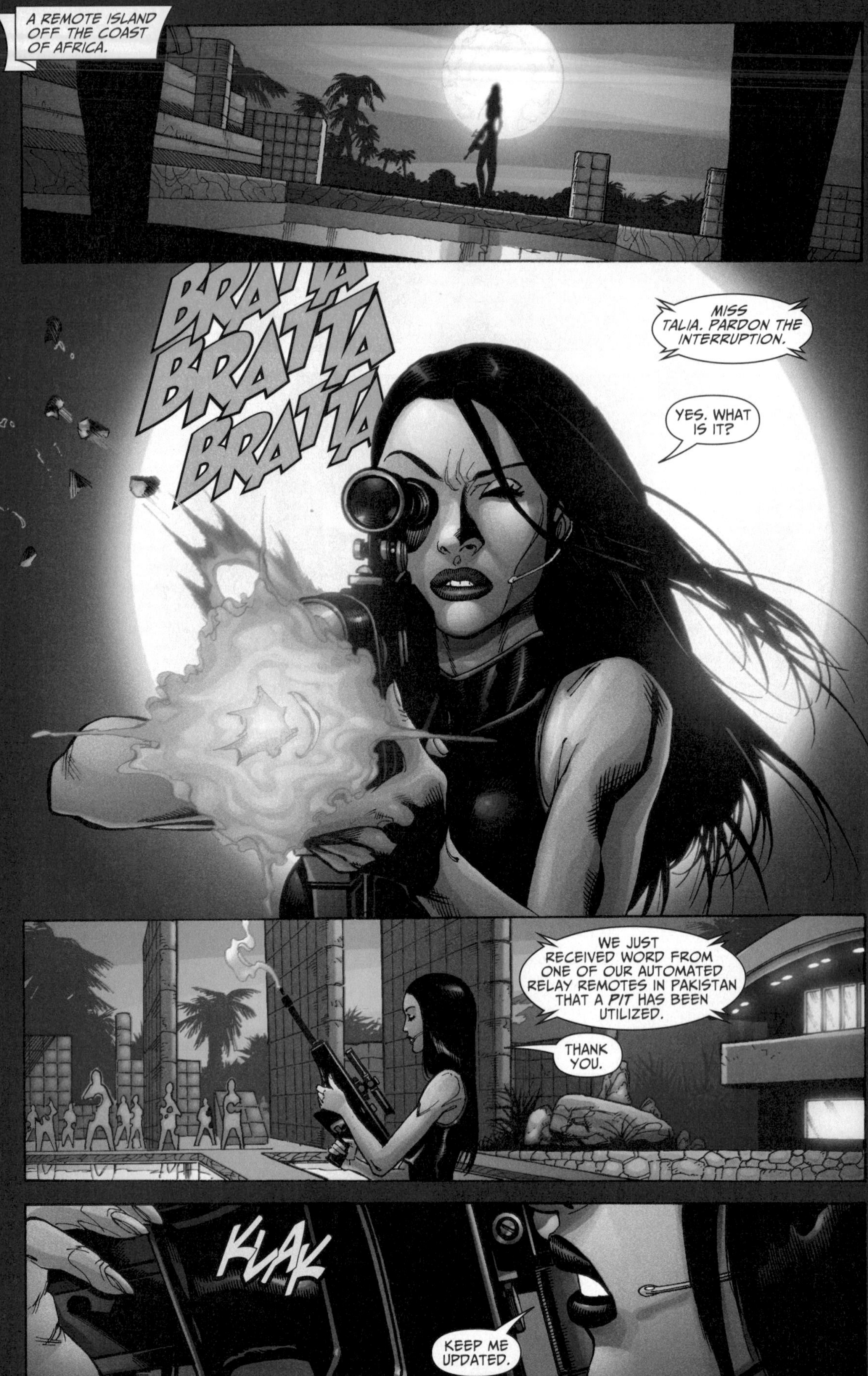
A REMOTE ISLAND OFF THE COAST OF AFRICA.
BRATTA BRATTA BRATTA
MISS TALIA. PARDON THE INTERRUPTION.
YES. WHAT IS IT?
WE JUST RECEIVED WORD FROM ONE OF OUR AUTOMATED RELAY REMOTES IN PAKISTAN THAT A PIT HAS BEEN UTILIZED.
THANK YOU.
KLAK
KEEP ME UPDATED.

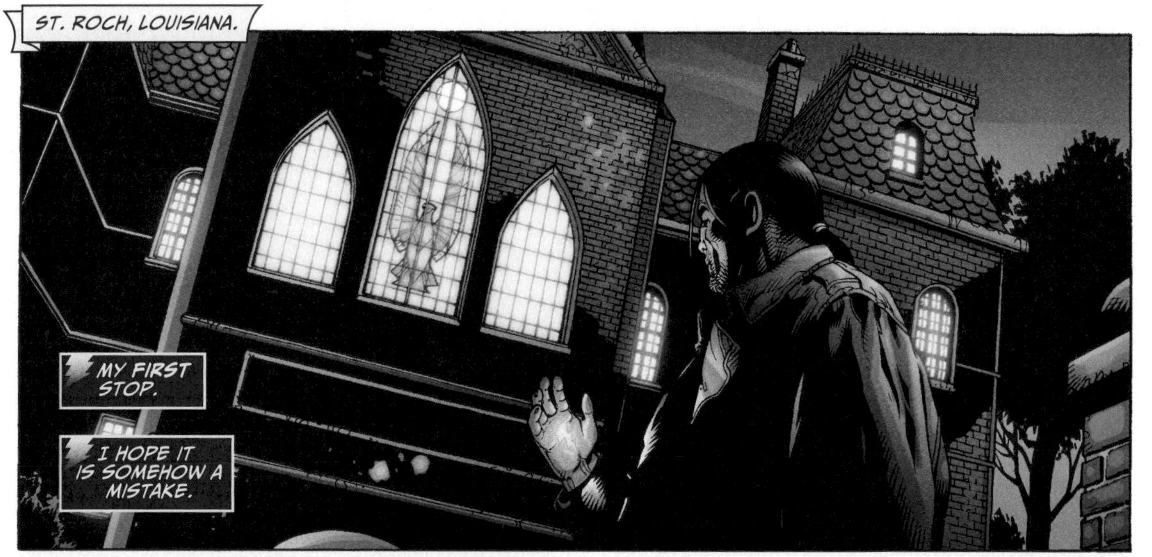
ST. ROCH, LOUISIANA.
MY FIRST STOP.
I HOPE IT IS SOMEHOW A MISTAKE.

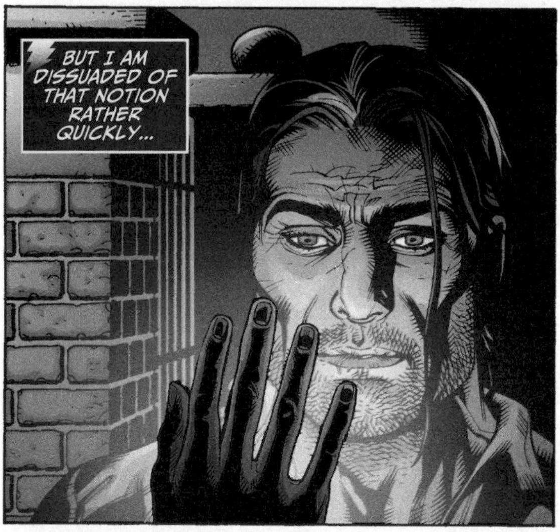
BUT I AM DISSUADED OF THAT NOTION RATHER QUICKLY...

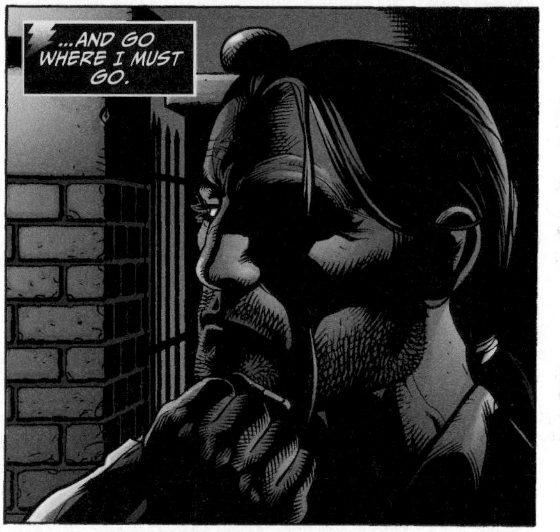
...AND GO WHERE I MUST GO.

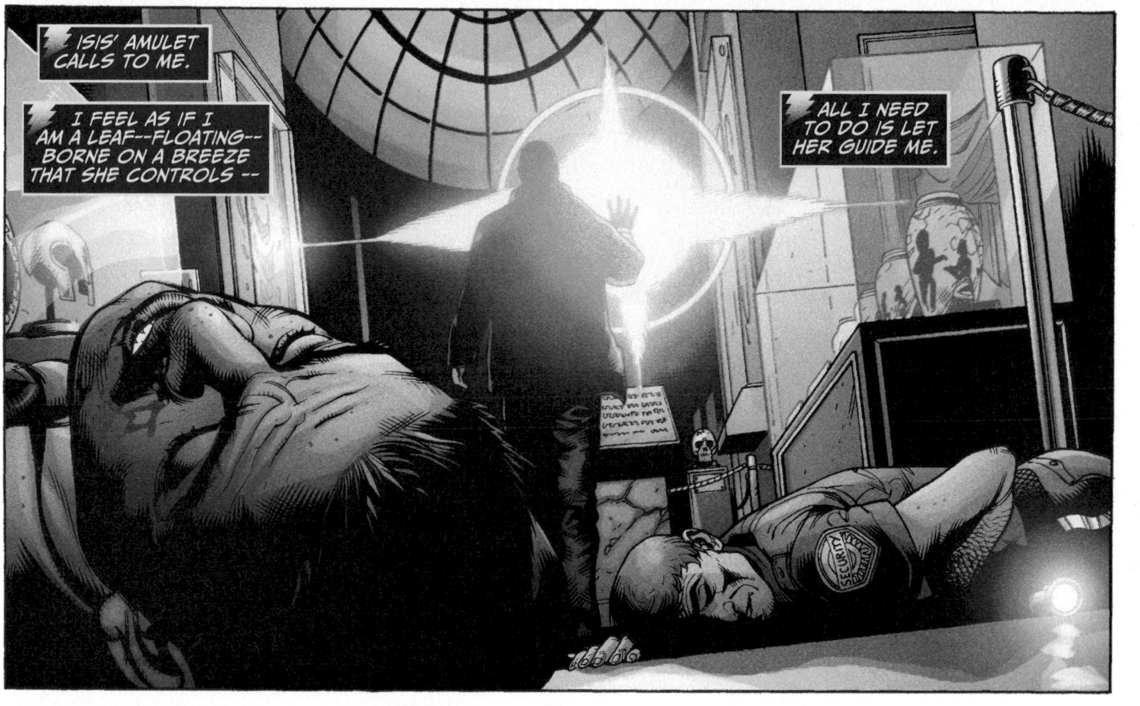
ISIS' AMULET CALLS TO ME.
I FEEL AS IF I AM A LEAF--FLOATING-- BORNE ON A BREEZE THAT SHE CONTROLS --
ALL I NEED TO DO IS LET HER GUIDE ME.

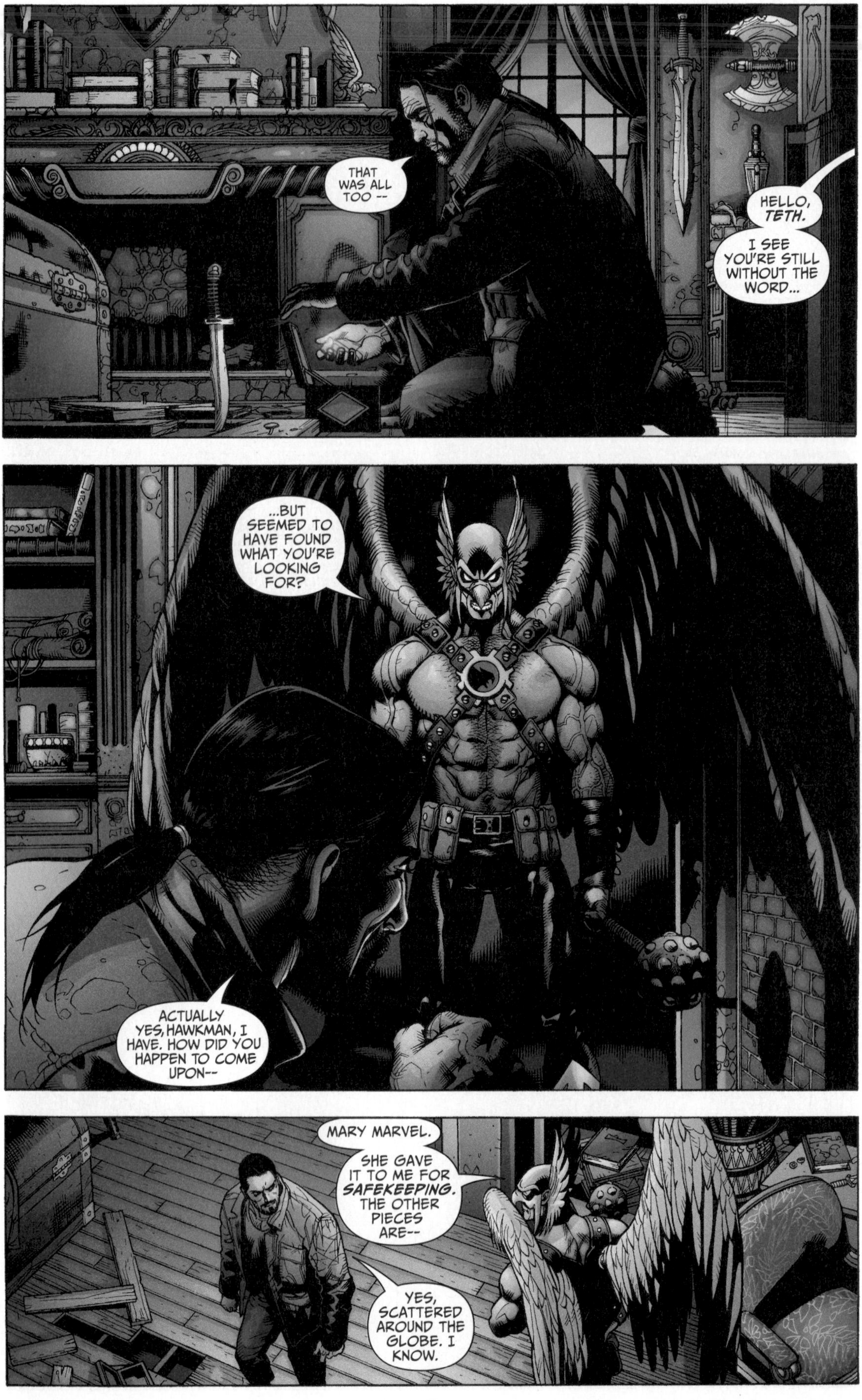
THAT WAS ALL TOO --
HELLO, *TETH.*
I SEE YOU'RE STILL WITHOUT THE WORD...
...BUT SEEMED TO HAVE FOUND WHAT YOU'RE LOOKING FOR?
ACTUALLY YES, HAWKMAN, I HAVE. HOW DID YOU HAPPEN TO COME UPON--
MARY MARVEL.
SHE GAVE IT TO ME FOR *SAFEKEEPING.* THE OTHER PIECES ARE--
YES, SCATTERED AROUND THE GLOBE. I KNOW.

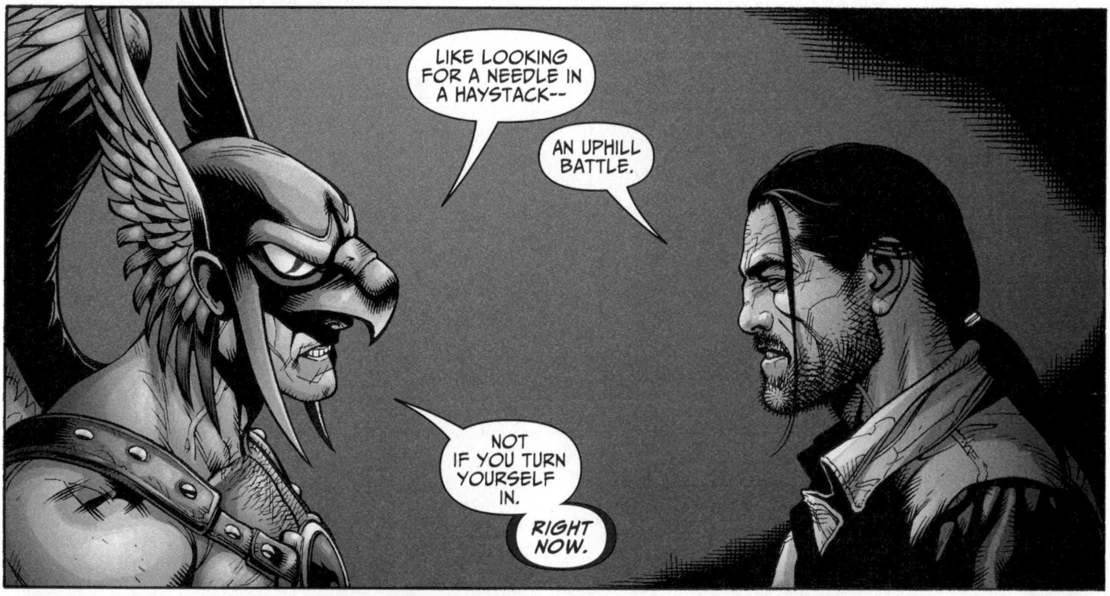

LIKE LOOKING FOR A NEEDLE IN A HAYSTACK--
AN UPHILL BATTLE.
NOT IF YOU TURN YOURSELF IN.
RIGHT NOW.

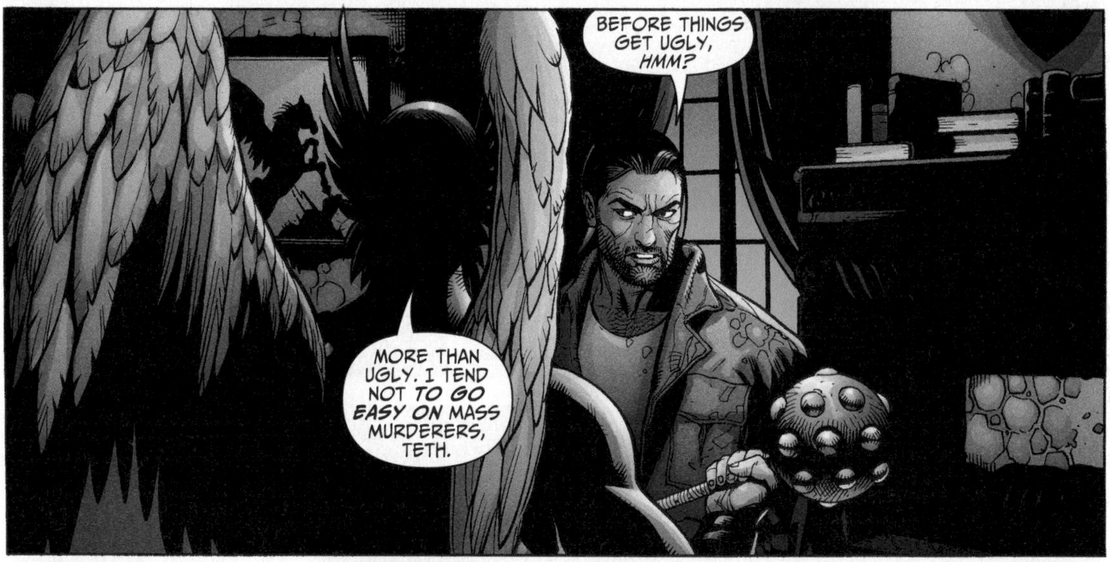

BEFORE THINGS GET UGLY, HMM?
MORE THAN UGLY. I TEND NOT TO GO EASY ON MASS MURDERERS, TETH.

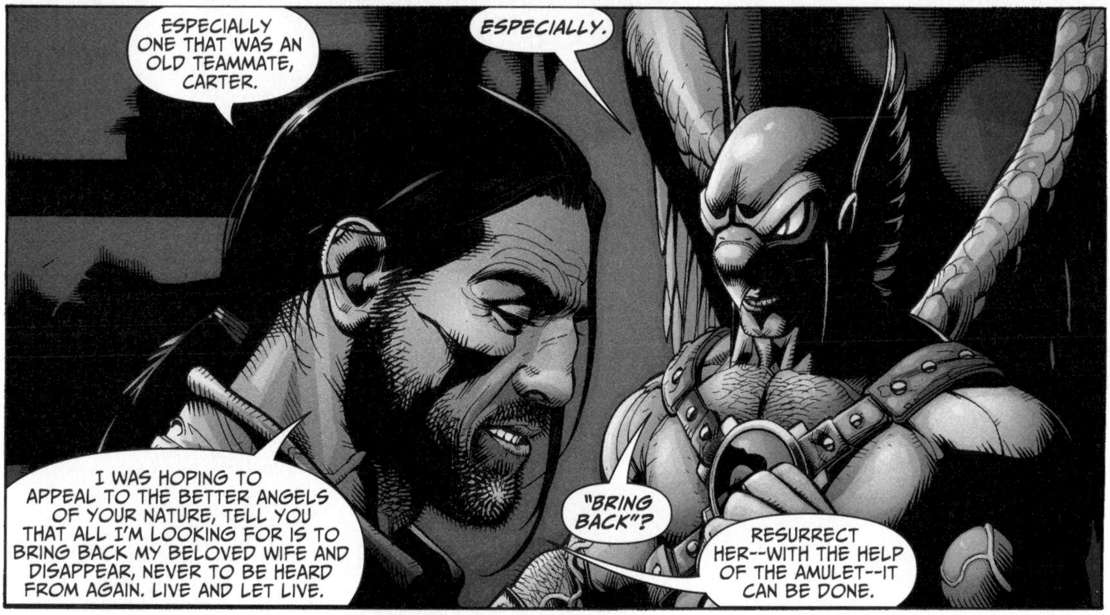

ESPECIALLY ONE THAT WAS AN OLD TEAMMATE, CARTER.
ESPECIALLY.
I WAS HOPING TO APPEAL TO THE BETTER ANGELS OF YOUR NATURE, TELL YOU THAT ALL I'M LOOKING FOR IS TO BRING BACK MY BELOVED WIFE AND DISAPPEAR, NEVER TO BE HEARD FROM AGAIN. LIVE AND LET LIVE.
"BRING BACK"?
RESURRECT HER--WITH THE HELP OF THE AMULET--IT CAN BE DONE.

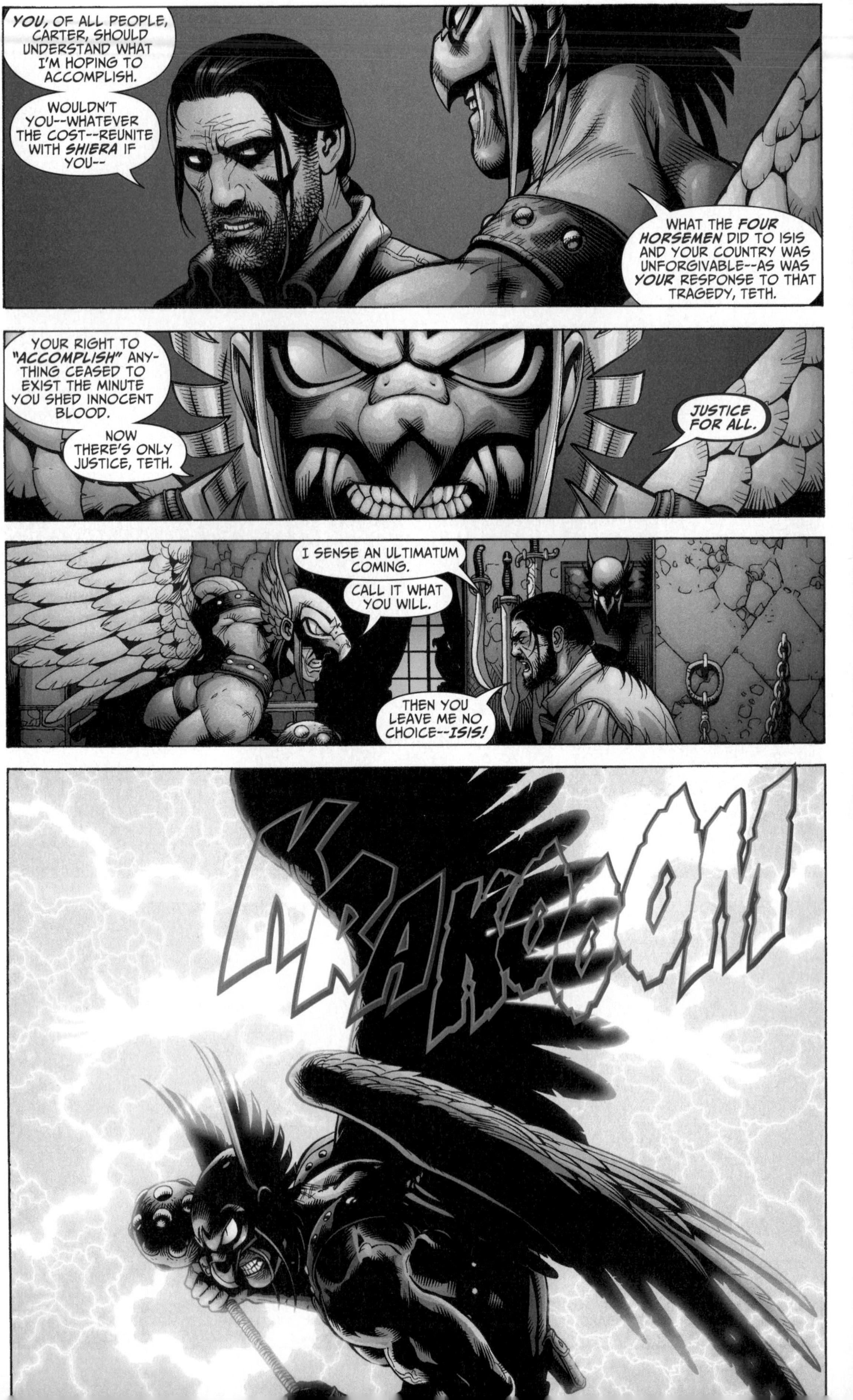
YOU, OF ALL PEOPLE, CARTER, SHOULD UNDERSTAND WHAT I'M HOPING TO ACCOMPLISH.
WOULDN'T YOU--WHATEVER THE COST--REUNITE WITH SHIERA IF YOU--
WHAT THE FOUR HORSEMEN DID TO ISIS AND YOUR COUNTRY WAS UNFORGIVABLE--AS WAS YOUR RESPONSE TO THAT TRAGEDY, TETH.
YOUR RIGHT TO "ACCOMPLISH" ANYTHING CEASED TO EXIST THE MINUTE YOU SHED INNOCENT BLOOD.
NOW THERE'S ONLY JUSTICE, TETH.
JUSTICE FOR ALL.
I SENSE AN ULTIMATUM COMING.
CALL IT WHAT YOU WILL.
THEN YOU LEAVE ME NO CHOICE--ISIS!
KRAKOOM

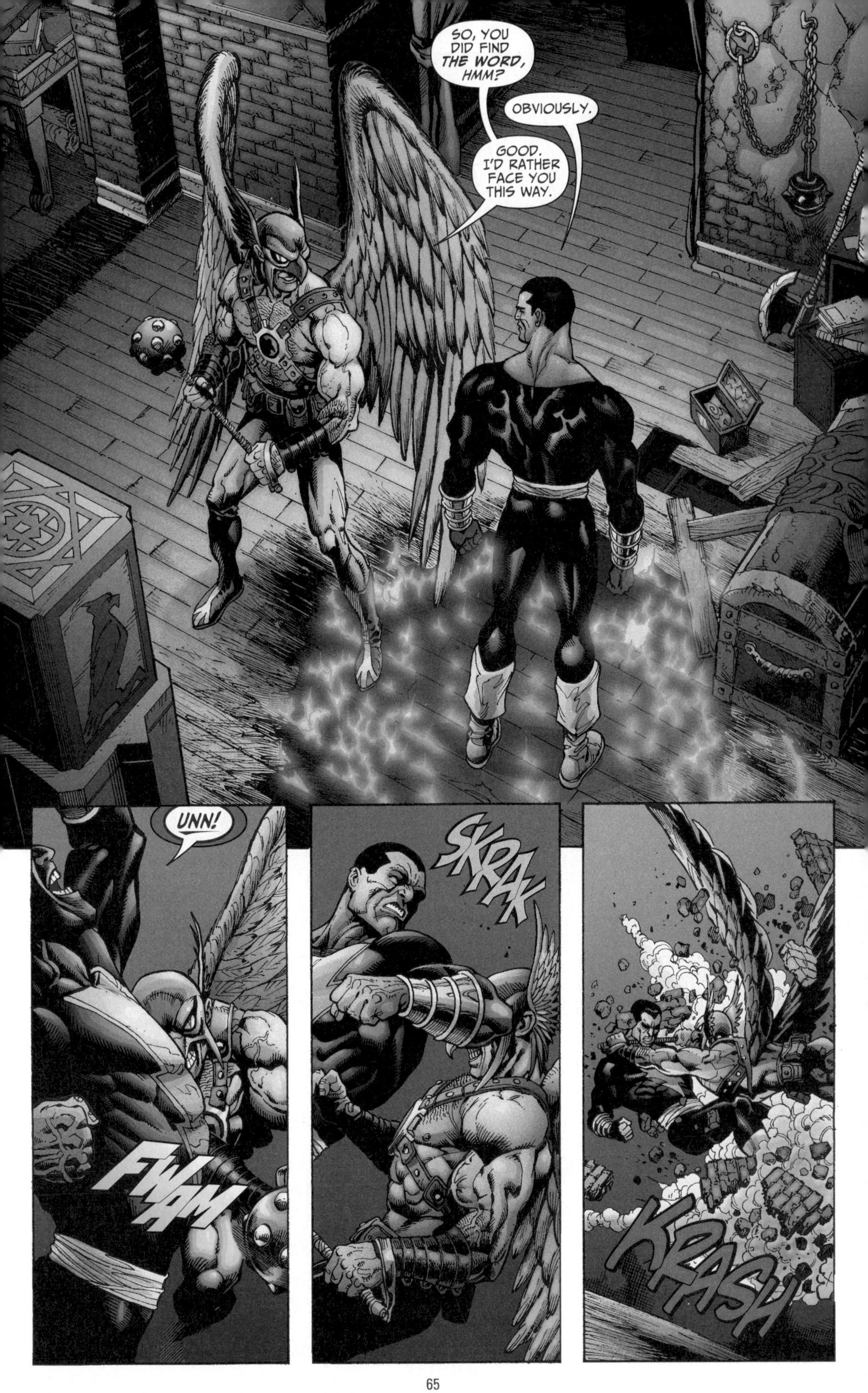
SO, YOU DID FIND THE WORD, HMM?
OBVIOUSLY.
GOOD. I'D RATHER FACE YOU THIS WAY.
UNN!
FWAM
SKRAK
KRASH

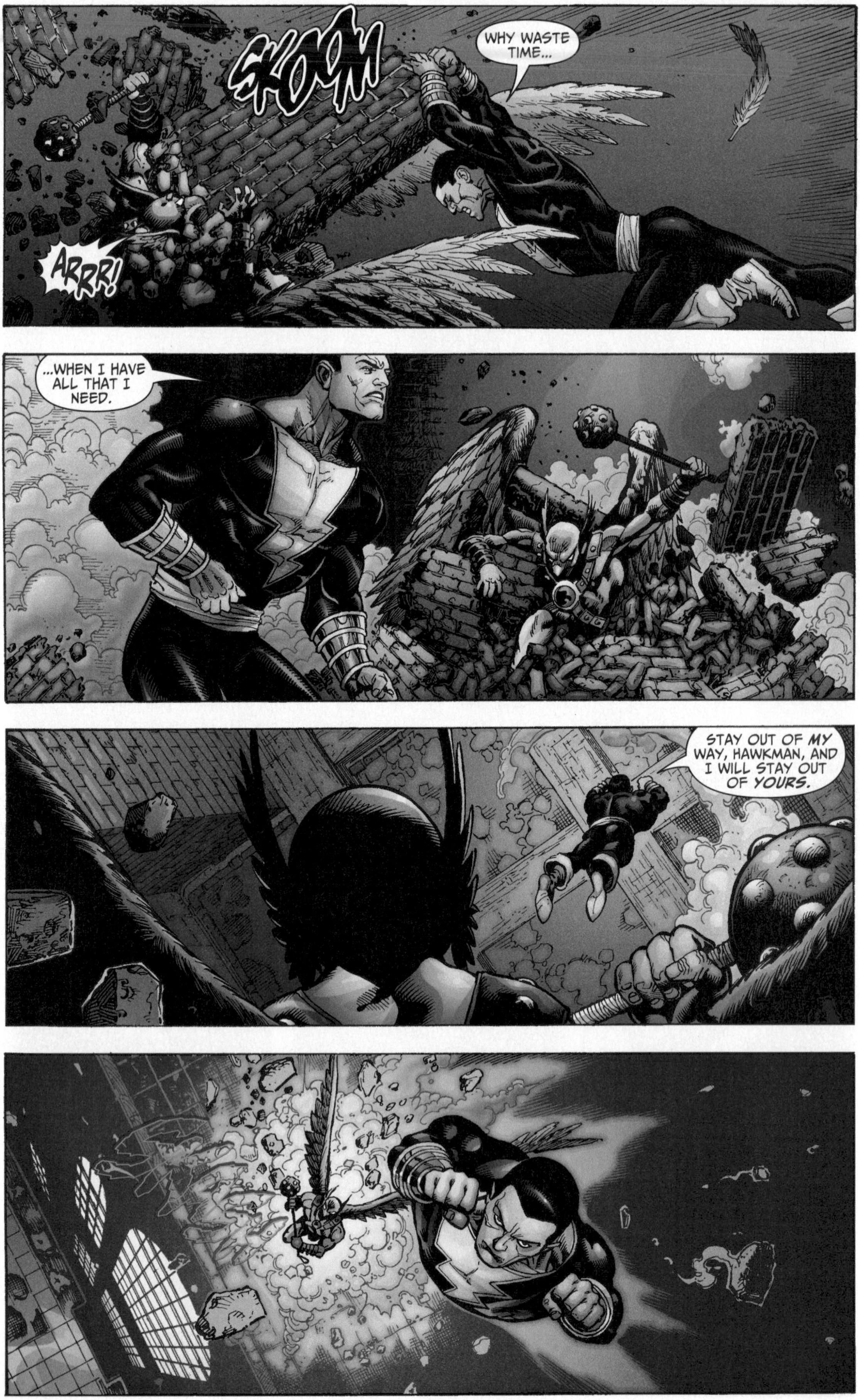
SKOOM
WHY WASTE TIME...
ARRR!
...WHEN I HAVE ALL THAT I NEED.
STAY OUT OF *MY* WAY, HAWKMAN, AND I WILL STAY OUT OF *YOURS*.

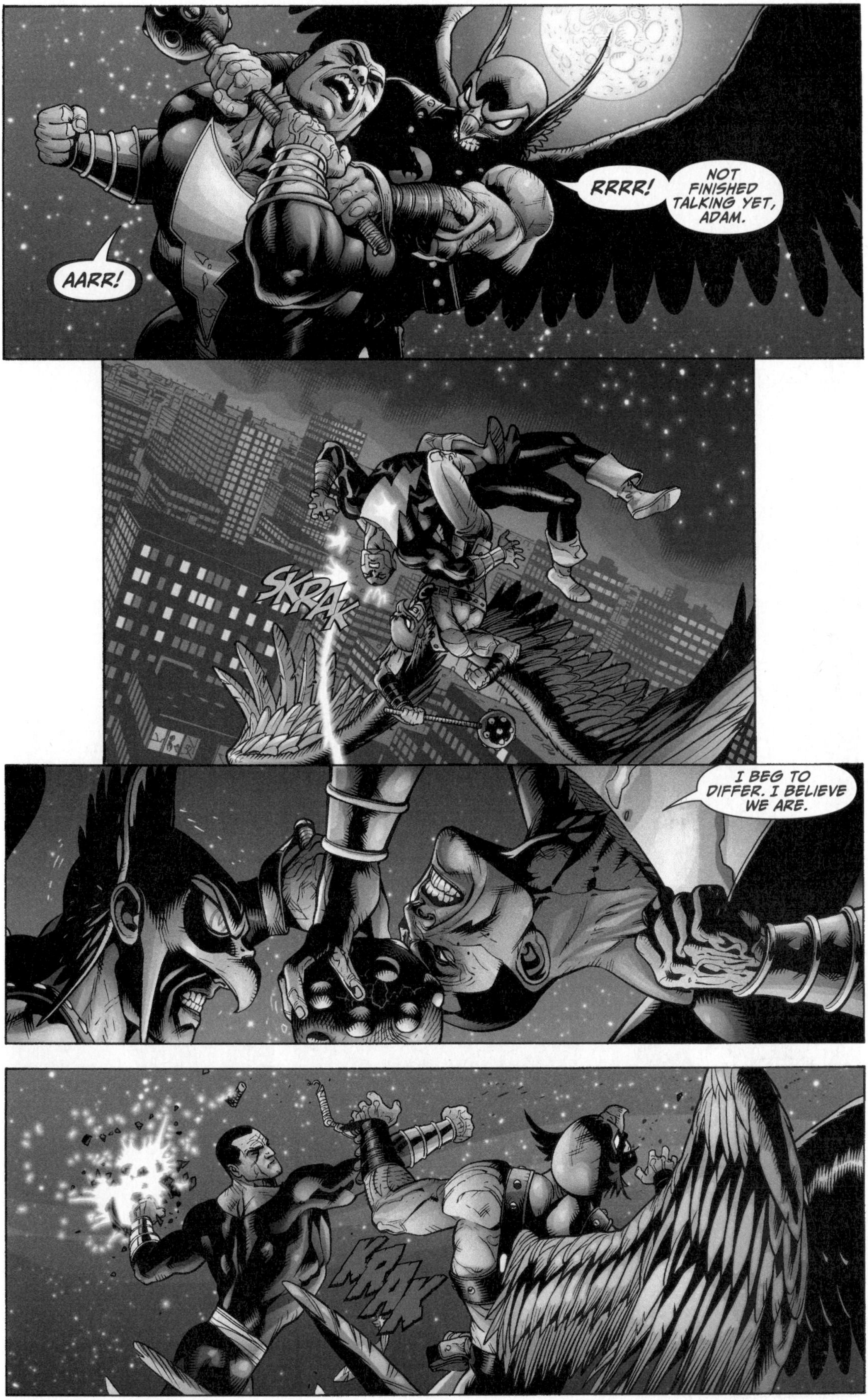
RRRR!
NOT FINISHED TALKING YET, ADAM.
AARR!
SKRAK
I BEG TO DIFFER. I BELIEVE WE ARE.
KRAK

SHRRAPP

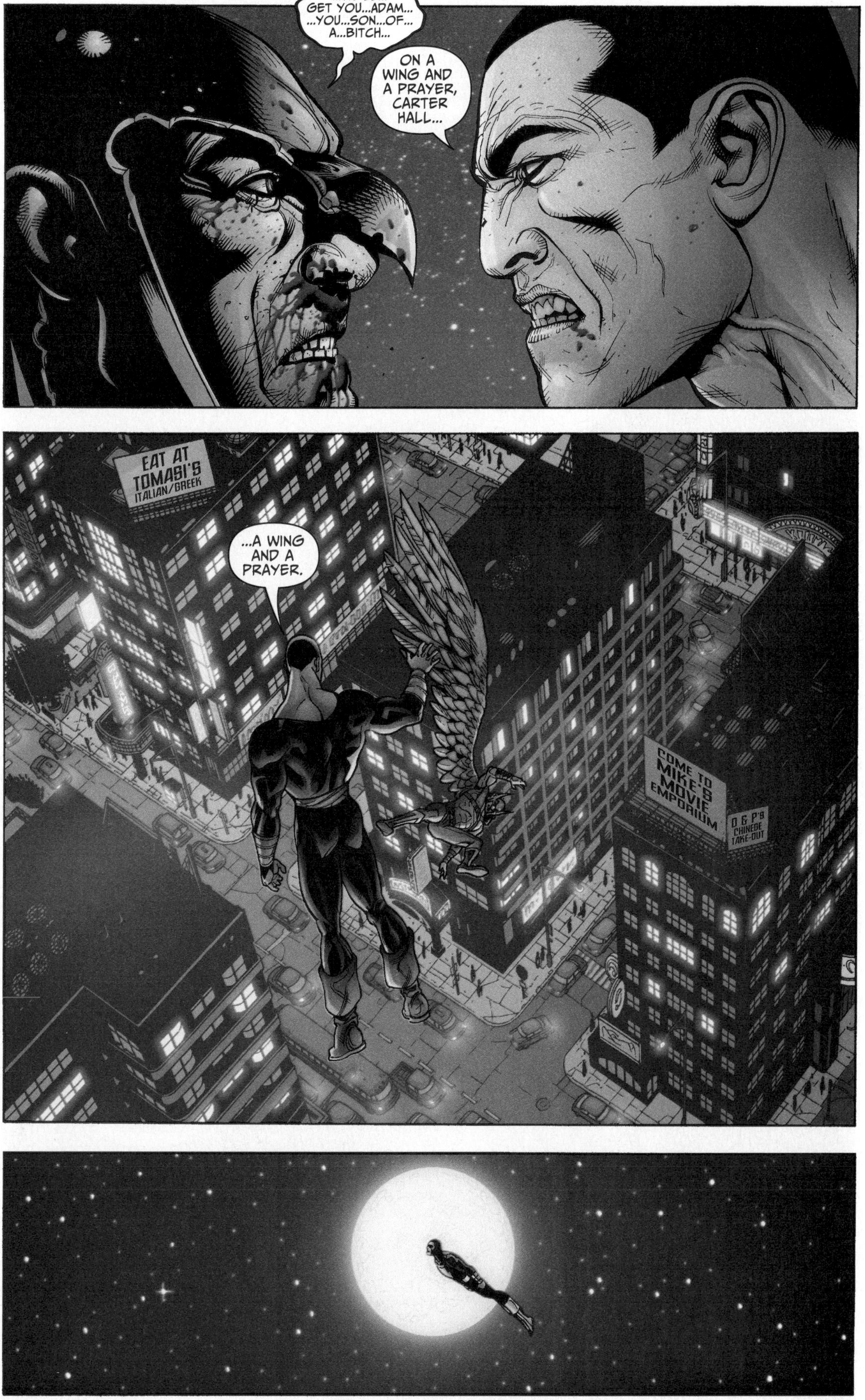
...WE'LL... GET YOU...ADAM... ...YOU...SON...OF... A...BITCH...
ON A WING AND A PRAYER, CARTER HALL...
EAT AT TOMASI'S ITALIAN/GREEK
...A WING AND A PRAYER.
COME TO MIKE'S MOVIE EMPORIUM
D & P's CHINESE TAKE-OUT

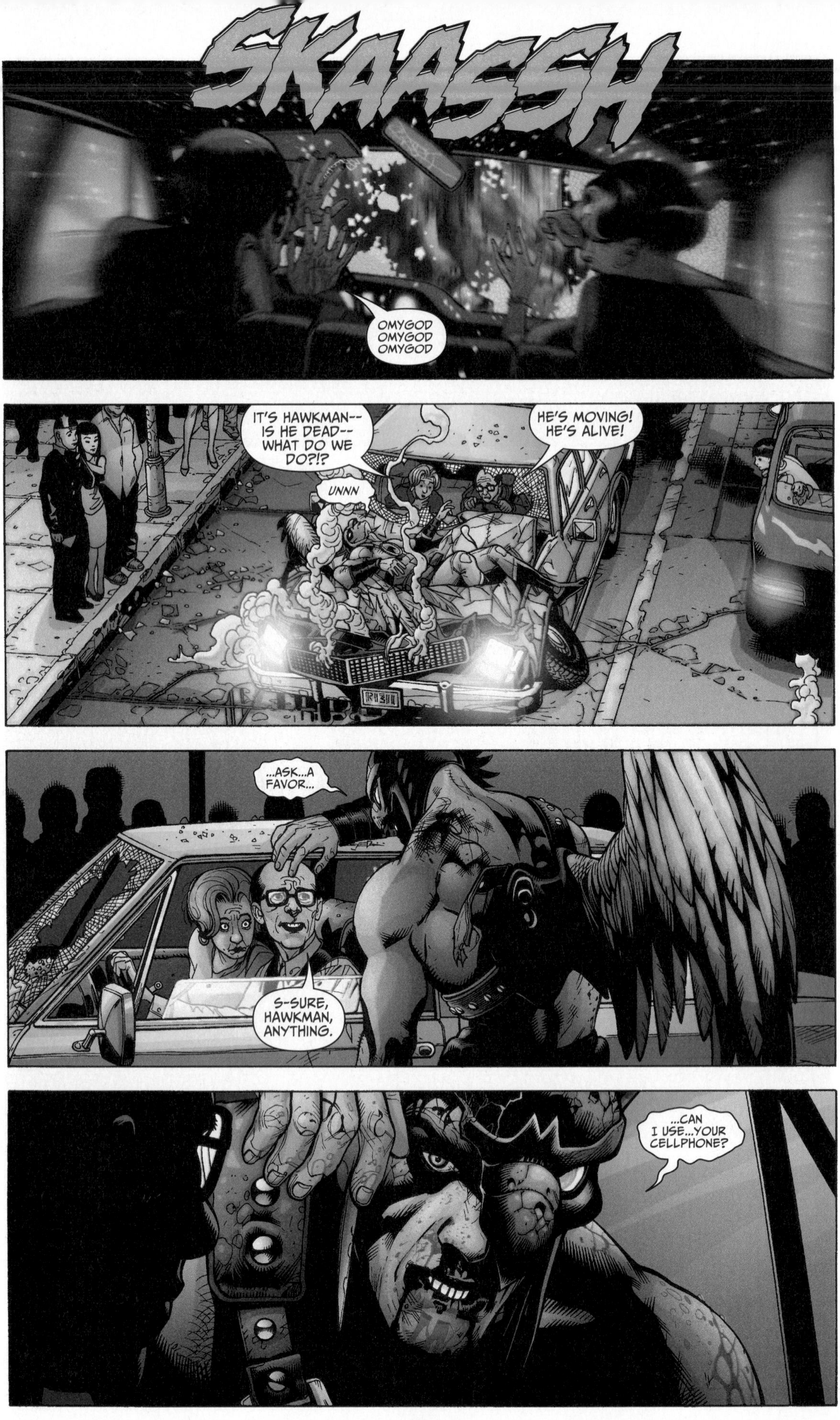
SKAASSH
OMYGOD OMYGOD OMYGOD
IT'S HAWKMAN-- IS HE DEAD-- WHAT DO WE DO?!?
HE'S MOVING! HE'S ALIVE!
UNNN
...ASK...A FAVOR...
S-SURE, HAWKMAN, ANYTHING.
...CAN I USE...YOUR CELLPHONE?

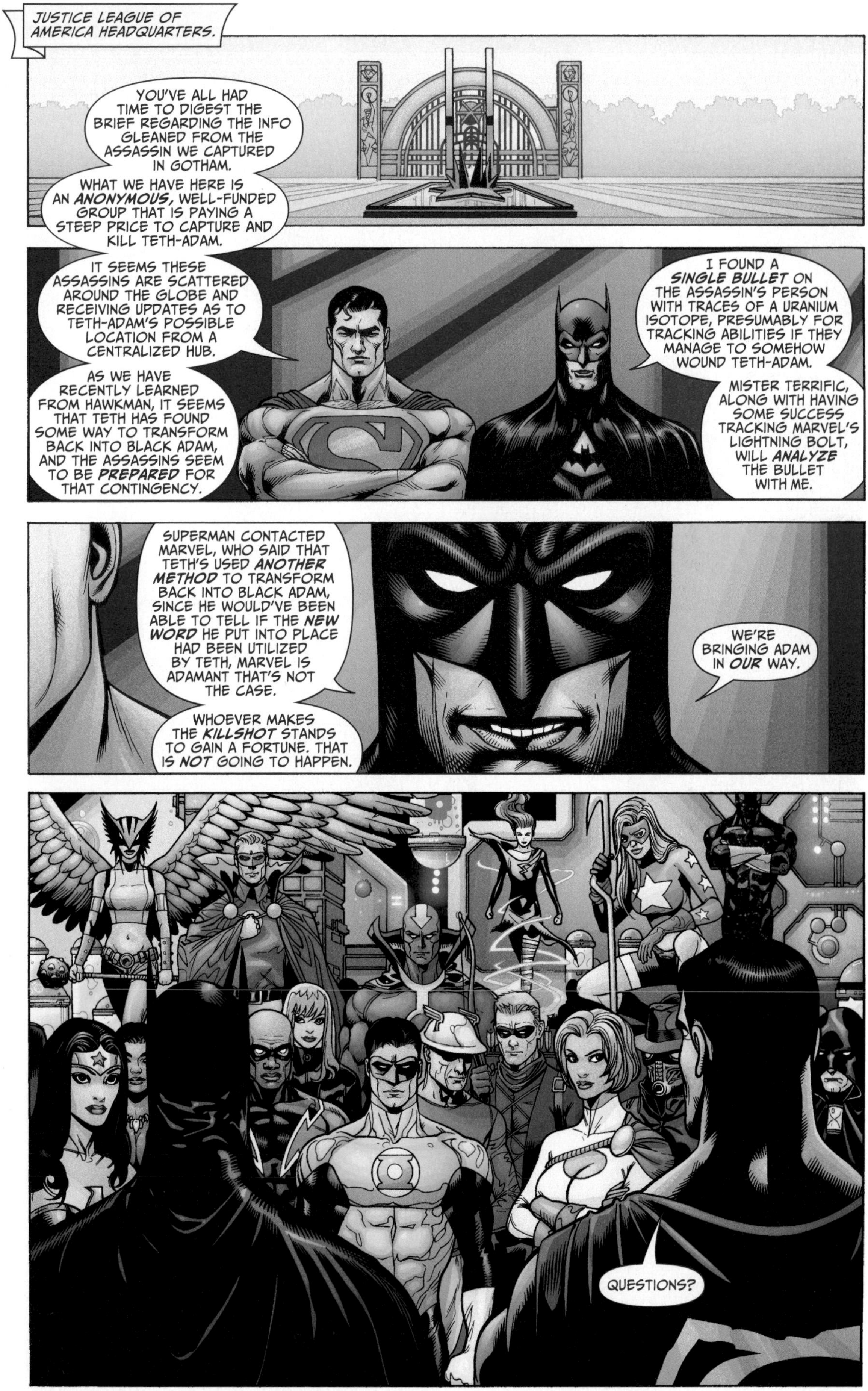
JUSTICE LEAGUE OF AMERICA HEADQUARTERS.
YOU'VE ALL HAD TIME TO DIGEST THE BRIEF REGARDING THE INFO GLEANED FROM THE ASSASSIN WE CAPTURED IN GOTHAM.
WHAT WE HAVE HERE IS AN ANONYMOUS, WELL-FUNDED GROUP THAT IS PAYING A STEEP PRICE TO CAPTURE AND KILL TETH-ADAM.
IT SEEMS THESE ASSASSINS ARE SCATTERED AROUND THE GLOBE AND RECEIVING UPDATES AS TO TETH-ADAM'S POSSIBLE LOCATION FROM A CENTRALIZED HUB.
AS WE HAVE RECENTLY LEARNED FROM HAWKMAN, IT SEEMS THAT TETH HAS FOUND SOME WAY TO TRANSFORM BACK INTO BLACK ADAM, AND THE ASSASSINS SEEM TO BE PREPARED FOR THAT CONTINGENCY.
I FOUND A SINGLE BULLET ON THE ASSASSIN'S PERSON WITH TRACES OF A URANIUM ISOTOPE, PRESUMABLY FOR TRACKING ABILITIES IF THEY MANAGE TO SOMEHOW WOUND TETH-ADAM.
MISTER TERRIFIC, ALONG WITH HAVING SOME SUCCESS TRACKING MARVEL'S LIGHTNING BOLT, WILL ANALYZE THE BULLET WITH ME.
SUPERMAN CONTACTED MARVEL, WHO SAID THAT TETH'S USED ANOTHER METHOD TO TRANSFORM BACK INTO BLACK ADAM, SINCE HE WOULD'VE BEEN ABLE TO TELL IF THE NEW WORD HE PUT INTO PLACE HAD BEEN UTILIZED BY TETH, MARVEL IS ADAMANT THAT'S NOT THE CASE.
WHOEVER MAKES THE KILLSHOT STANDS TO GAIN A FORTUNE. THAT IS NOT GOING TO HAPPEN.
WE'RE BRINGING ADAM IN OUR WAY.
QUESTIONS?

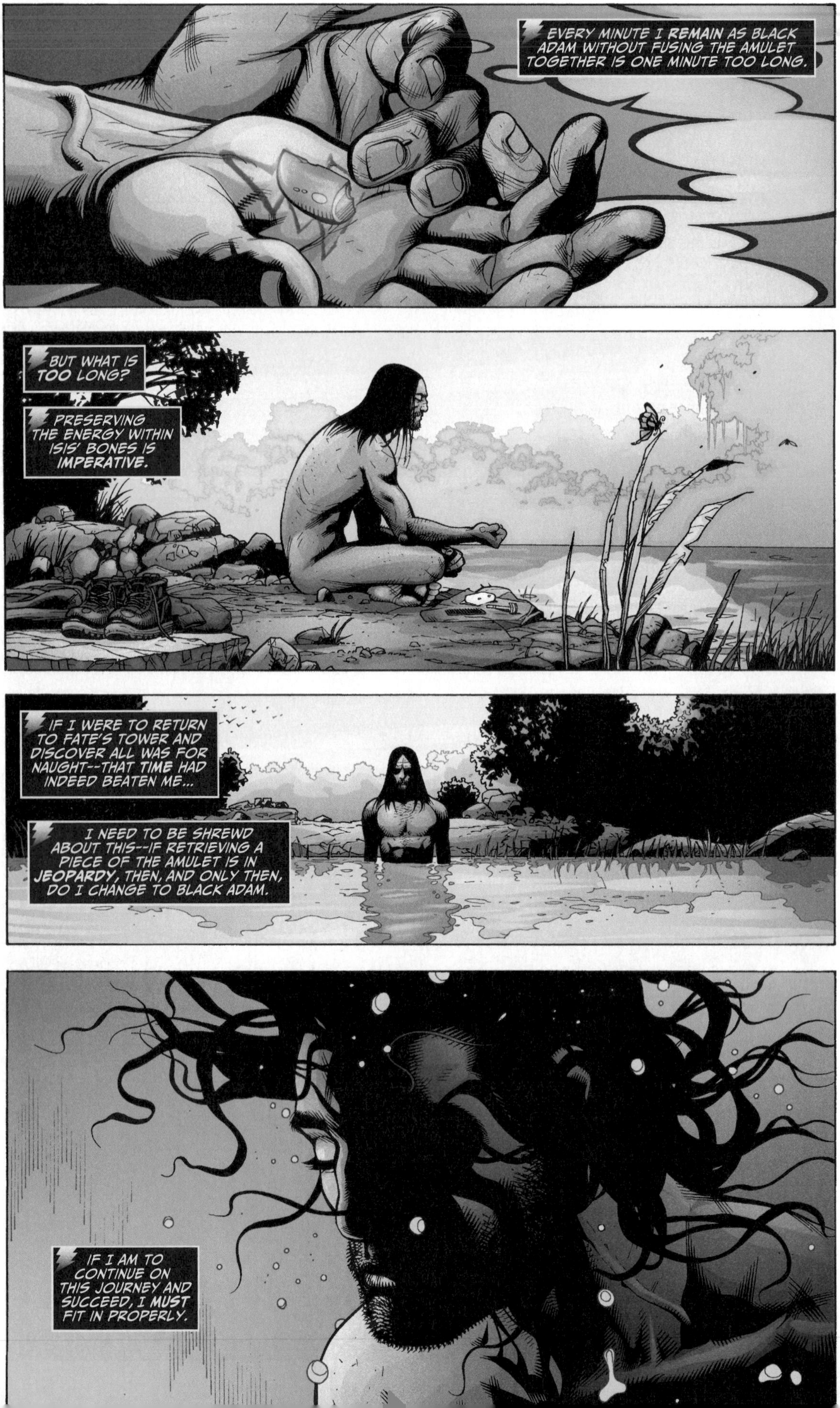
EVERY MINUTE I REMAIN AS BLACK ADAM WITHOUT FUSING THE AMULET TOGETHER IS ONE MINUTE TOO LONG.
BUT WHAT IS TOO LONG?
PRESERVING THE ENERGY WITHIN ISIS' BONES IS IMPERATIVE.
IF I WERE TO RETURN TO FATE'S TOWER AND DISCOVER ALL WAS FOR NAUGHT--THAT TIME HAD INDEED BEATEN ME...
I NEED TO BE SHREWD ABOUT THIS--IF RETRIEVING A PIECE OF THE AMULET IS IN JEOPARDY, THEN, AND ONLY THEN, DO I CHANGE TO BLACK ADAM.
IF I AM TO CONTINUE ON THIS JOURNEY AND SUCCEED, I MUST FIT IN PROPERLY.

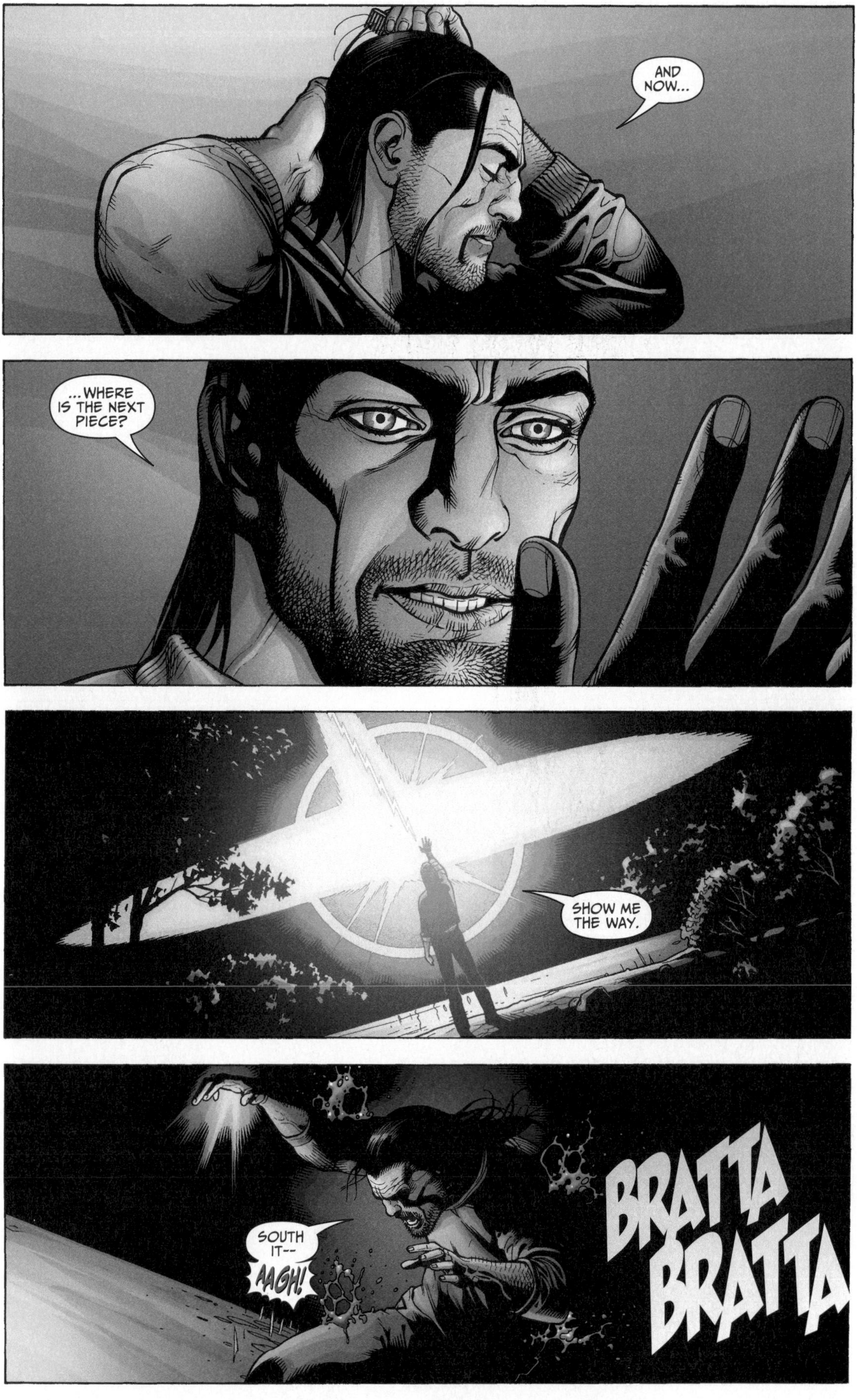
AND NOW...
...WHERE IS THE NEXT PIECE?
SHOW ME THE WAY.
BRATTA BRATTA
SOUTH IT--
AAGH!

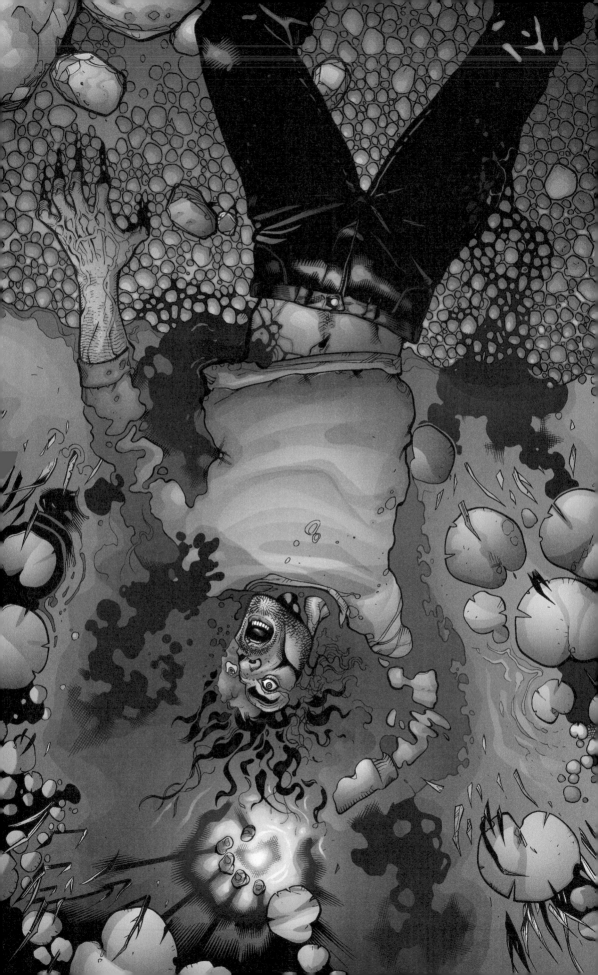

Chapter Four

This chapter inked by Christian Alamy

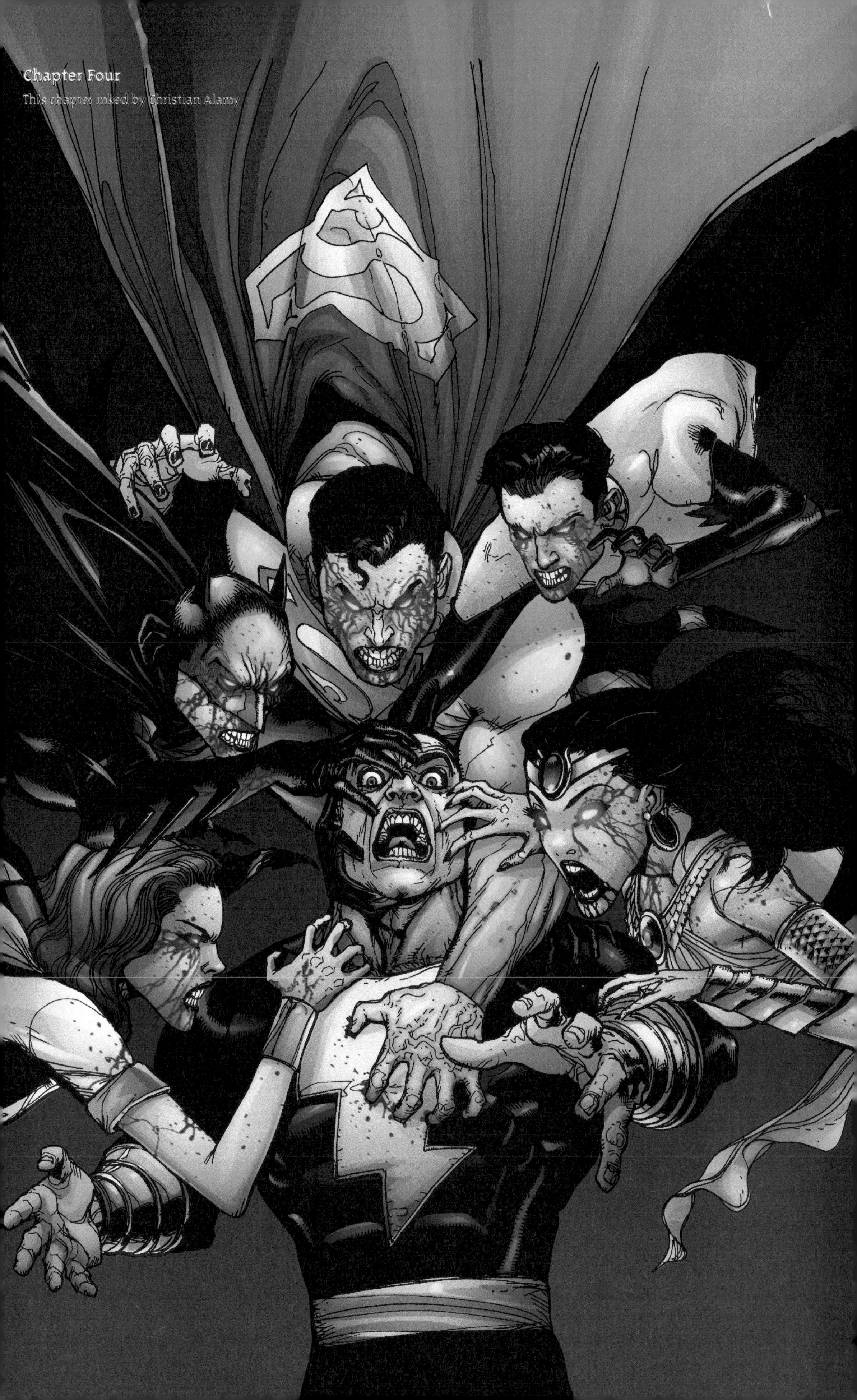

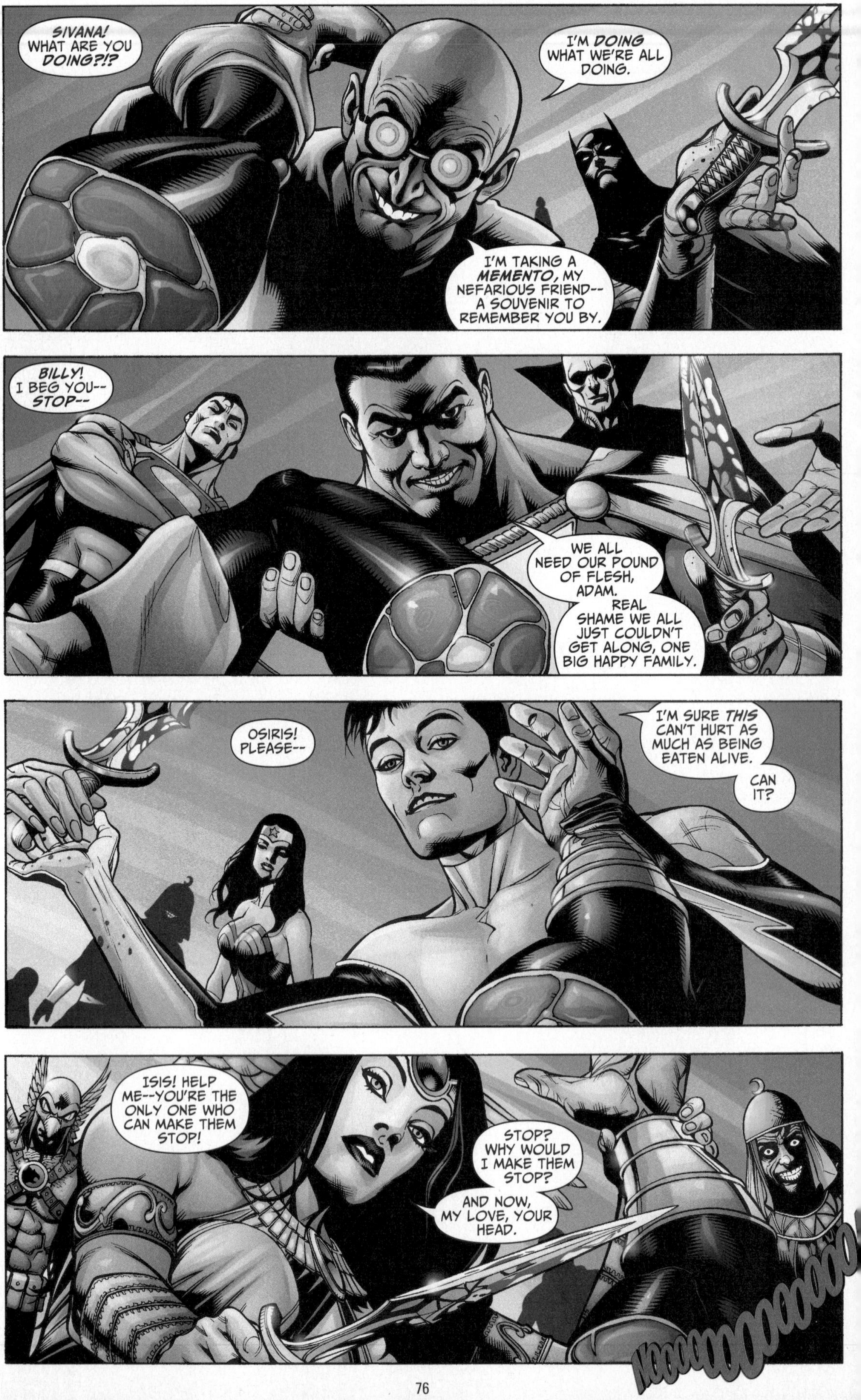
SIVANA! WHAT ARE YOU DOING?!?
I'M DOING WHAT WE'RE ALL DOING.
I'M TAKING A MEMENTO, MY NEFARIOUS FRIEND-- A SOUVENIR TO REMEMBER YOU BY.
BILLY! I BEG YOU-- STOP--
WE ALL NEED OUR POUND OF FLESH, ADAM.
REAL SHAME WE ALL JUST COULDN'T GET ALONG, ONE BIG HAPPY FAMILY.
OSIRIS! PLEASE--
I'M SURE THIS CAN'T HURT AS MUCH AS BEING EATEN ALIVE.
CAN IT?
ISIS! HELP ME--YOU'RE THE ONLY ONE WHO CAN MAKE THEM STOP!
STOP? WHY WOULD I MAKE THEM STOP?
AND NOW, MY LOVE, YOUR HEAD.
NOOOOOOOOOOOOOO

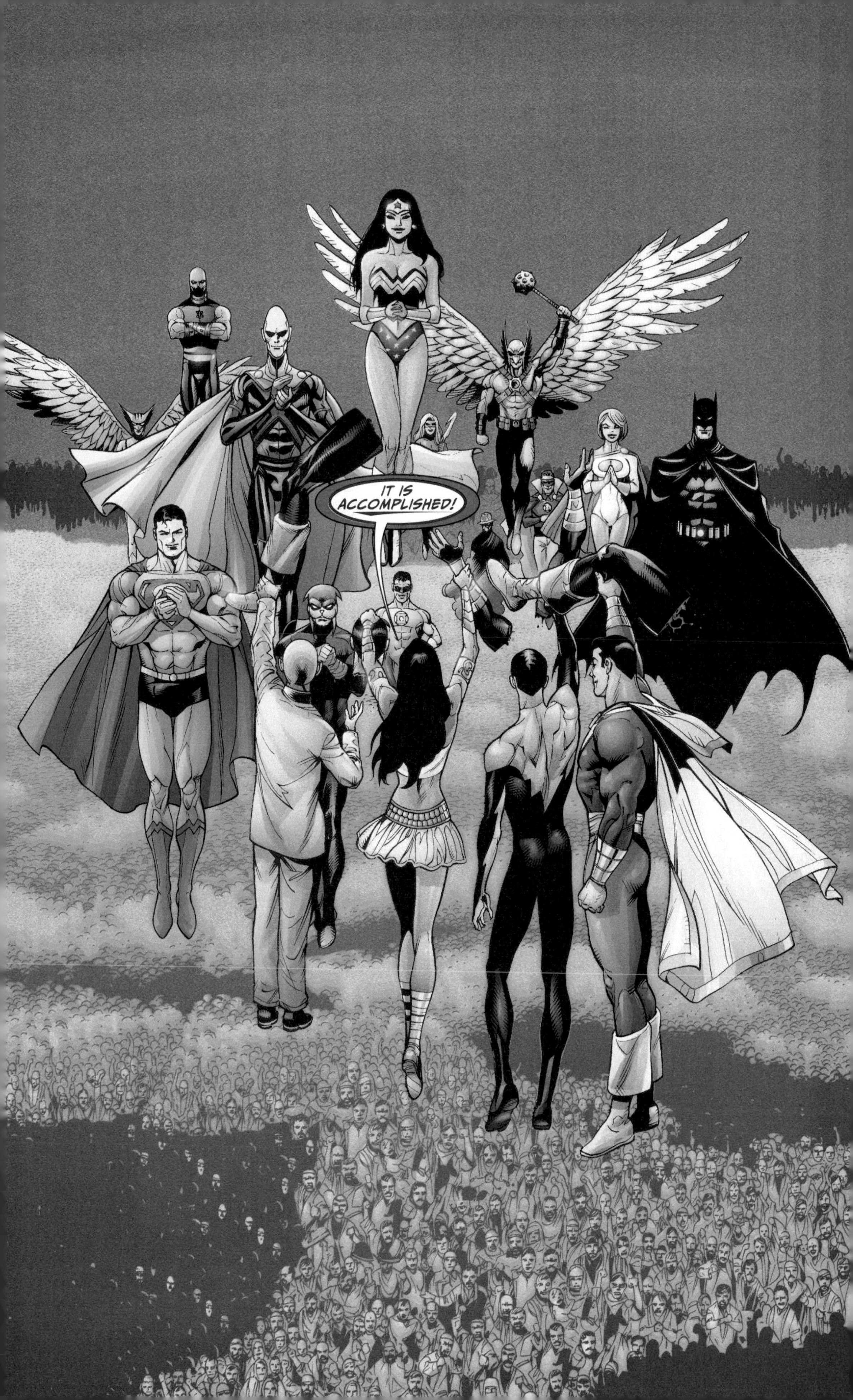
IT IS ACCOMPLISHED!

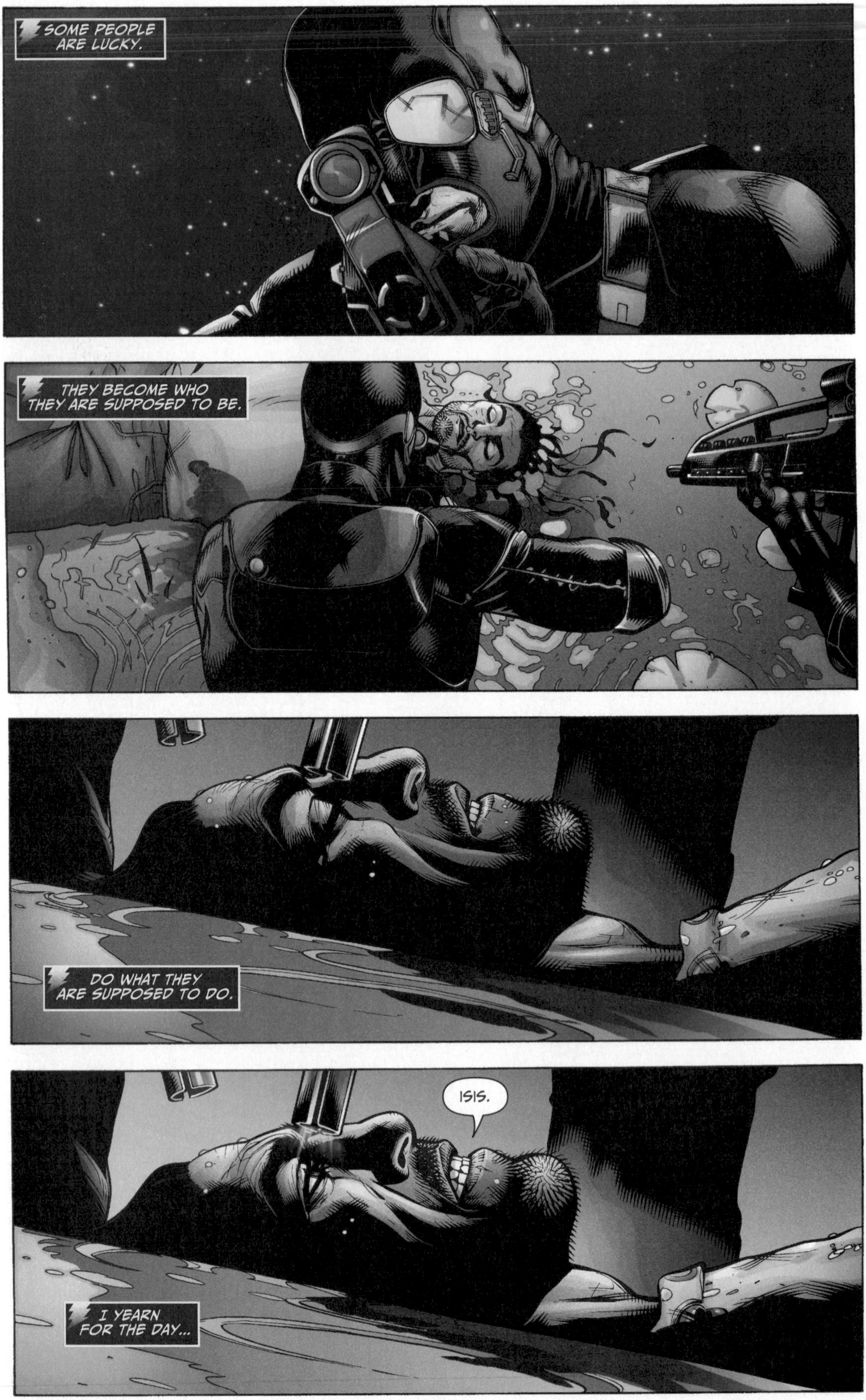
SOME PEOPLE ARE LUCKY.
THEY BECOME WHO THEY ARE SUPPOSED TO BE.
DO WHAT THEY ARE SUPPOSED TO DO.
ISIS.
I YEARN FOR THE DAY...

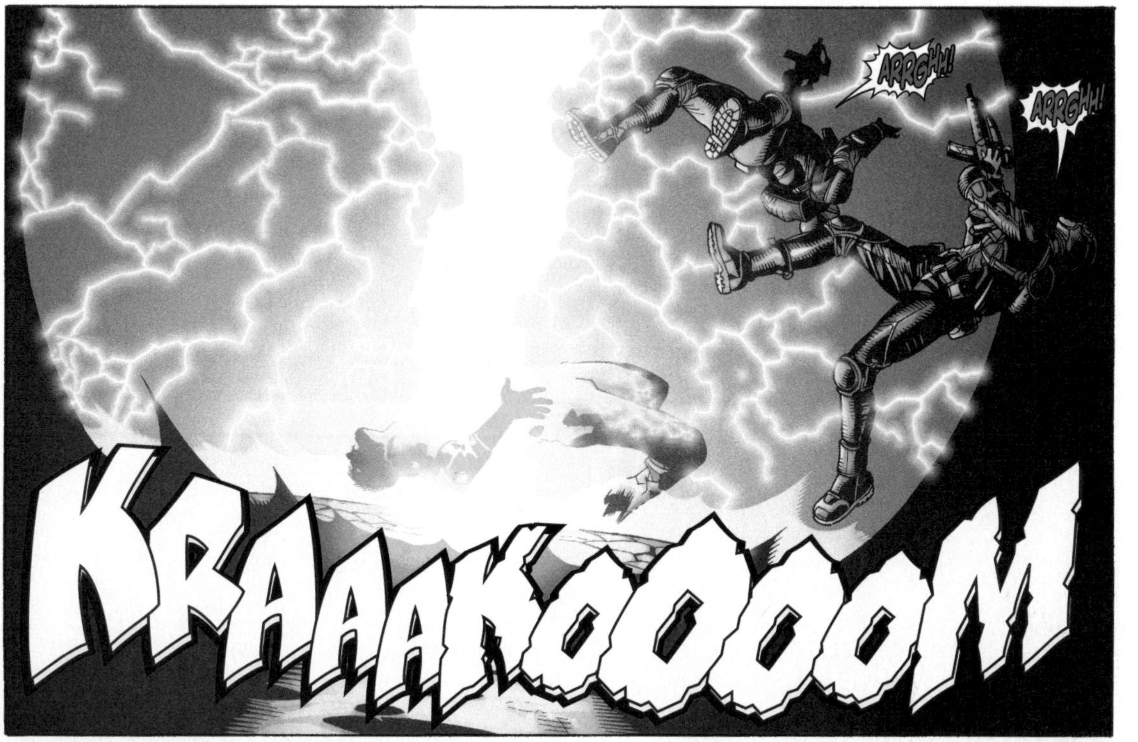
ARRGHH!
ARRGHH!
KRAAAKOOOOOM

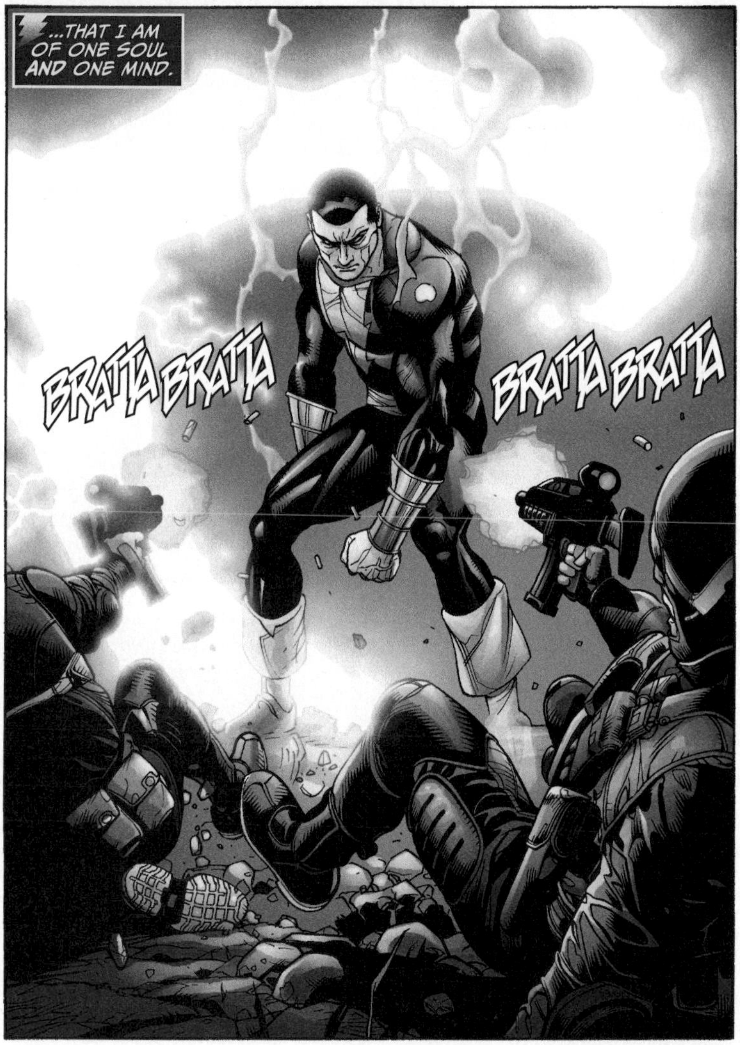
...THAT I AM OF ONE SOUL AND ONE MIND.
BRATTA BRATTA
BRATTA BRATTA

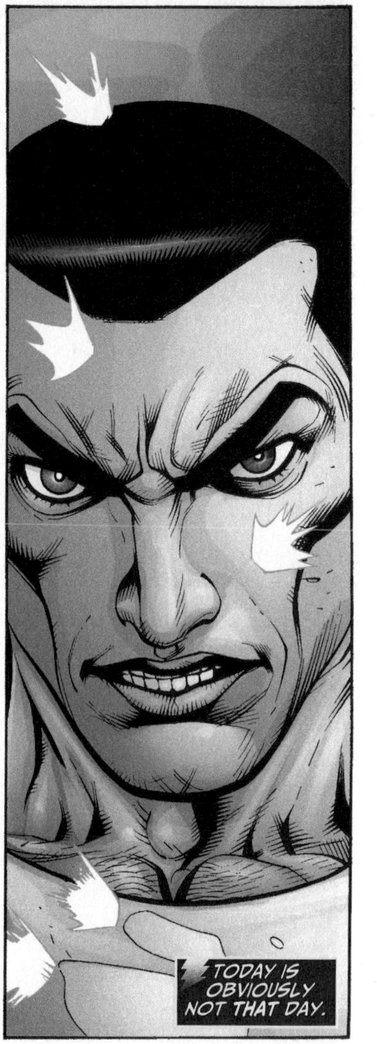
TODAY IS OBVIOUSLY NOT THAT DAY.

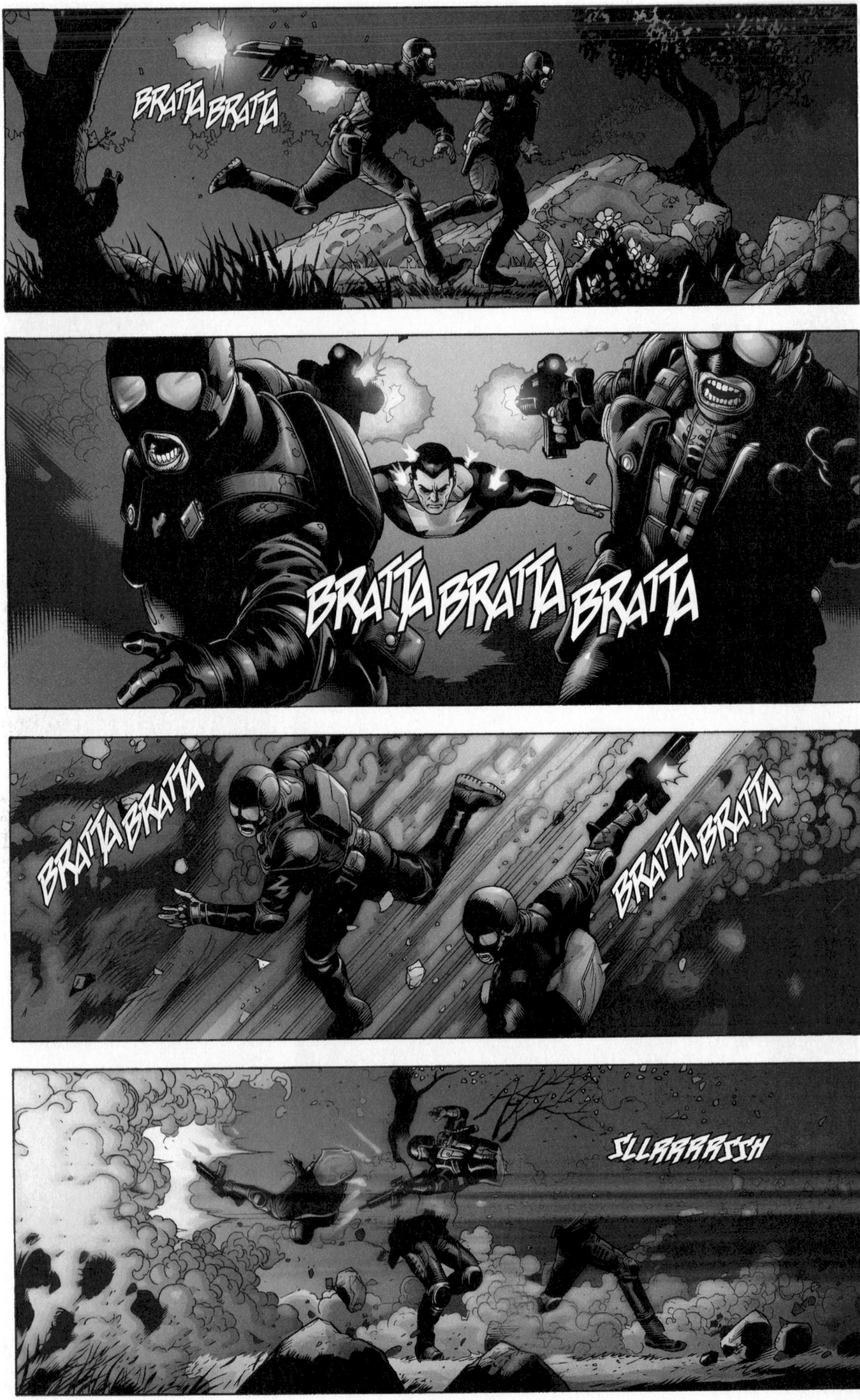
BRATTA BRATTA
BRATTA BRATTA BRATTA
BRATTA BRATTA
BRATTA BRATTA
SLLRRRRSSH

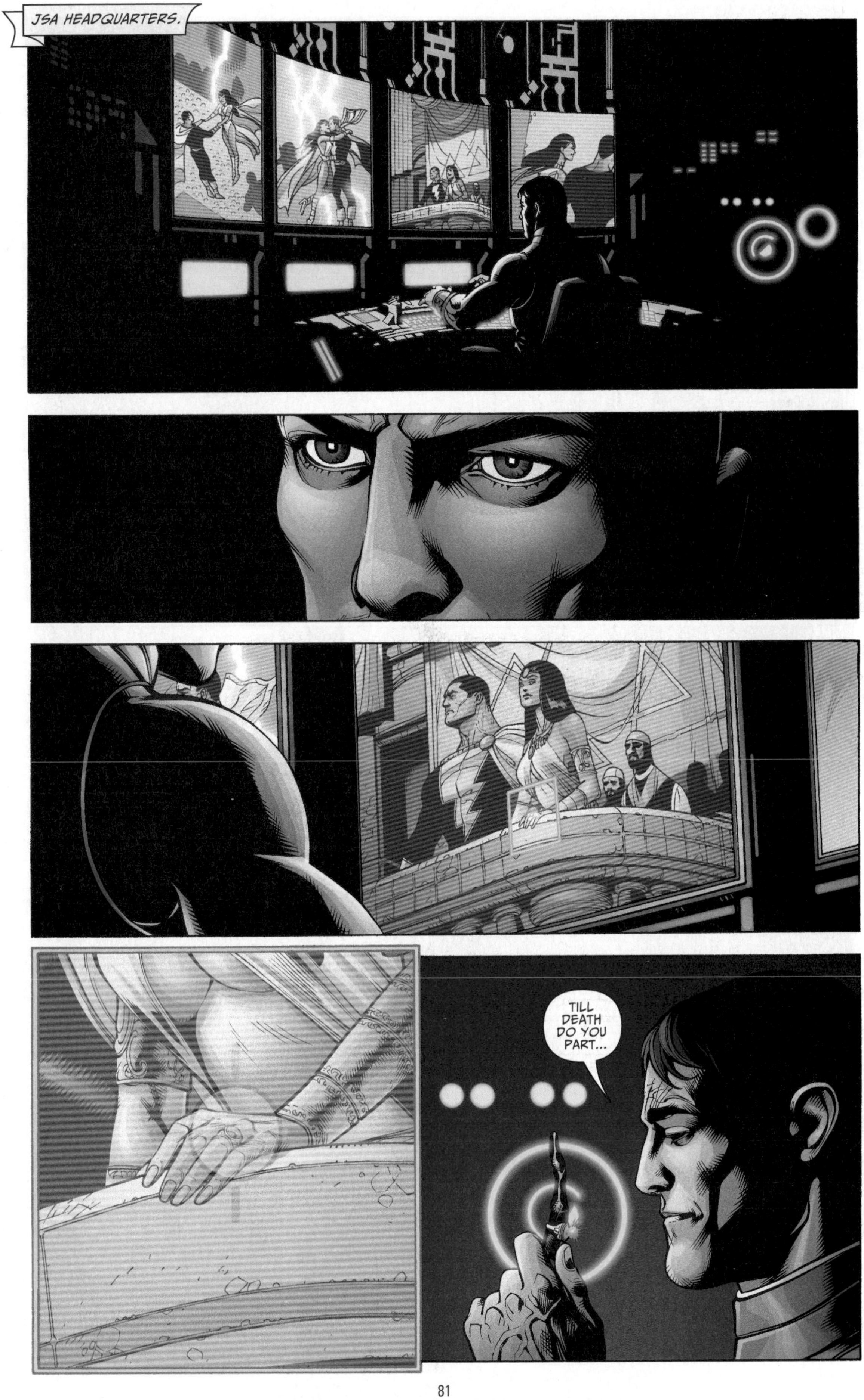
JSA HEADQUARTERS.
TILL DEATH DO YOU PART...

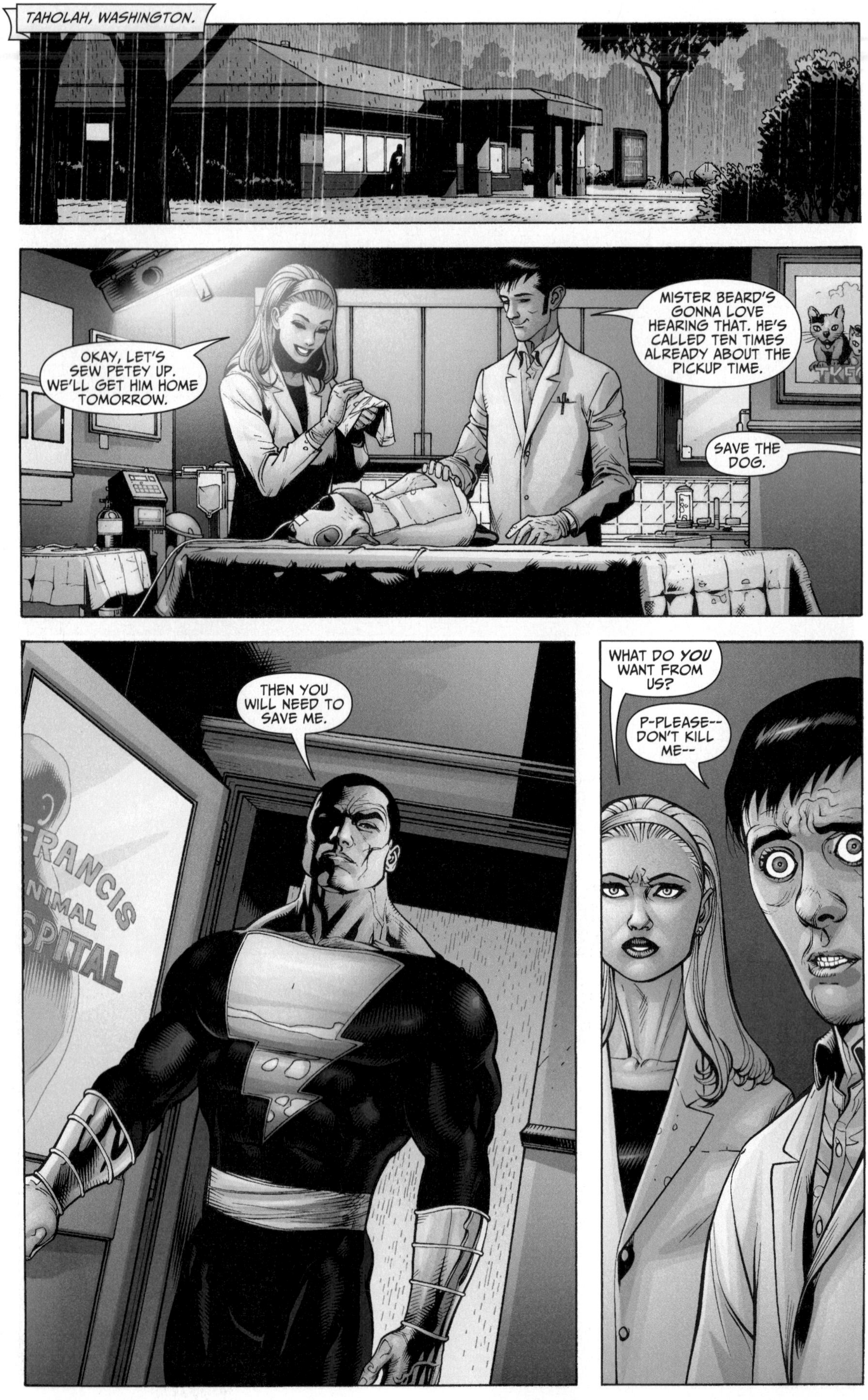
TAHOLAH, WASHINGTON.
OKAY, LET'S SEW PETEY UP. WE'LL GET HIM HOME TOMORROW.
MISTER BEARD'S GONNA LOVE HEARING THAT. HE'S CALLED TEN TIMES ALREADY ABOUT THE PICKUP TIME.
SAVE THE DOG.
THEN YOU WILL NEED TO SAVE ME.
WHAT DO *YOU* WANT FROM US?
P-PLEASE-- DON'T KILL ME--

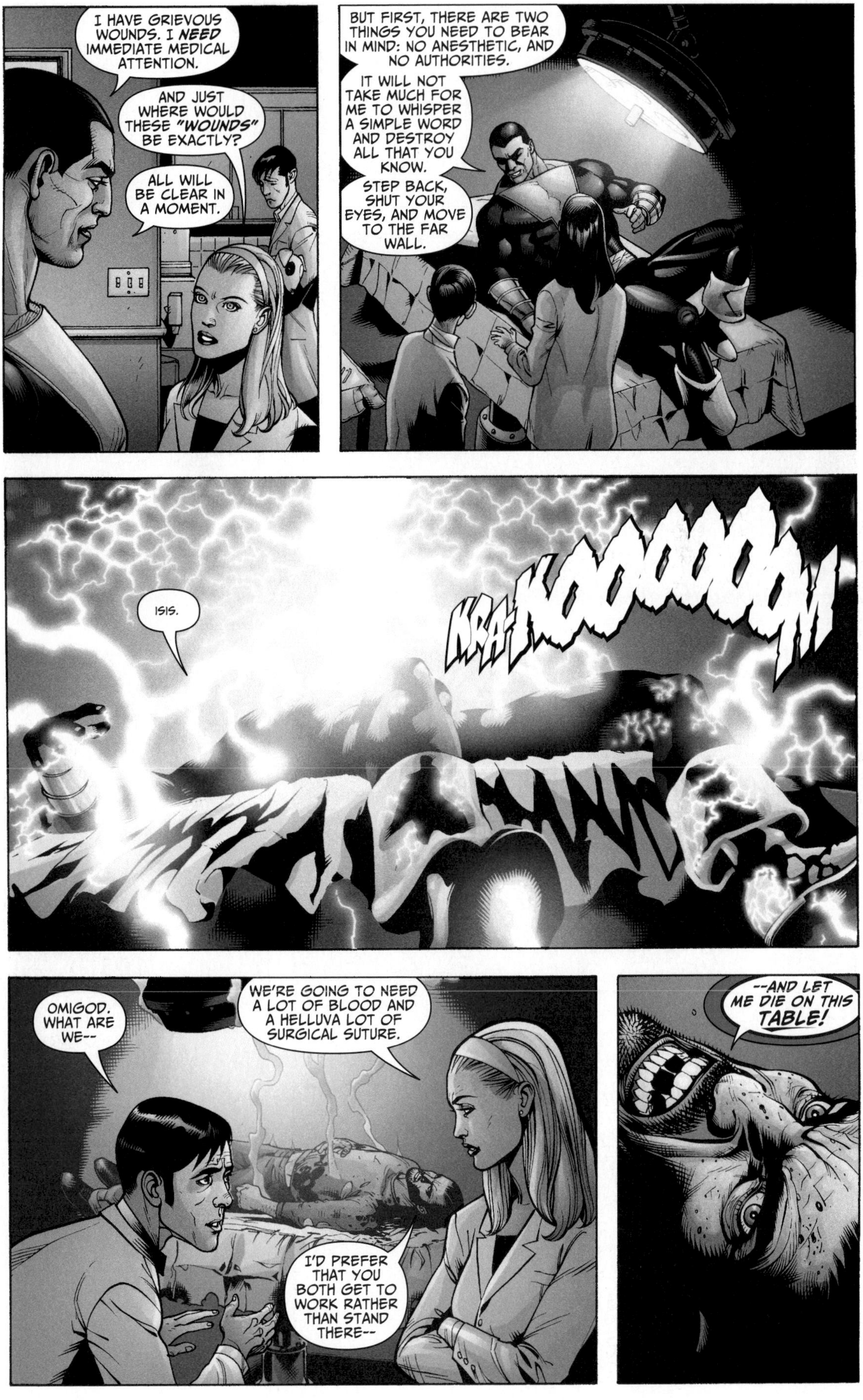
I HAVE GRIEVOUS WOUNDS. I NEED IMMEDIATE MEDICAL ATTENTION.
AND JUST WHERE WOULD THESE "WOUNDS" BE EXACTLY?
ALL WILL BE CLEAR IN A MOMENT.
BUT FIRST, THERE ARE TWO THINGS YOU NEED TO BEAR IN MIND: NO ANESTHETIC, AND NO AUTHORITIES.
IT WILL NOT TAKE MUCH FOR ME TO WHISPER A SIMPLE WORD AND DESTROY ALL THAT YOU KNOW.
STEP BACK, SHUT YOUR EYES, AND MOVE TO THE FAR WALL.
ISIS.
KRA-KOOOOOOM
OMIGOD. WHAT ARE WE--
WE'RE GOING TO NEED A LOT OF BLOOD AND A HELLUVA LOT OF SURGICAL SUTURE.
I'D PREFER THAT YOU BOTH GET TO WORK RATHER THAN STAND THERE--
--AND LET ME DIE ON THIS TABLE!

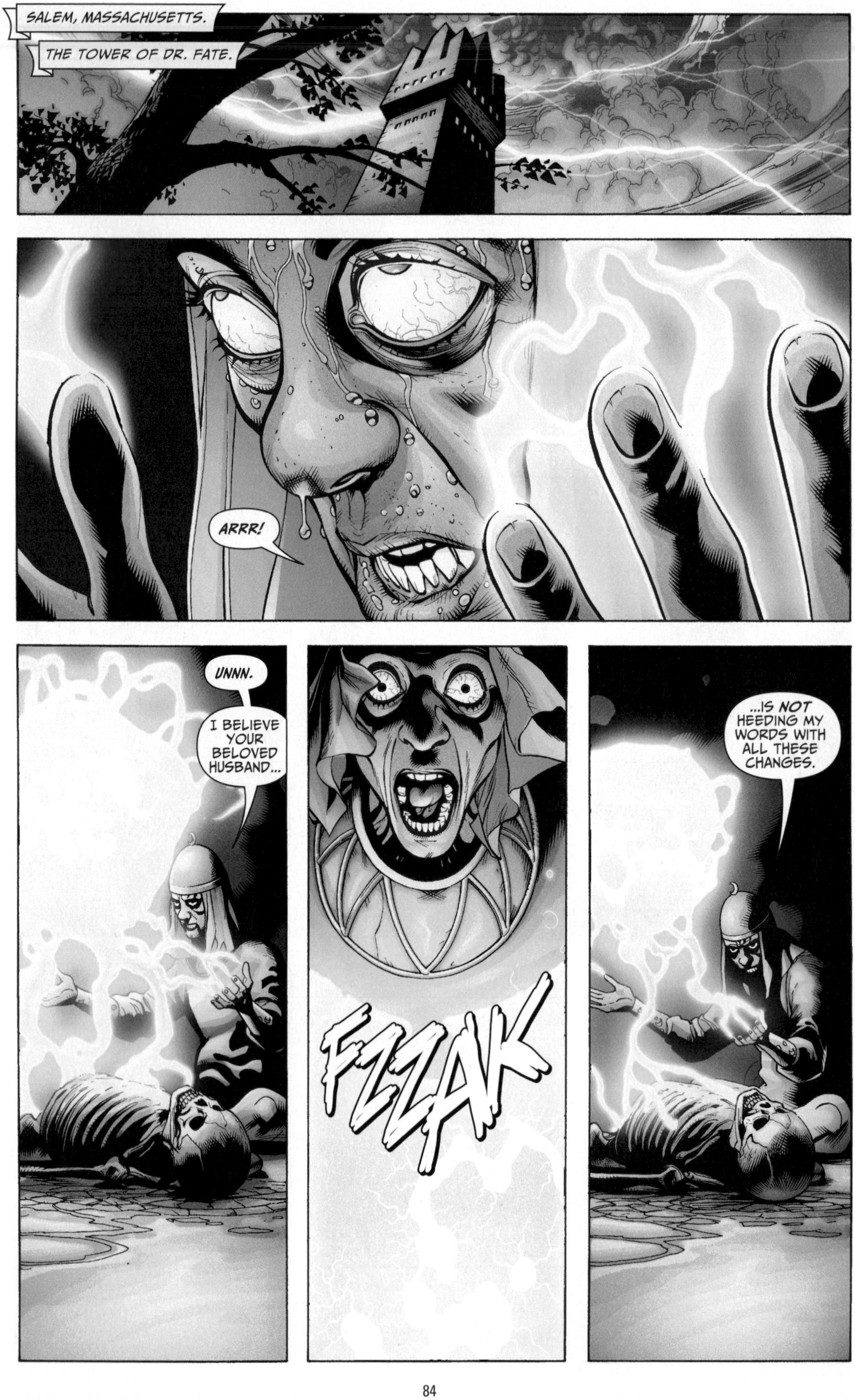
SALEM, MASSACHUSETTS.
THE TOWER OF DR. FATE.
ARRR!
UNNN.
I BELIEVE YOUR BELOVED HUSBAND...
FZZAK
...IS NOT HEEDING MY WORDS WITH ALL THESE CHANGES.

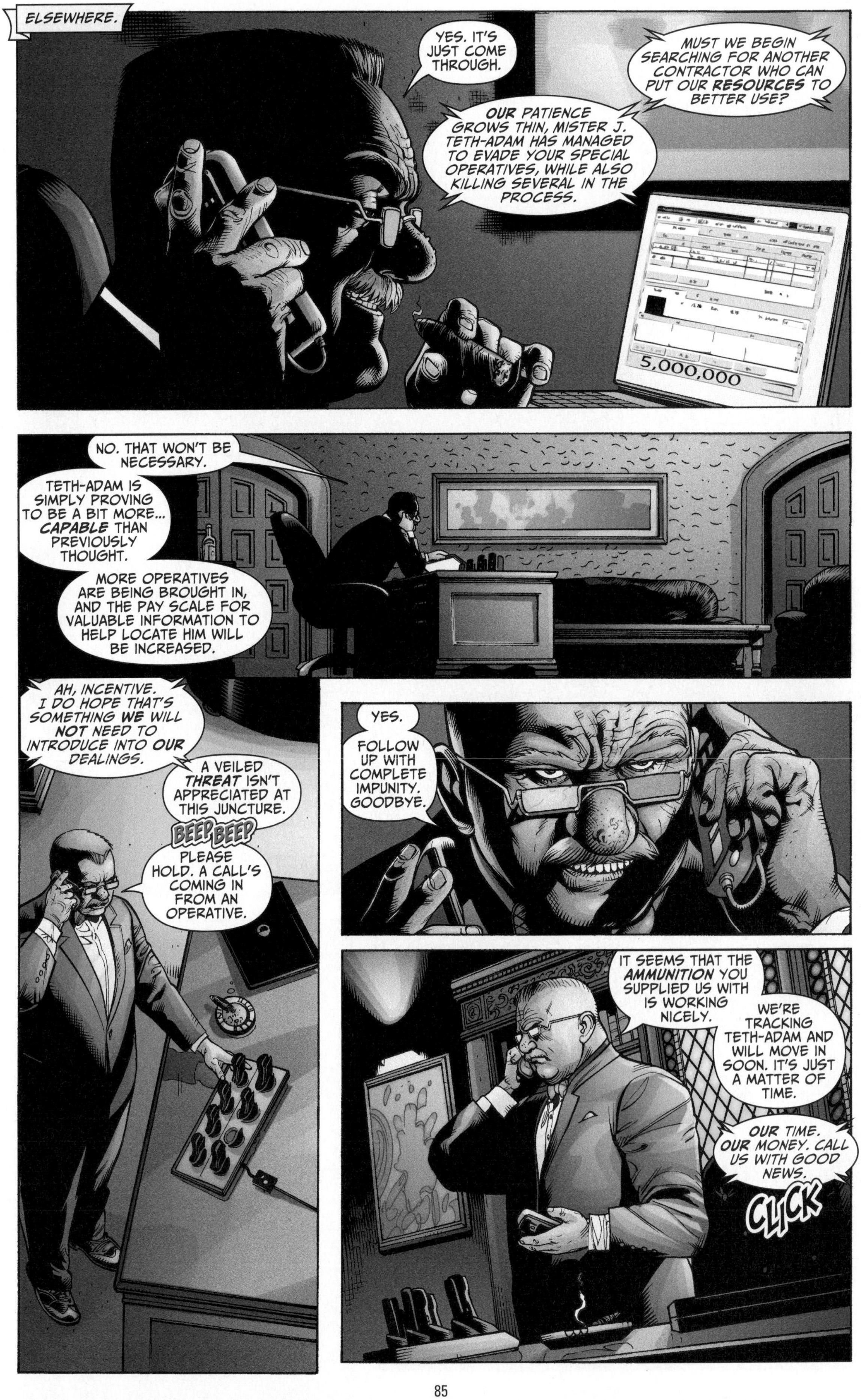
ELSEWHERE.
YES. IT'S JUST COME THROUGH.
OUR PATIENCE GROWS THIN, MISTER J. TETH-ADAM HAS MANAGED TO EVADE YOUR SPECIAL OPERATIVES, WHILE ALSO KILLING SEVERAL IN THE PROCESS.
MUST WE BEGIN SEARCHING FOR ANOTHER CONTRACTOR WHO CAN PUT OUR RESOURCES TO BETTER USE?
5,000,000
NO. THAT WON'T BE NECESSARY.
TETH-ADAM IS SIMPLY PROVING TO BE A BIT MORE... CAPABLE THAN PREVIOUSLY THOUGHT.
MORE OPERATIVES ARE BEING BROUGHT IN, AND THE PAY SCALE FOR VALUABLE INFORMATION TO HELP LOCATE HIM WILL BE INCREASED.
AH, INCENTIVE. I DO HOPE THAT'S SOMETHING WE WILL NOT NEED TO INTRODUCE INTO OUR DEALINGS.
A VEILED THREAT ISN'T APPRECIATED AT THIS JUNCTURE.
BEEP BEEP
PLEASE HOLD. A CALL'S COMING IN FROM AN OPERATIVE.
YES.
FOLLOW UP WITH COMPLETE IMPUNITY. GOODBYE.
IT SEEMS THAT THE AMMUNITION YOU SUPPLIED US WITH IS WORKING NICELY.
WE'RE TRACKING TETH-ADAM AND WILL MOVE IN SOON. IT'S JUST A MATTER OF TIME.
OUR TIME. OUR MONEY. CALL US WITH GOOD NEWS.
CLICK

ARRR--

WHAT-- WHERE--HOW LONG--

RELAX.

YOU'VE BEEN OUT FOR OVER TWO HOURS.

TWO HOURS?

AND I'D APPRECIATE IT IF YOU WAITED TILL YOU LEFT TO POP OPEN ALL MY SUTURES, 'CAUSE WE'RE ALL OUT OF BLOOD.

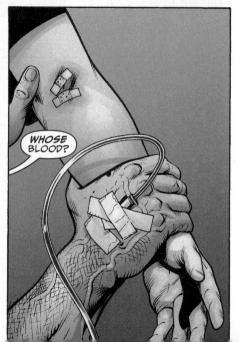

WHOSE BLOOD?

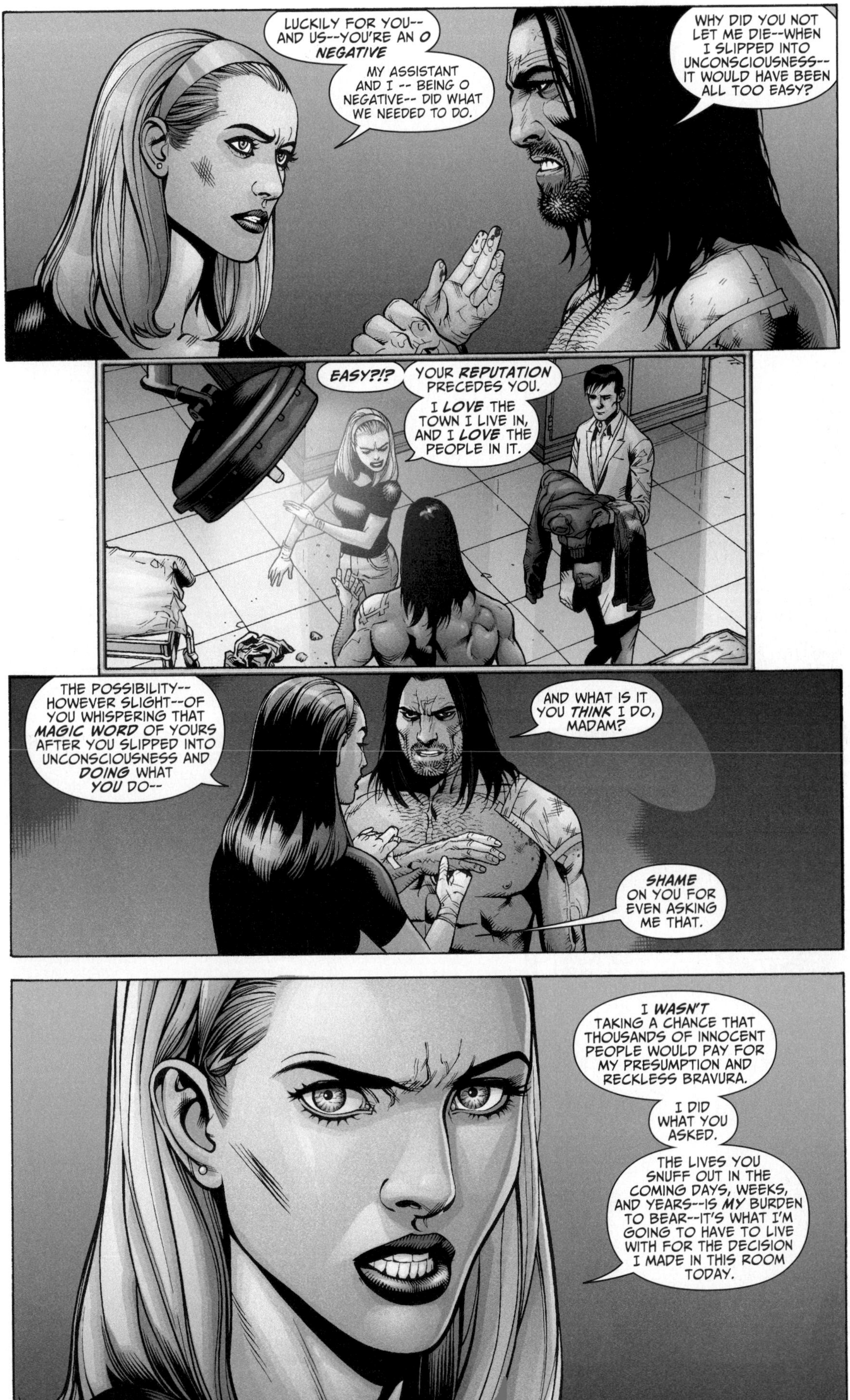
LUCKILY FOR YOU-- AND US--YOU'RE AN O NEGATIVE
MY ASSISTANT AND I -- BEING O NEGATIVE-- DID WHAT WE NEEDED TO DO.
WHY DID YOU NOT LET ME DIE--WHEN I SLIPPED INTO UNCONSCIOUSNESS-- IT WOULD HAVE BEEN ALL TOO EASY?
EASY?!?
YOUR REPUTATION PRECEDES YOU.
I LOVE THE TOWN I LIVE IN, AND I LOVE THE PEOPLE IN IT.
THE POSSIBILITY-- HOWEVER SLIGHT--OF YOU WHISPERING THAT MAGIC WORD OF YOURS AFTER YOU SLIPPED INTO UNCONSCIOUSNESS AND DOING WHAT YOU DO--
AND WHAT IS IT YOU THINK I DO, MADAM?
SHAME ON YOU FOR EVEN ASKING ME THAT.
I WASN'T TAKING A CHANCE THAT THOUSANDS OF INNOCENT PEOPLE WOULD PAY FOR MY PRESUMPTION AND RECKLESS BRAVURA.
I DID WHAT YOU ASKED.
THE LIVES YOU SNUFF OUT IN THE COMING DAYS, WEEKS, AND YEARS--IS MY BURDEN TO BEAR--IT'S WHAT I'M GOING TO HAVE TO LIVE WITH FOR THE DECISION I MADE IN THIS ROOM TODAY.

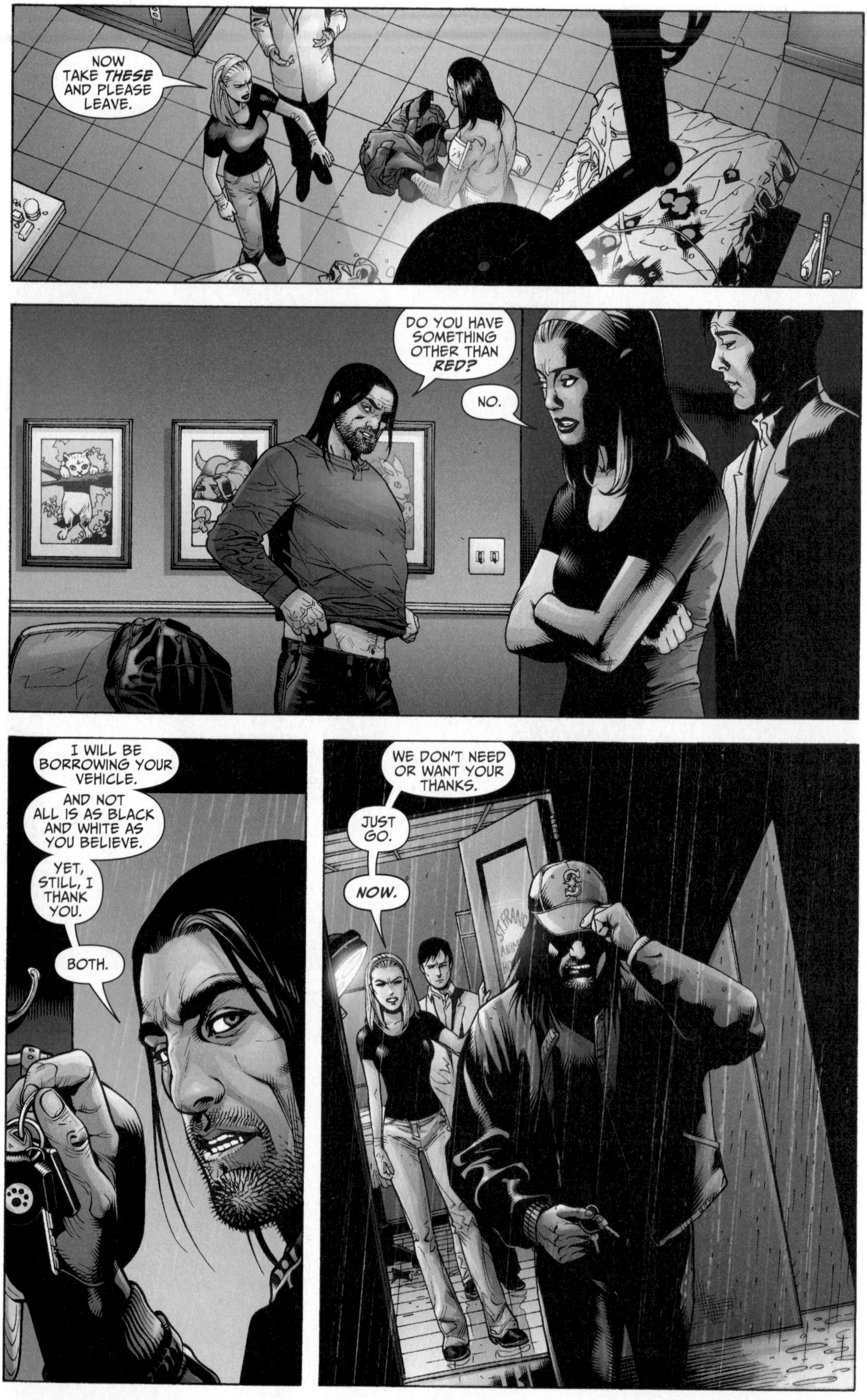
NOW TAKE THESE AND PLEASE LEAVE.
DO YOU HAVE SOMETHING OTHER THAN RED?
NO.
I WILL BE BORROWING YOUR VEHICLE.
AND NOT ALL IS AS BLACK AND WHITE AS YOU BELIEVE.
YET, STILL, I THANK YOU.
BOTH.
WE DON'T NEED OR WANT YOUR THANKS.
JUST GO.
NOW.

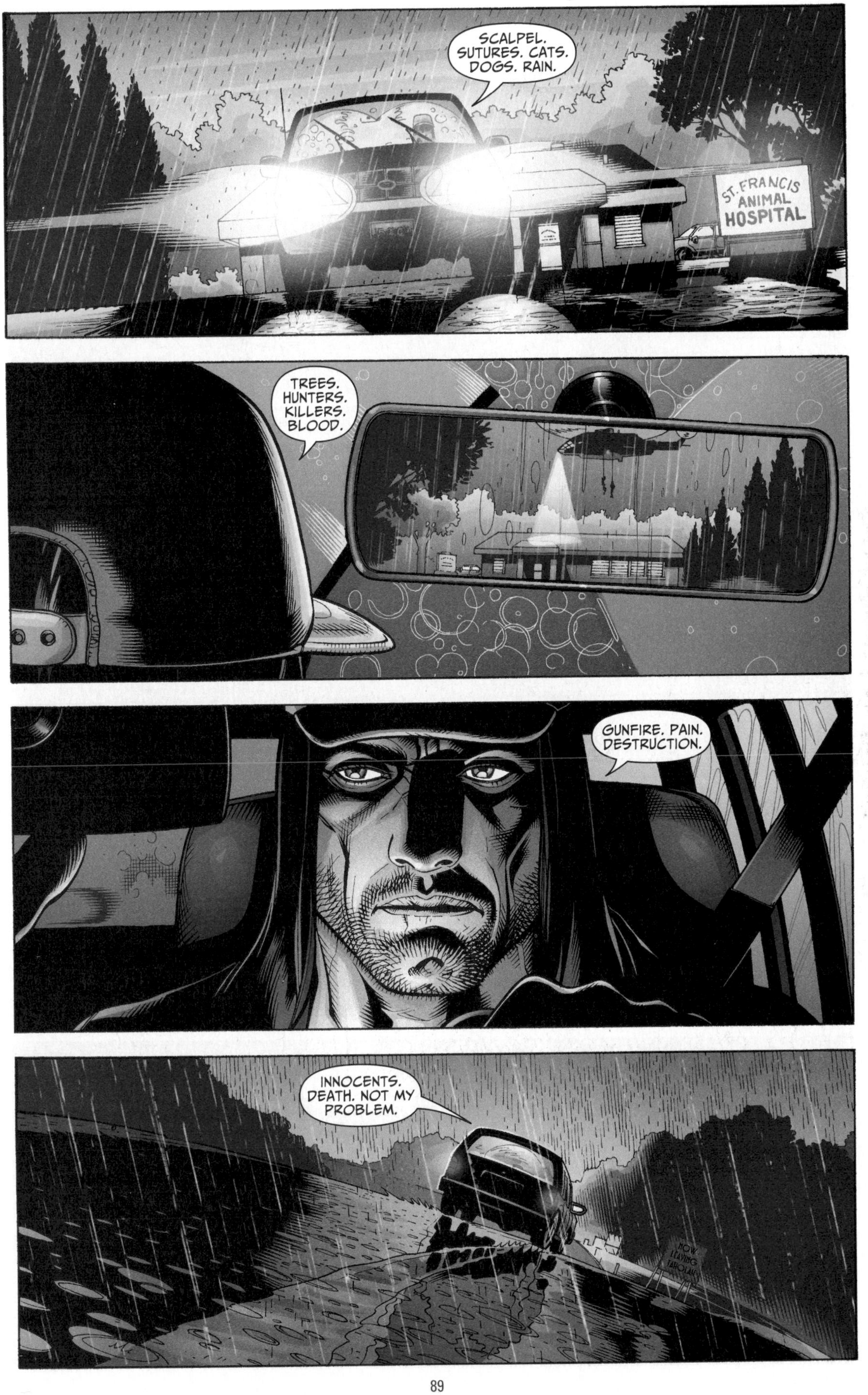
SCALPEL. SUTURES. CATS. DOGS. RAIN.
ST. FRANCIS ANIMAL HOSPITAL
TREES. HUNTERS. KILLERS. BLOOD.
GUNFIRE. PAIN. DESTRUCTION.
INNOCENTS. DEATH. NOT MY PROBLEM.
NOW LEAVING TAHOLAH

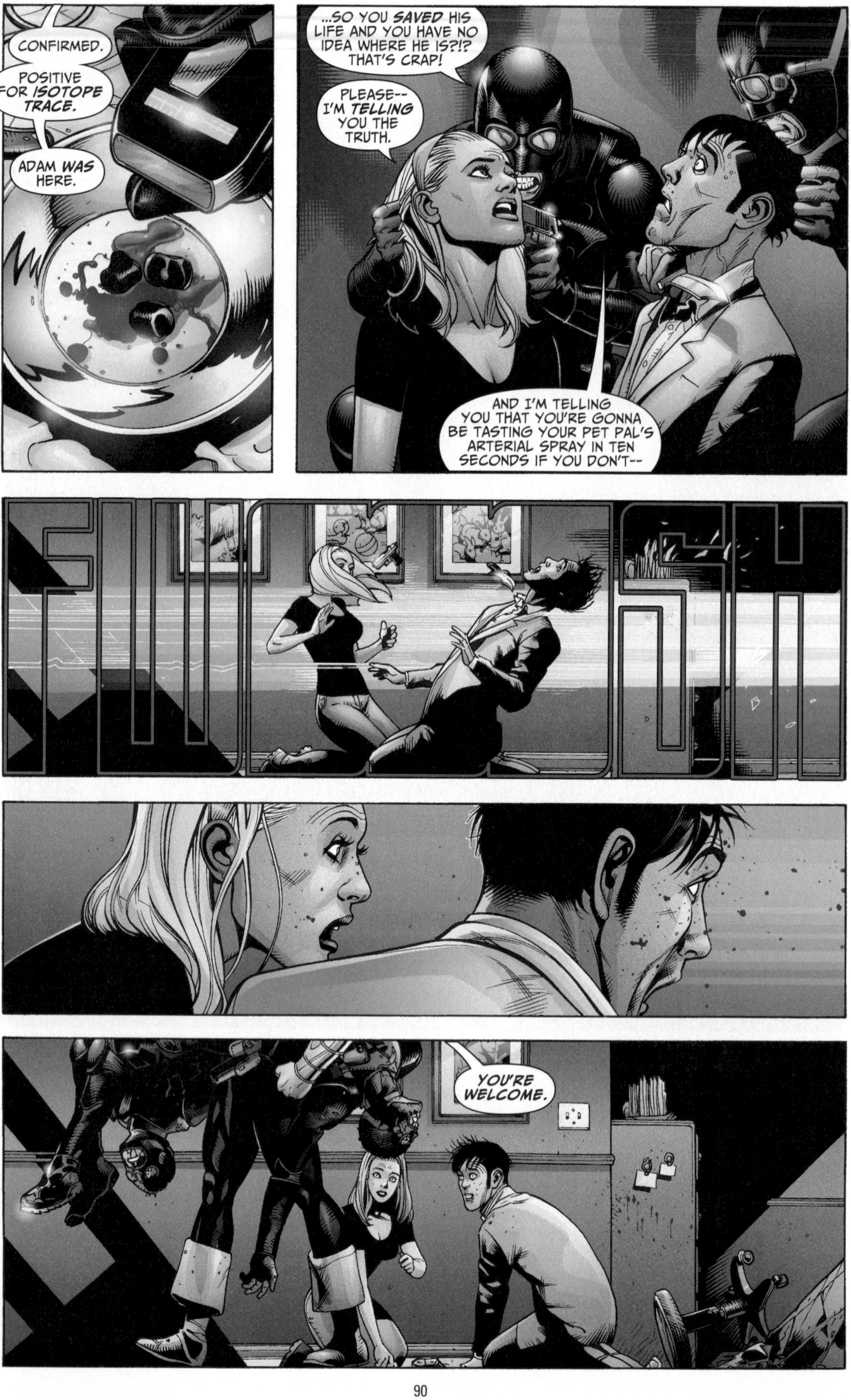
CONFIRMED.
POSITIVE FOR ISOTOPE TRACE.
ADAM WAS HERE.
...SO YOU SAVED HIS LIFE AND YOU HAVE NO IDEA WHERE HE IS?!? THAT'S CRAP!
PLEASE-- I'M TELLING YOU THE TRUTH.
AND I'M TELLING YOU THAT YOU'RE GONNA BE TASTING YOUR PET PAL'S ARTERIAL SPRAY IN TEN SECONDS IF YOU DON'T--
FWOOSH
YOU'RE WELCOME.

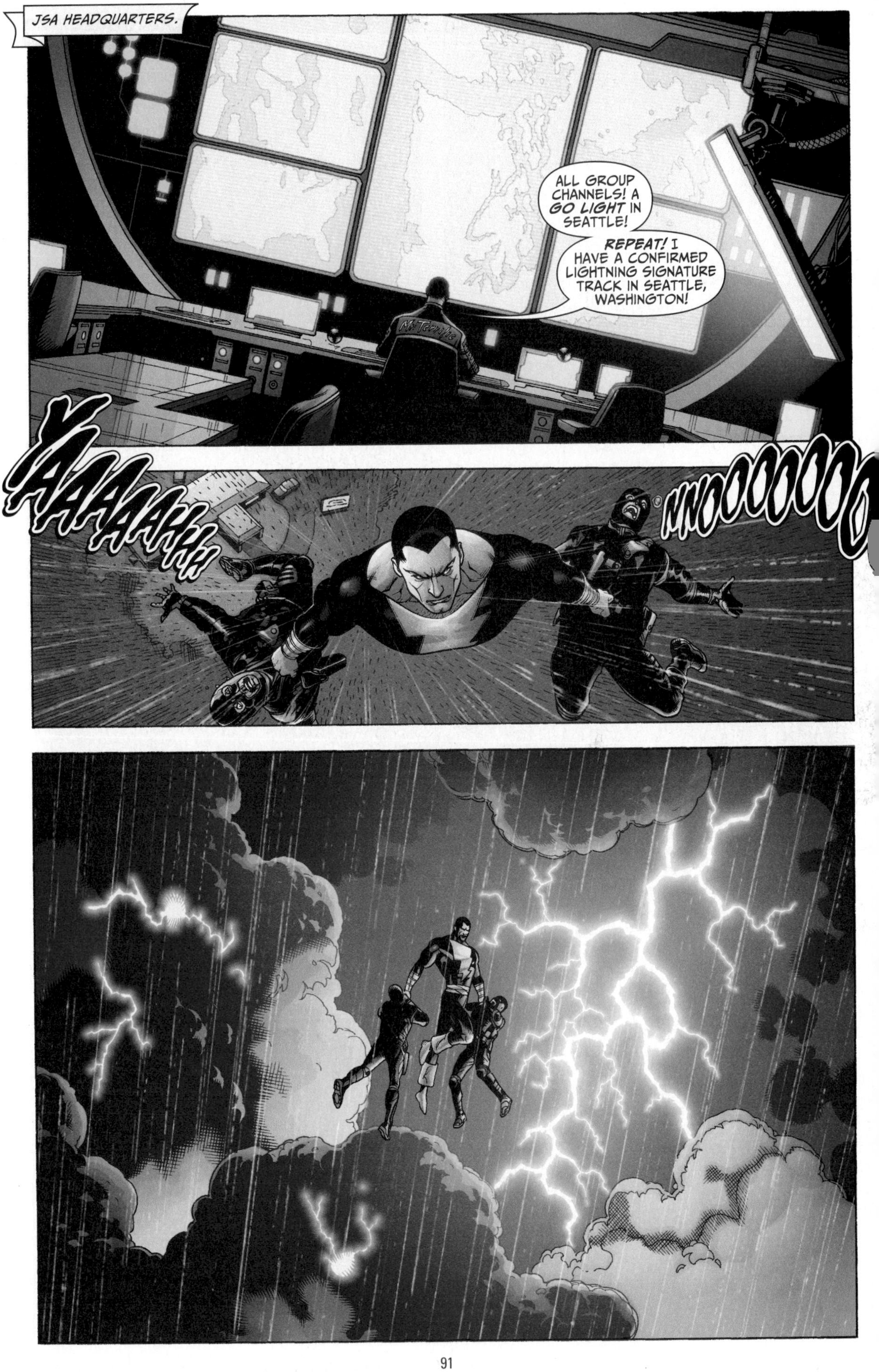
JSA HEADQUARTERS.
ALL GROUP CHANNELS! A GO LIGHT IN SEATTLE!
REPEAT! I HAVE A CONFIRMED LIGHTNING SIGNATURE TRACK IN SEATTLE, WASHINGTON!
YAAAAAHHH
NNOOOOOOO

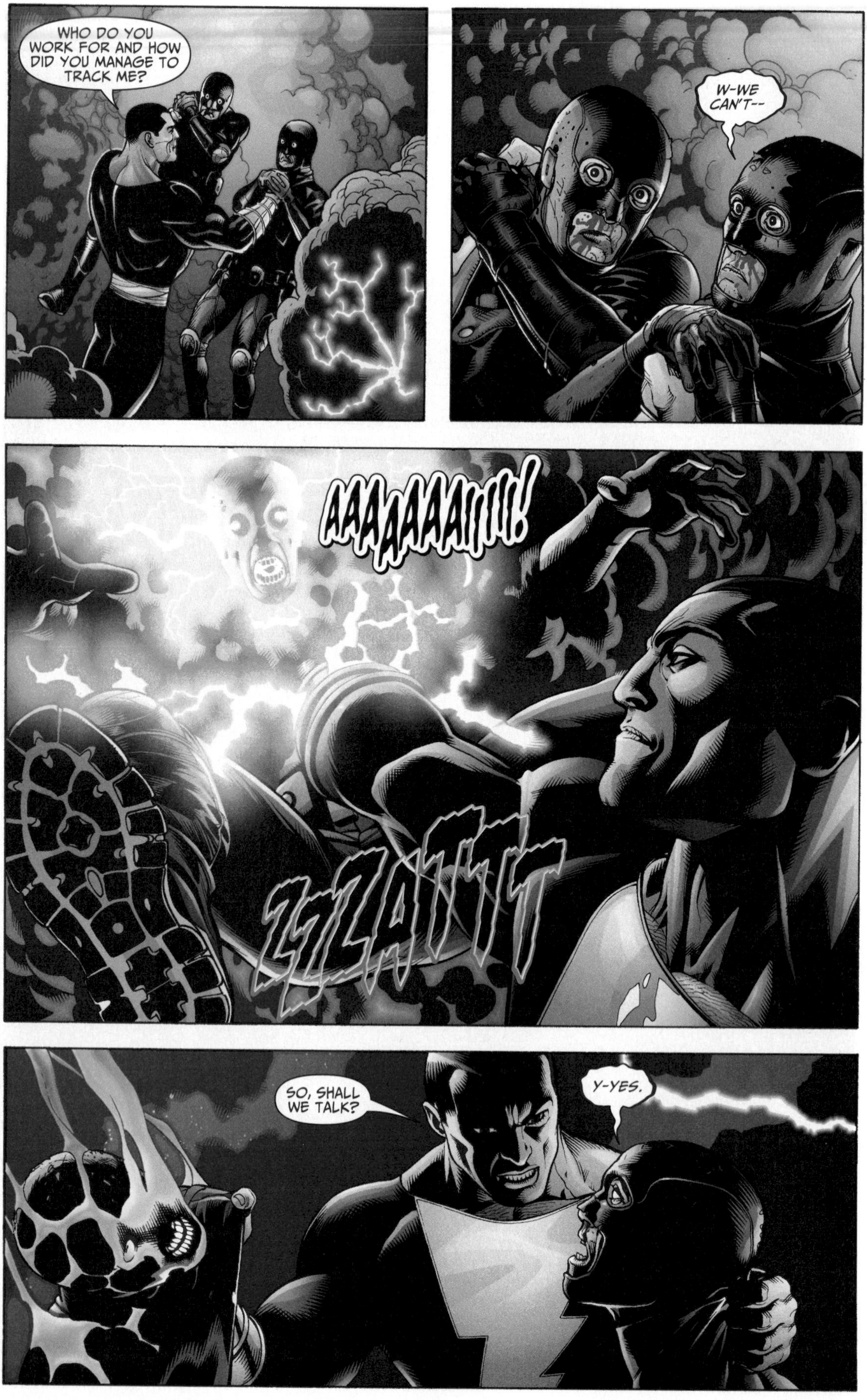
WHO DO YOU WORK FOR AND HOW DID YOU MANAGE TO TRACK ME?
W-WE CAN'T--
AAAAAAAIIIII!
ZZZATTT
SO, SHALL WE TALK?
Y-YES.

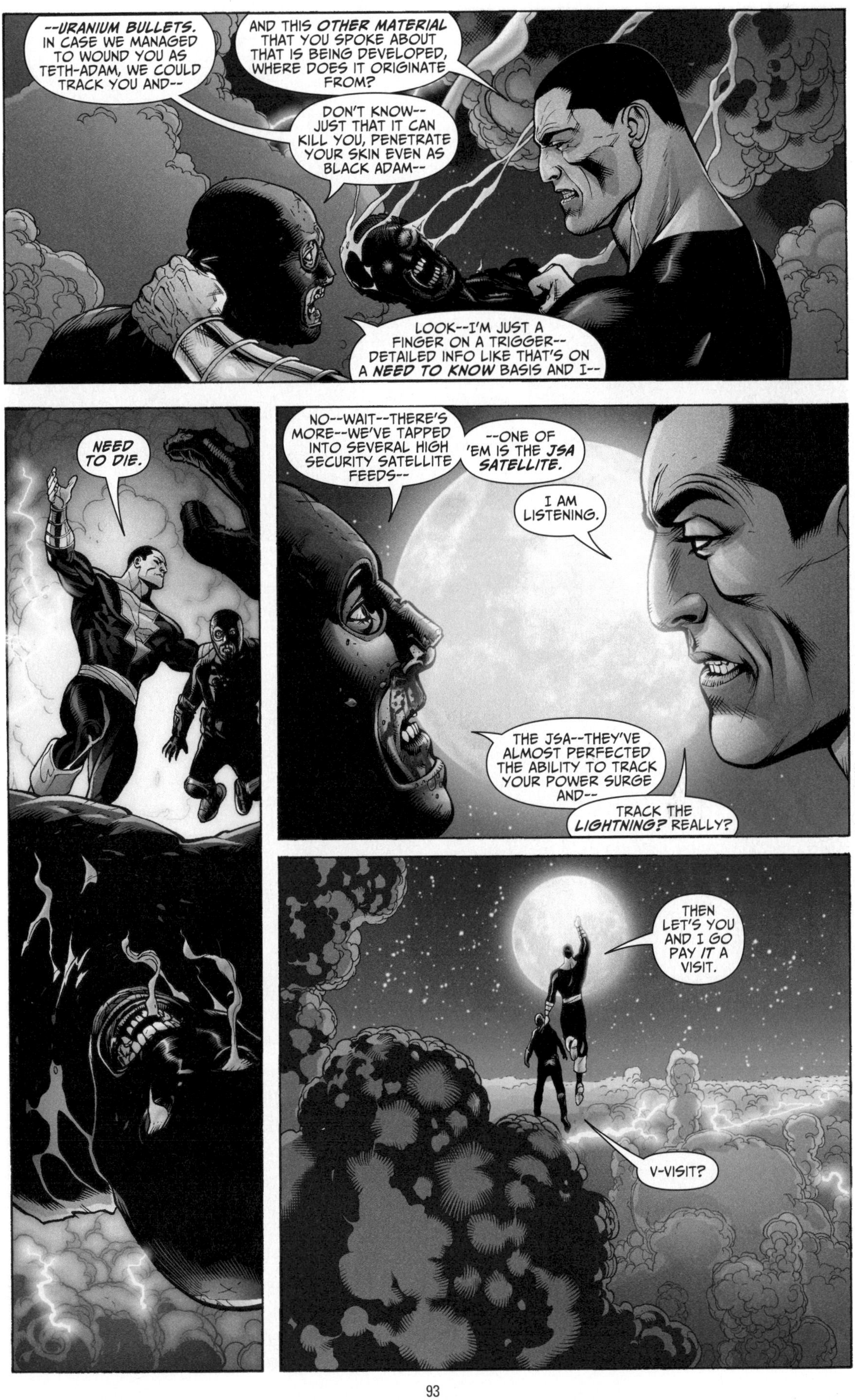
--URANIUM BULLETS. IN CASE WE MANAGED TO WOUND YOU AS TETH-ADAM, WE COULD TRACK YOU AND--
AND THIS OTHER MATERIAL THAT YOU SPOKE ABOUT THAT IS BEING DEVELOPED, WHERE DOES IT ORIGINATE FROM?
DON'T KNOW-- JUST THAT IT CAN KILL YOU, PENETRATE YOUR SKIN EVEN AS BLACK ADAM--
LOOK--I'M JUST A FINGER ON A TRIGGER-- DETAILED INFO LIKE THAT'S ON A NEED TO KNOW BASIS AND I--
NEED TO DIE.
NO--WAIT--THERE'S MORE--WE'VE TAPPED INTO SEVERAL HIGH SECURITY SATELLITE FEEDS--
--ONE OF 'EM IS THE JSA SATELLITE.
I AM LISTENING.
THE JSA--THEY'VE ALMOST PERFECTED THE ABILITY TO TRACK YOUR POWER SURGE AND--
TRACK THE LIGHTNING? REALLY?
THEN LET'S YOU AND I GO PAY IT A VISIT.
V-VISIT?

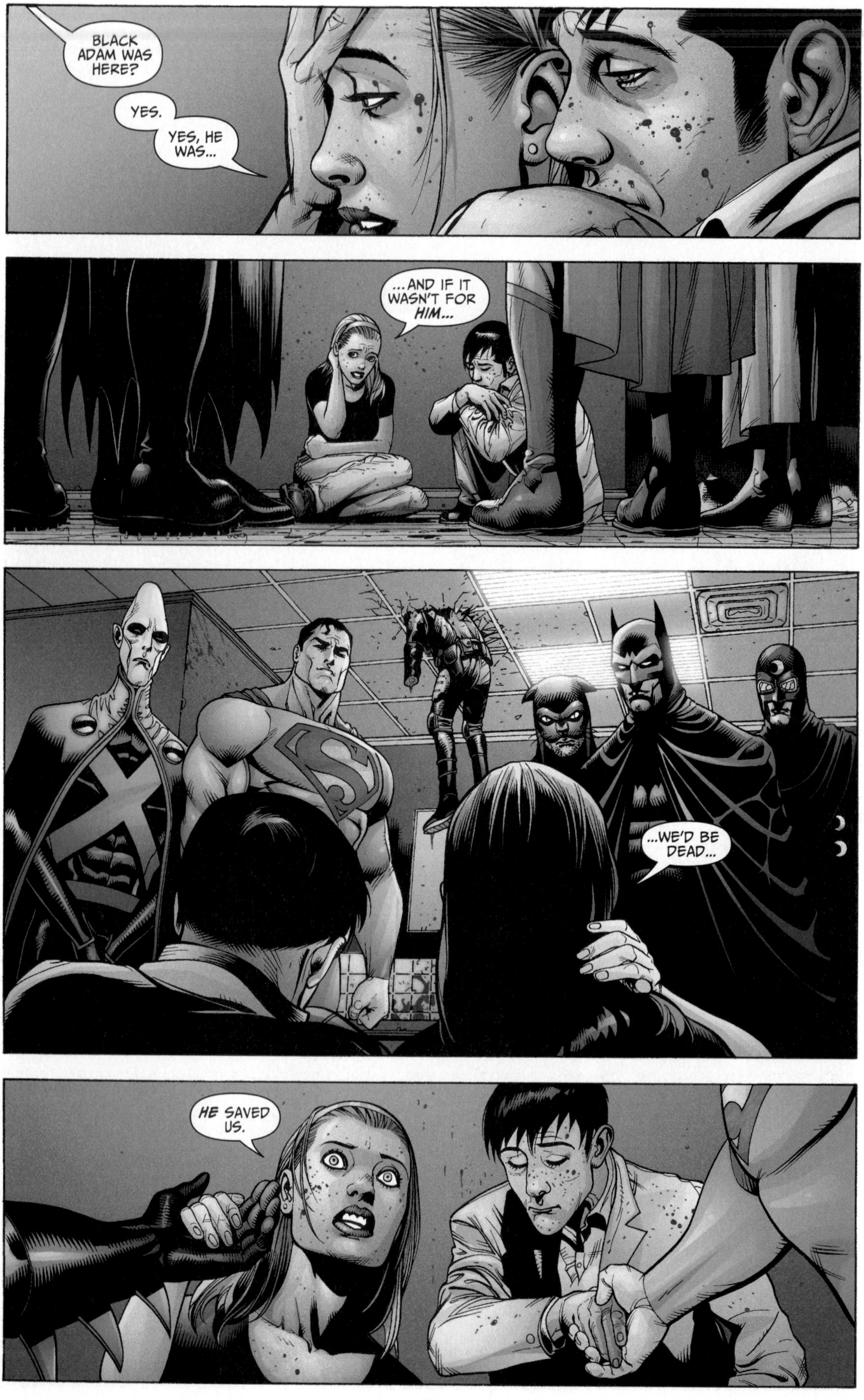
BLACK ADAM WAS HERE?
YES.
YES, HE WAS...
...AND IF IT WASN'T FOR HIM...
...WE'D BE DEAD...
HE SAVED US.

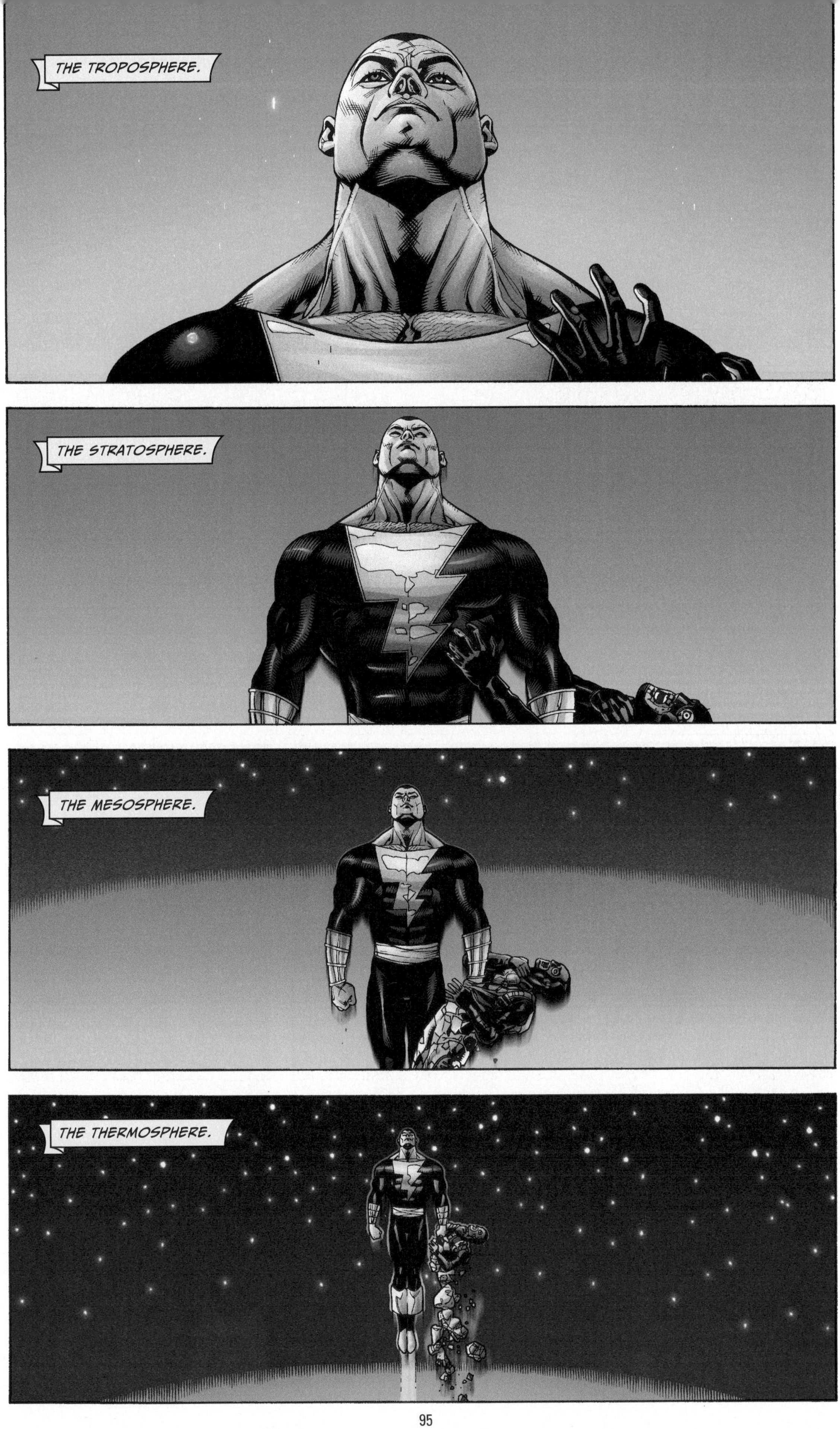
THE TROPOSPHERE.
THE STRATOSPHERE.
THE MESOSPHERE.
THE THERMOSPHERE.

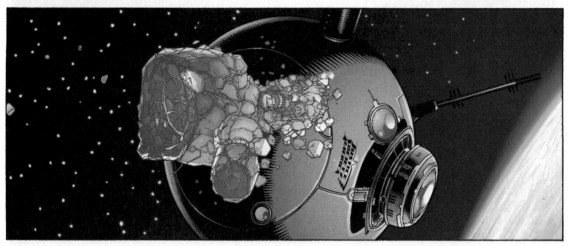

DAMN IT.

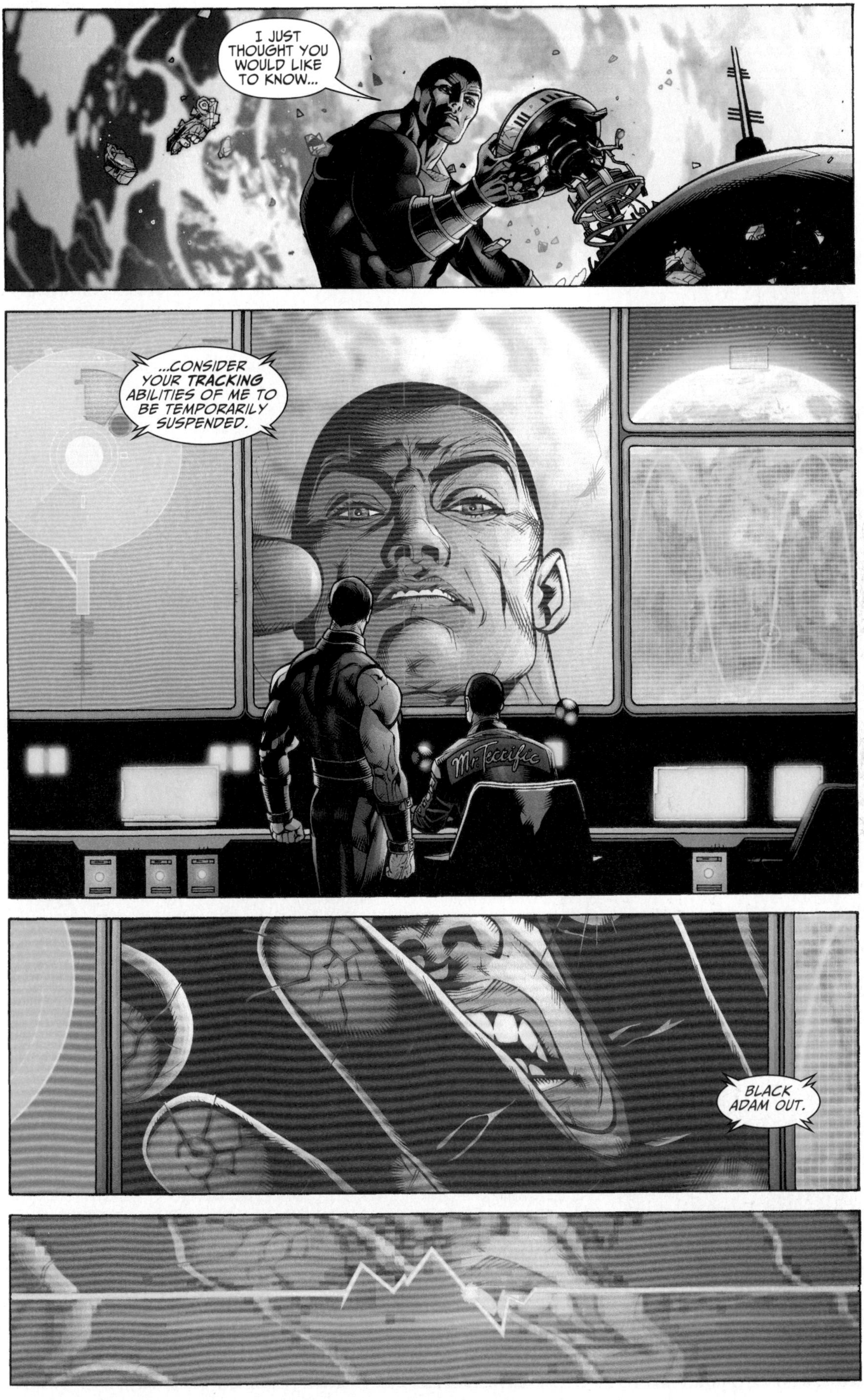
I JUST THOUGHT YOU WOULD LIKE TO KNOW...
...CONSIDER YOUR TRACKING ABILITIES OF ME TO BE TEMPORARILY SUSPENDED.
Mr. Terrific
BLACK ADAM OUT.

Chapter Five

This chapter inked by Christian Alamy and Rodney Ramos

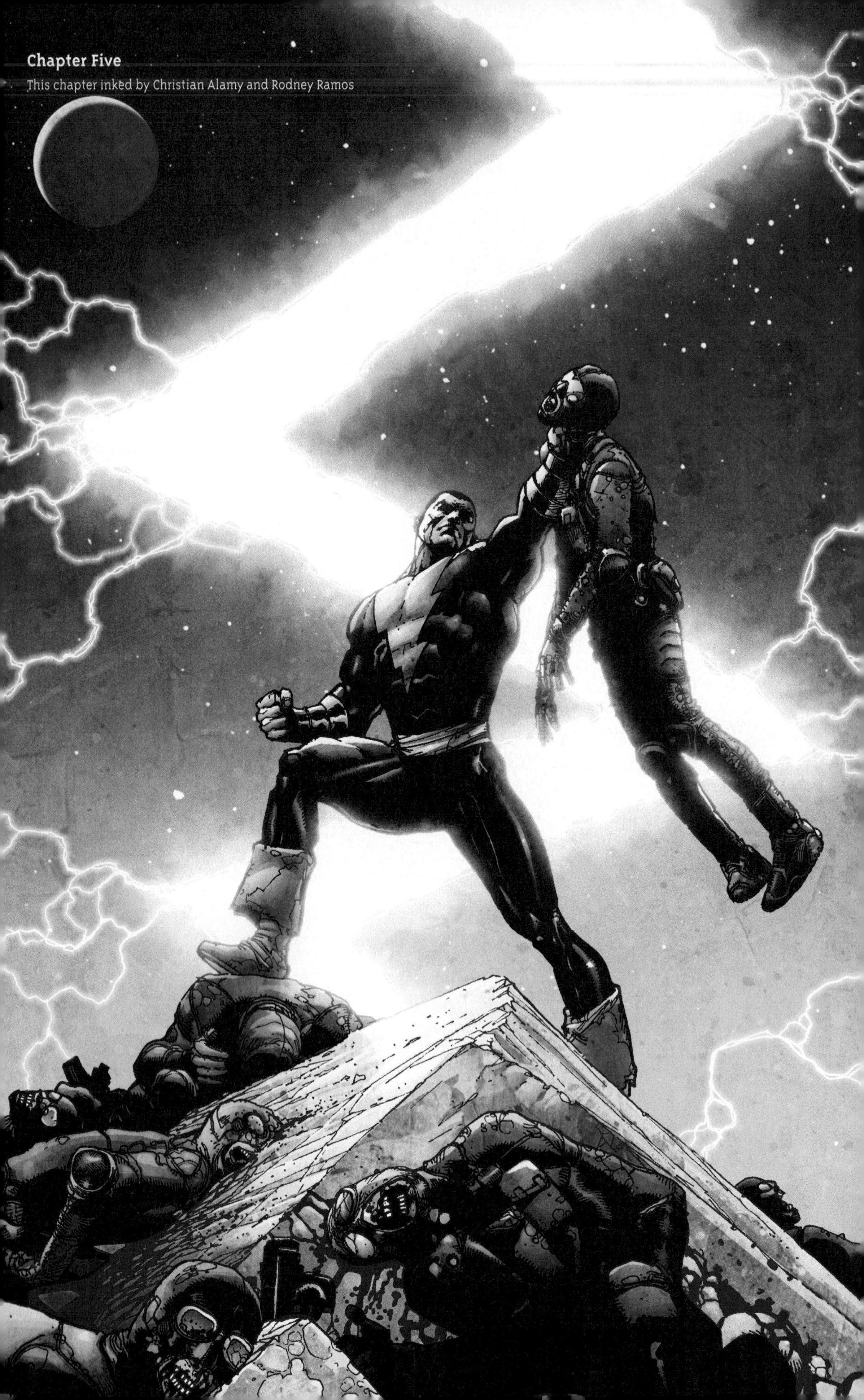

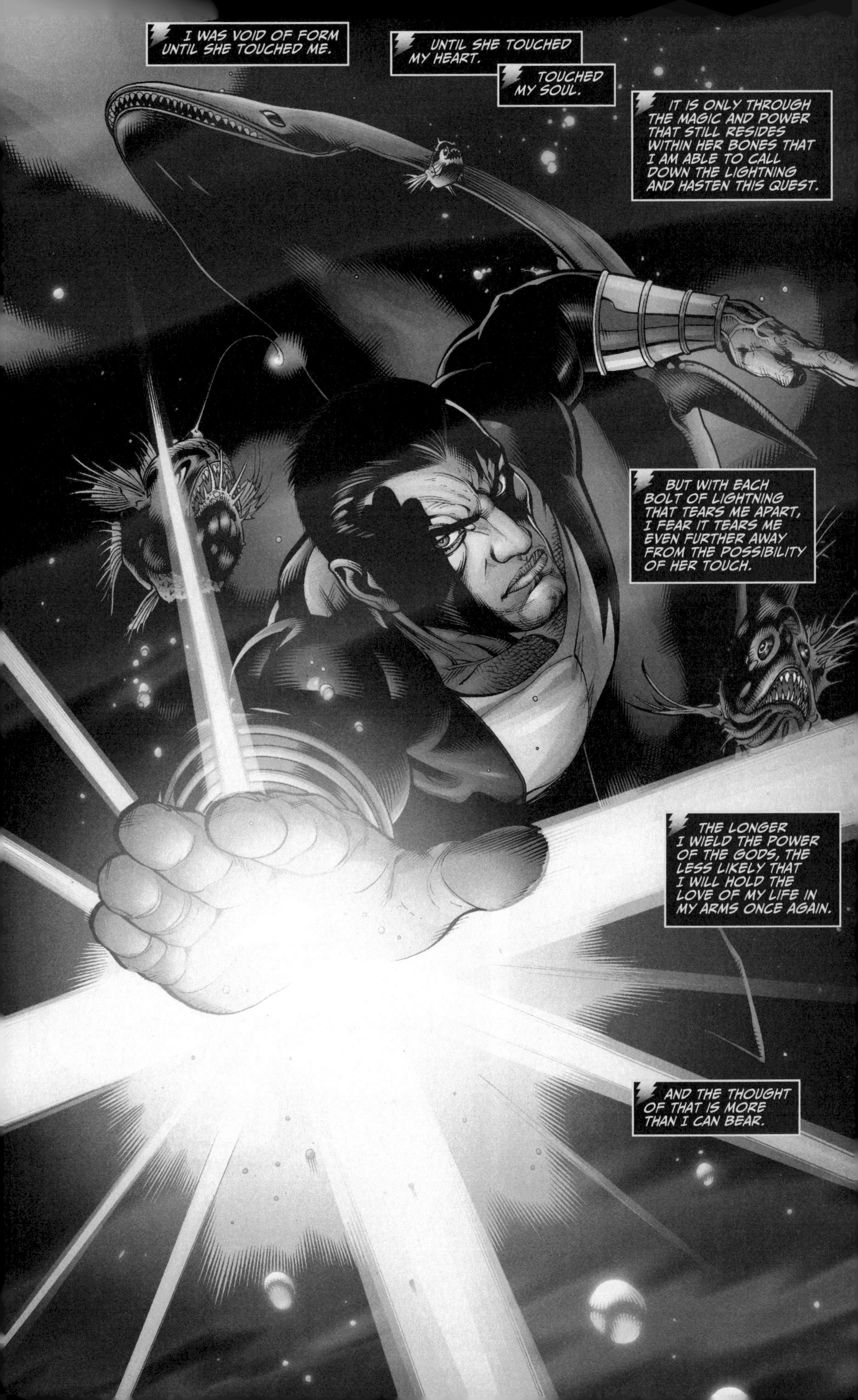
I WAS VOID OF FORM UNTIL SHE TOUCHED ME.
UNTIL SHE TOUCHED MY HEART.
TOUCHED MY SOUL.
IT IS ONLY THROUGH THE MAGIC AND POWER THAT STILL RESIDES WITHIN HER BONES THAT I AM ABLE TO CALL DOWN THE LIGHTNING AND HASTEN THIS QUEST.
BUT WITH EACH BOLT OF LIGHTNING THAT TEARS ME APART, I FEAR IT TEARS ME EVEN FURTHER AWAY FROM THE POSSIBILITY OF HER TOUCH.
THE LONGER I WIELD THE POWER OF THE GODS, THE LESS LIKELY THAT I WILL HOLD THE LOVE OF MY LIFE IN MY ARMS ONCE AGAIN.
AND THE THOUGHT OF THAT IS MORE THAN I CAN BEAR.

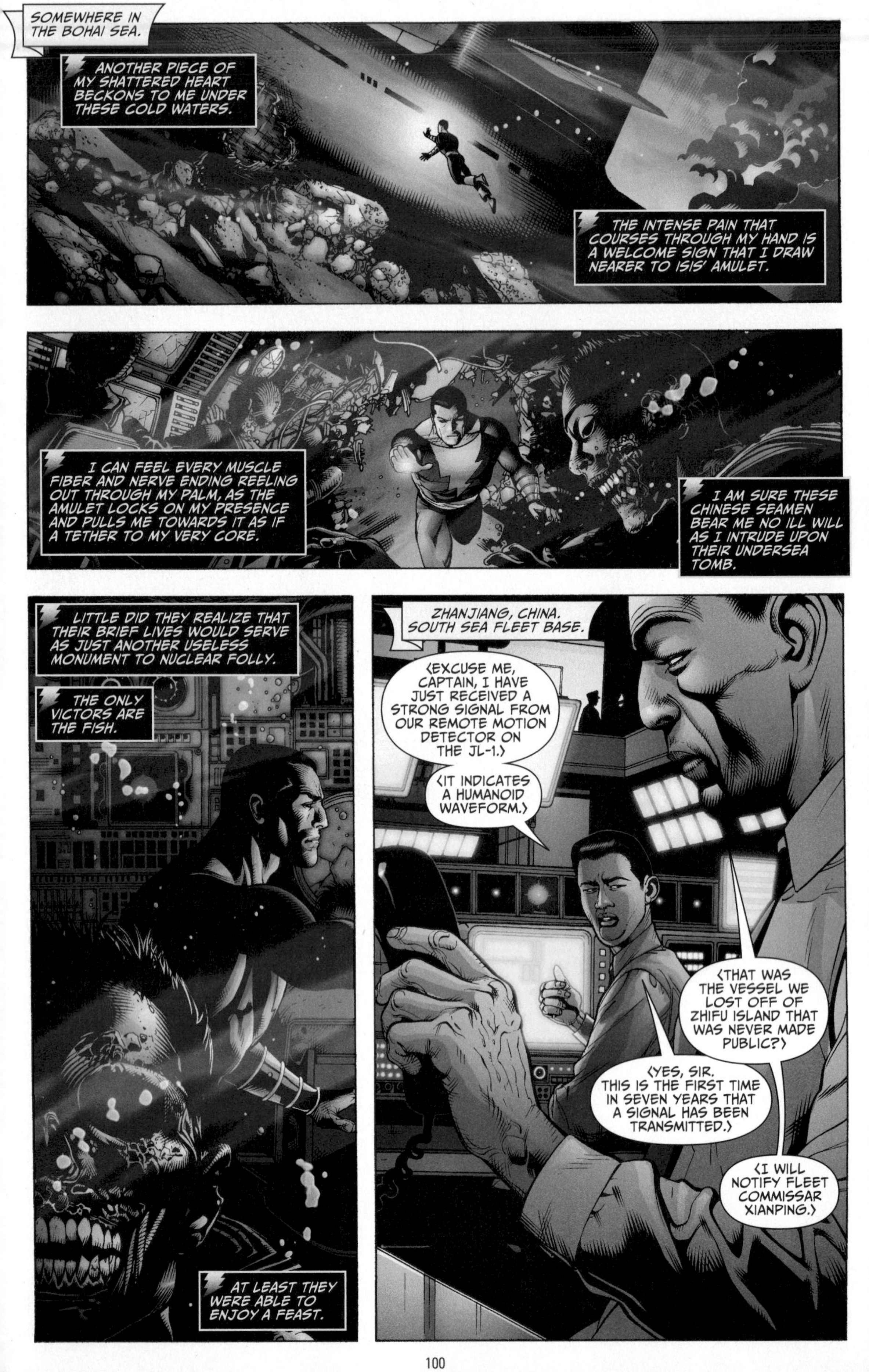
SOMEWHERE IN THE BOHAI SEA.
ANOTHER PIECE OF MY SHATTERED HEART BECKONS TO ME UNDER THESE COLD WATERS.
THE INTENSE PAIN THAT COURSES THROUGH MY HAND IS A WELCOME SIGN THAT I DRAW NEARER TO ISIS' AMULET.
I CAN FEEL EVERY MUSCLE FIBER AND NERVE ENDING REELING OUT THROUGH MY PALM, AS THE AMULET LOCKS ON MY PRESENCE AND PULLS ME TOWARDS IT AS IF A TETHER TO MY VERY CORE.
I AM SURE THESE CHINESE SEAMEN BEAR ME NO ILL WILL AS I INTRUDE UPON THEIR UNDERSEA TOMB.
LITTLE DID THEY REALIZE THAT THEIR BRIEF LIVES WOULD SERVE AS JUST ANOTHER USELESS MONUMENT TO NUCLEAR FOLLY.
THE ONLY VICTORS ARE THE FISH.
AT LEAST THEY WERE ABLE TO ENJOY A FEAST.
ZHANJIANG, CHINA. SOUTH SEA FLEET BASE.
〈EXCUSE ME, CAPTAIN, I HAVE JUST RECEIVED A STRONG SIGNAL FROM OUR REMOTE MOTION DETECTOR ON THE JL-1.〉
〈IT INDICATES A HUMANOID WAVEFORM.〉
〈THAT WAS THE VESSEL WE LOST OFF OF ZHIFU ISLAND THAT WAS NEVER MADE PUBLIC?〉
〈YES, SIR. THIS IS THE FIRST TIME IN SEVEN YEARS THAT A SIGNAL HAS BEEN TRANSMITTED.〉
〈I WILL NOTIFY FLEET COMMISSAR XIANPING.〉

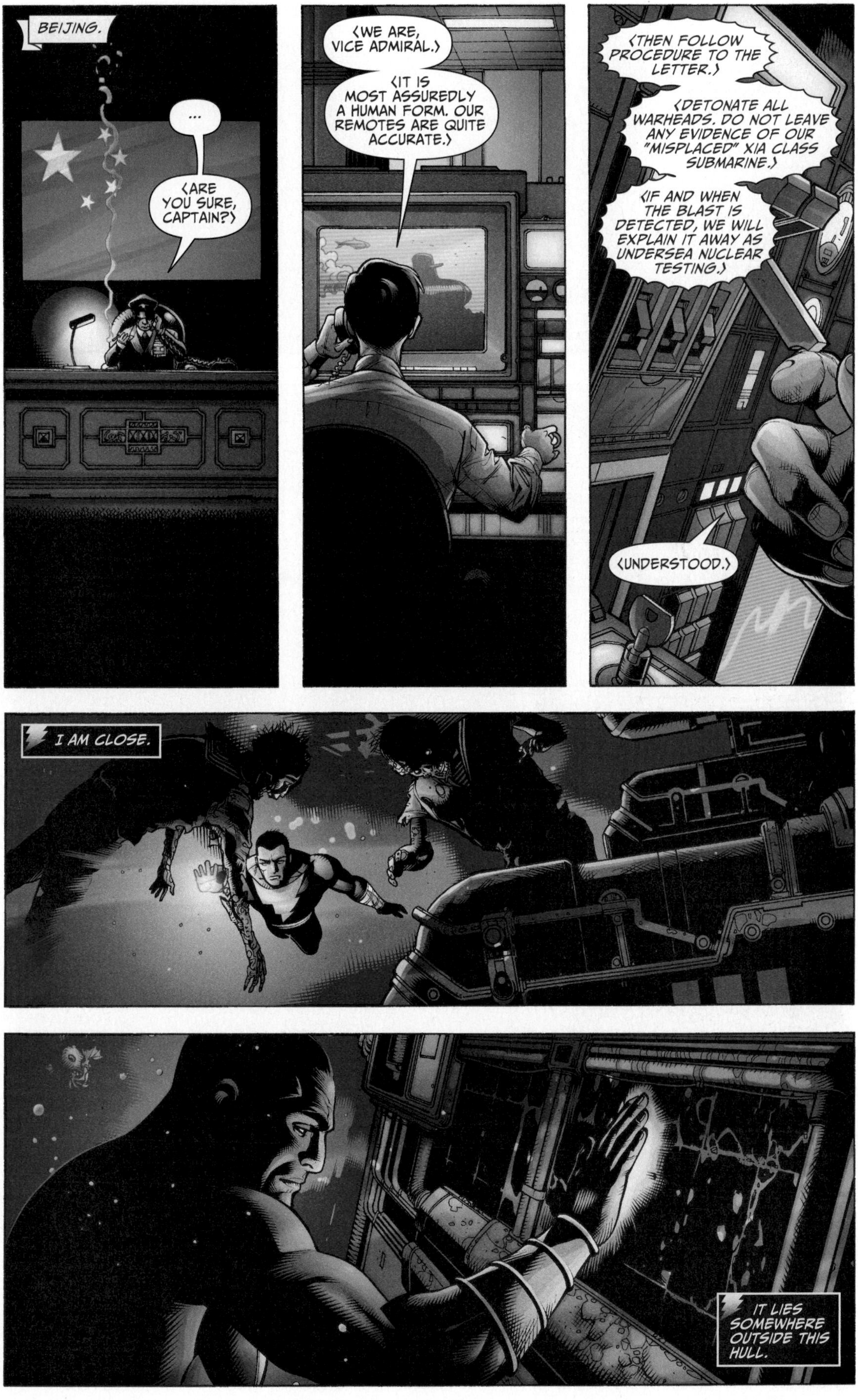
BEIJING.
...
‹ARE YOU SURE, CAPTAIN?›
‹WE ARE, VICE ADMIRAL.›
‹IT IS MOST ASSUREDLY A HUMAN FORM. OUR REMOTES ARE QUITE ACCURATE.›
‹THEN FOLLOW PROCEDURE TO THE LETTER.›
‹DETONATE ALL WARHEADS. DO NOT LEAVE ANY EVIDENCE OF OUR "MISPLACED" XIA CLASS SUBMARINE.›
‹IF AND WHEN THE BLAST IS DETECTED, WE WILL EXPLAIN IT AWAY AS UNDERSEA NUCLEAR TESTING.›
‹UNDERSTOOD.›
I AM CLOSE.
IT LIES SOMEWHERE OUTSIDE THIS HULL.

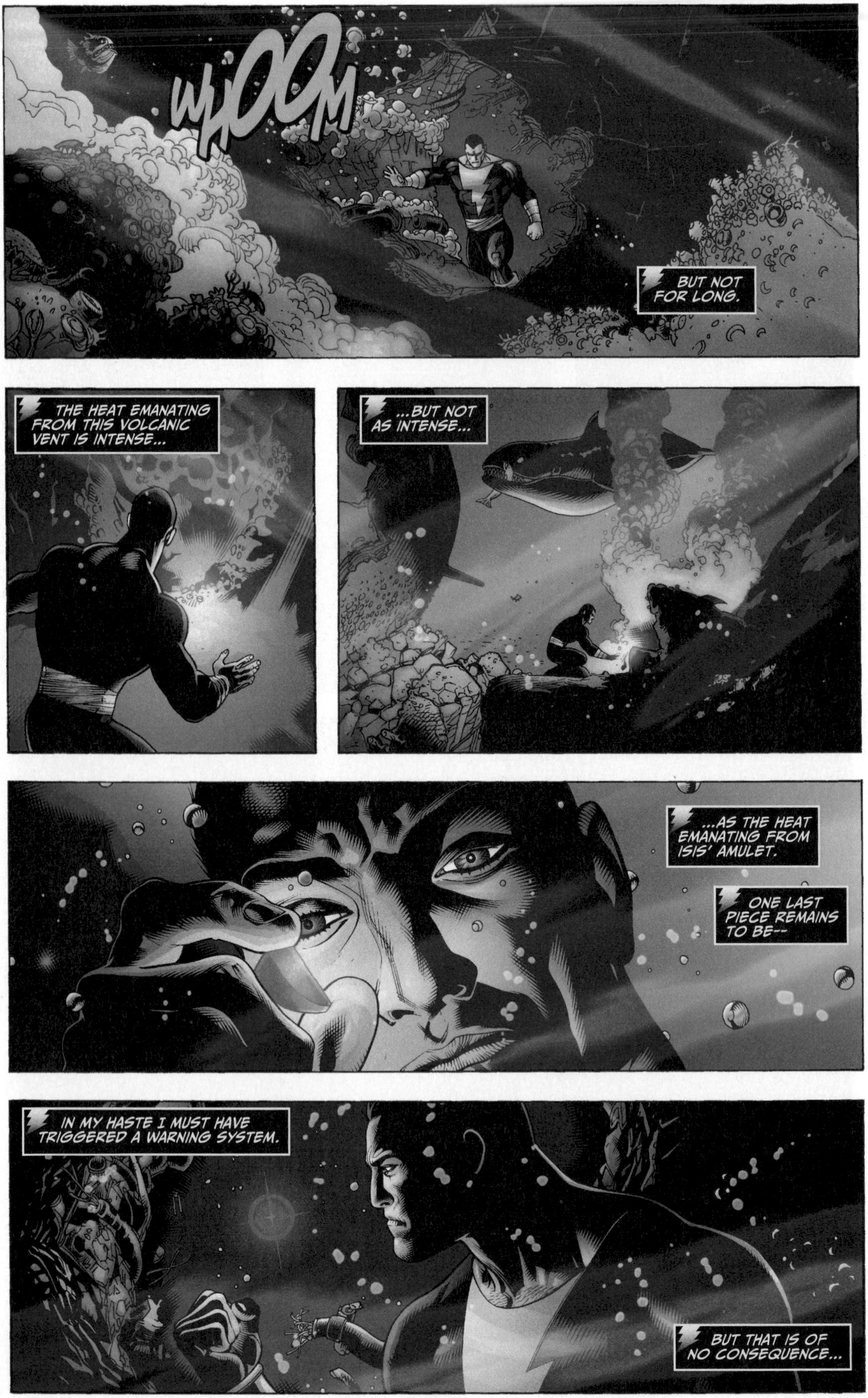
WHOOM
BUT NOT FOR LONG.
THE HEAT EMANATING FROM THIS VOLCANIC VENT IS INTENSE...
...BUT NOT AS INTENSE...
...AS THE HEAT EMANATING FROM ISIS' AMULET.
ONE LAST PIECE REMAINS TO BE--
IN MY HASTE I MUST HAVE TRIGGERED A WARNING SYSTEM.
BUT THAT IS OF NO CONSEQUENCE...

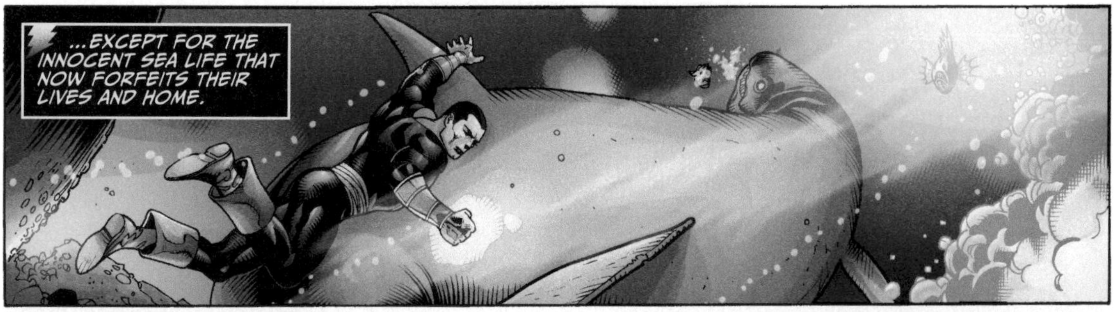
...EXCEPT FOR THE INNOCENT SEA LIFE THAT NOW FORFEITS THEIR LIVES AND HOME.

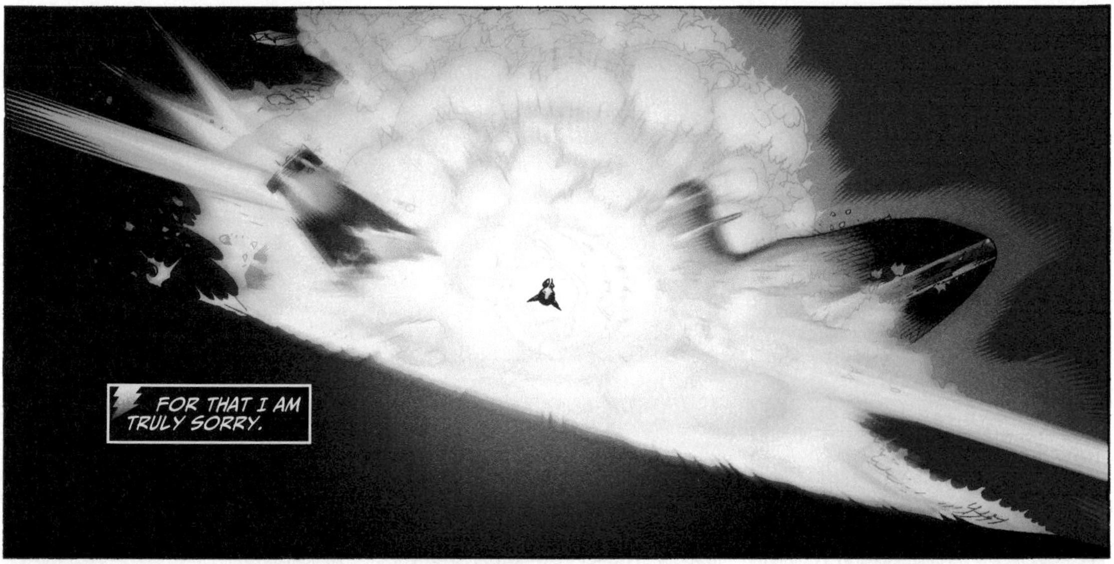
FOR THAT I AM TRULY SORRY.

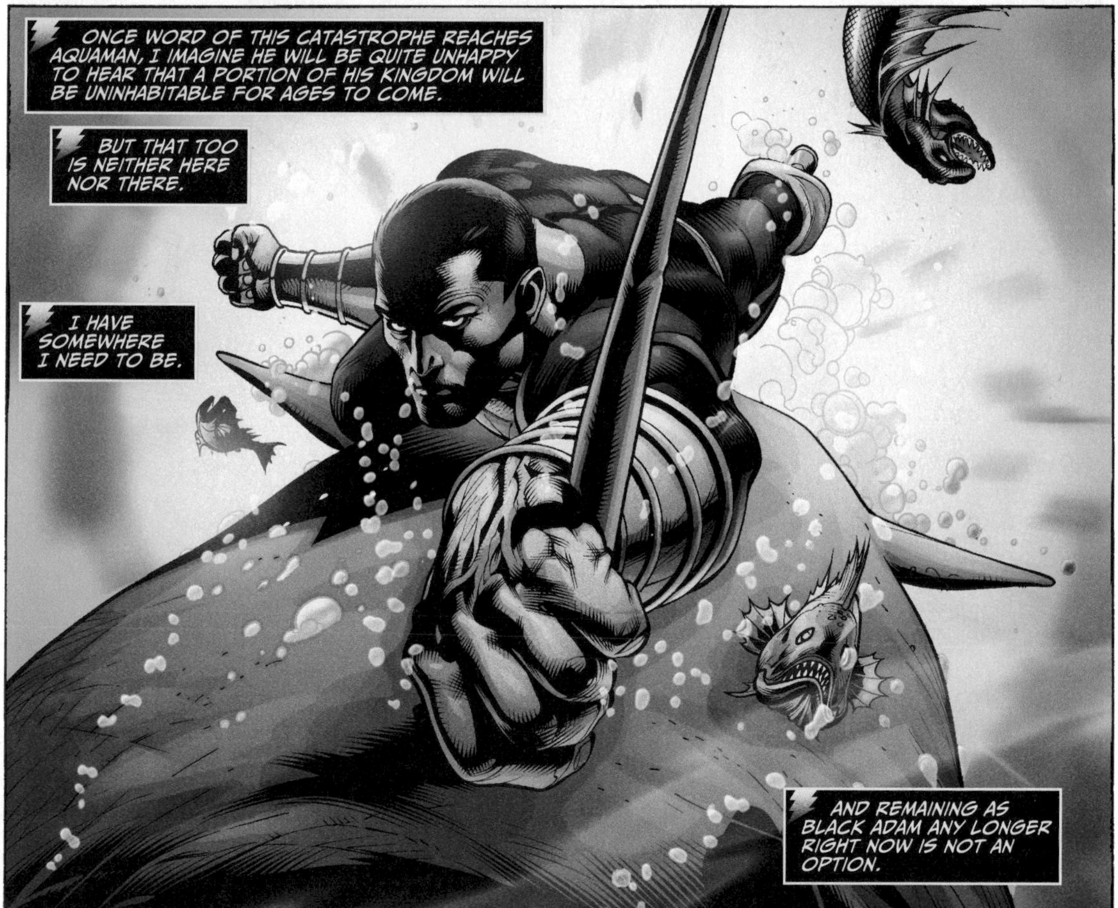
ONCE WORD OF THIS CATASTROPHE REACHES AQUAMAN, I IMAGINE HE WILL BE QUITE UNHAPPY TO HEAR THAT A PORTION OF HIS KINGDOM WILL BE UNINHABITABLE FOR AGES TO COME.
BUT THAT TOO IS NEITHER HERE NOR THERE.
I HAVE SOMEWHERE I NEED TO BE.
AND REMAINING AS BLACK ADAM ANY LONGER RIGHT NOW IS NOT AN OPTION.

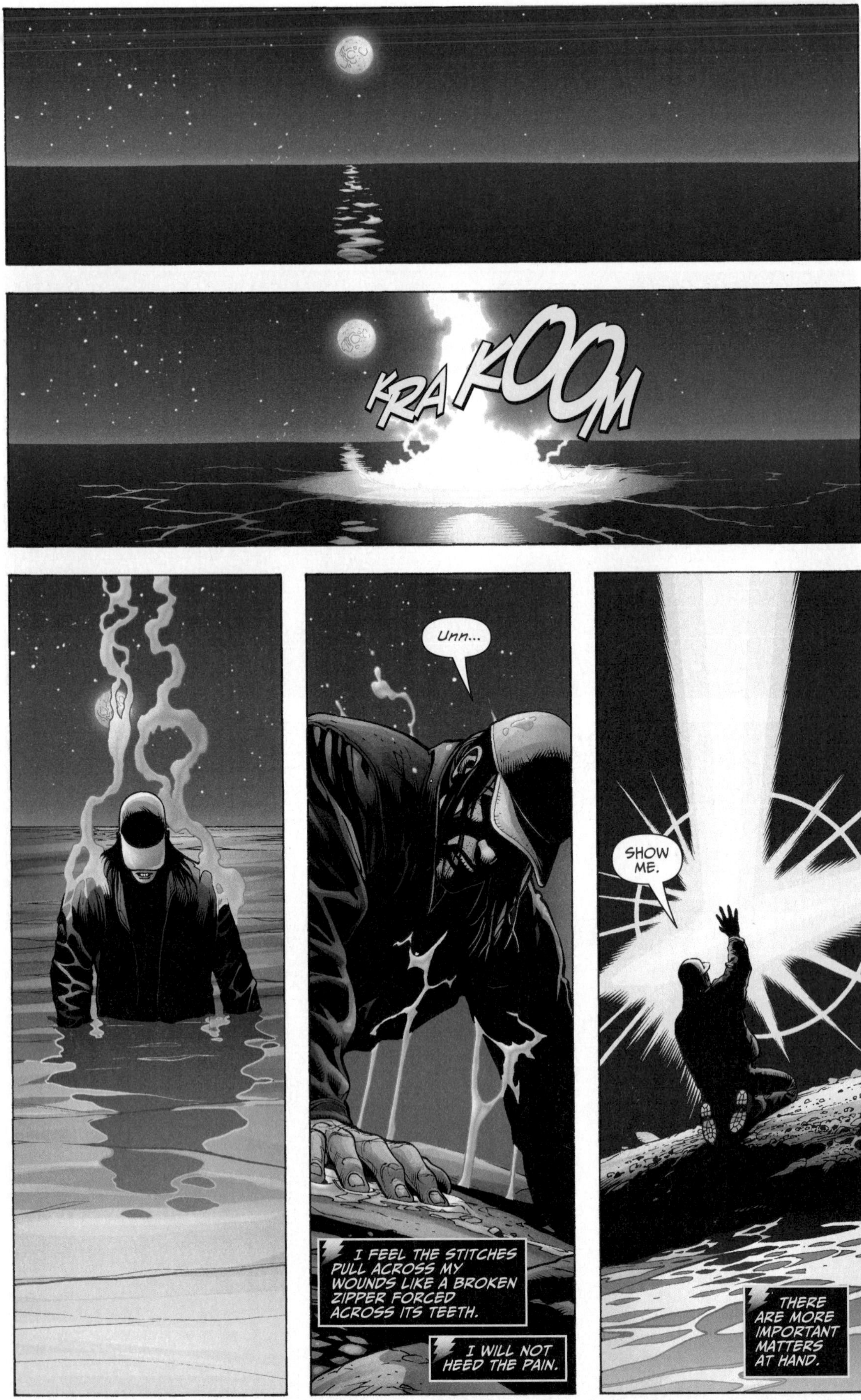
KRA KOOM
Unn...
I FEEL THE STITCHES PULL ACROSS MY WOUNDS LIKE A BROKEN ZIPPER FORCED ACROSS ITS TEETH.
I WILL NOT HEED THE PAIN.
SHOW ME.
THERE ARE MORE IMPORTANT MATTERS AT HAND.

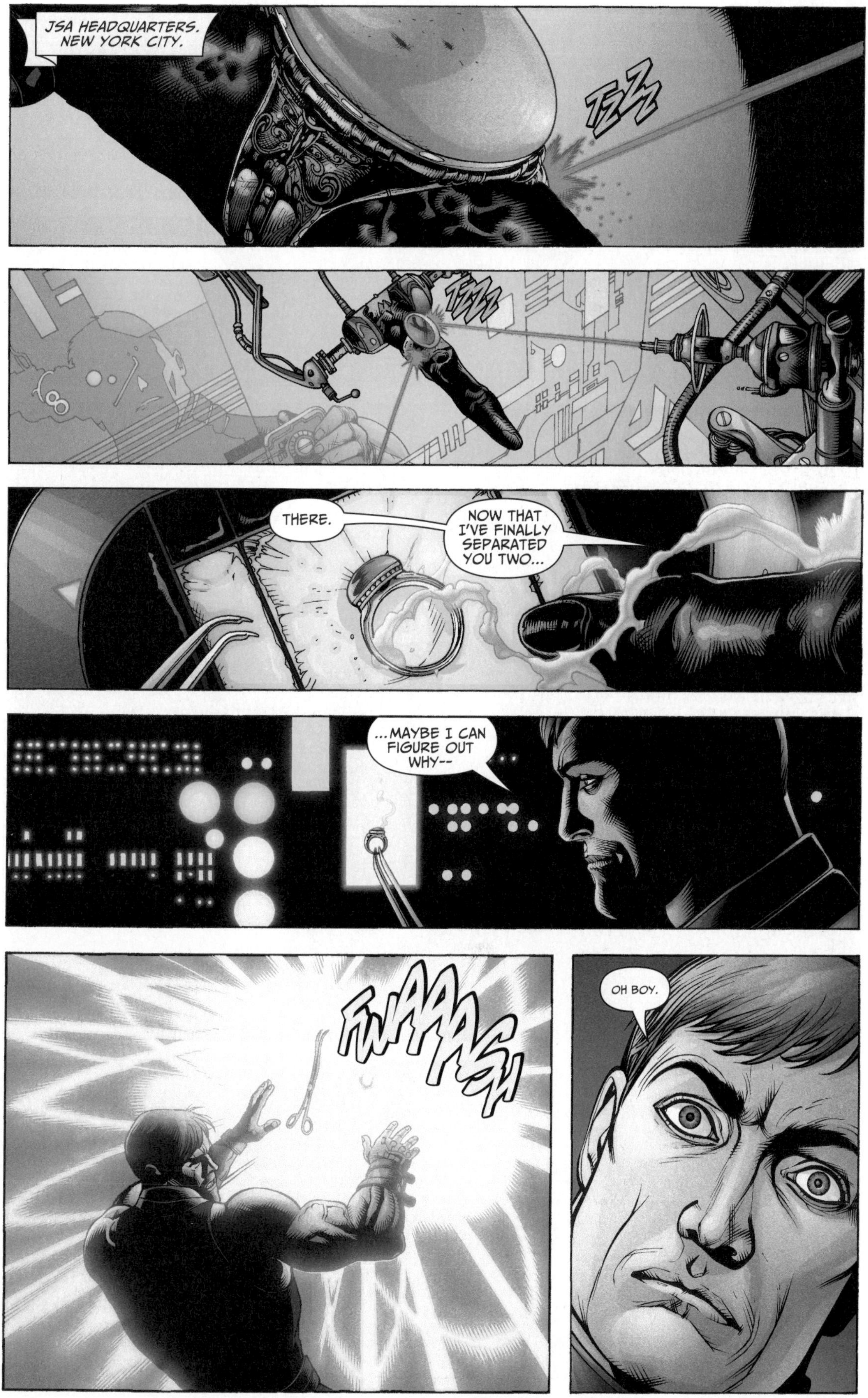
JSA HEADQUARTERS. NEW YORK CITY.
TZZZ
TZZZ
THERE.
NOW THAT I'VE FINALLY SEPARATED YOU TWO...
...MAYBE I CAN FIGURE OUT WHY--
FWAAASH
OH BOY.

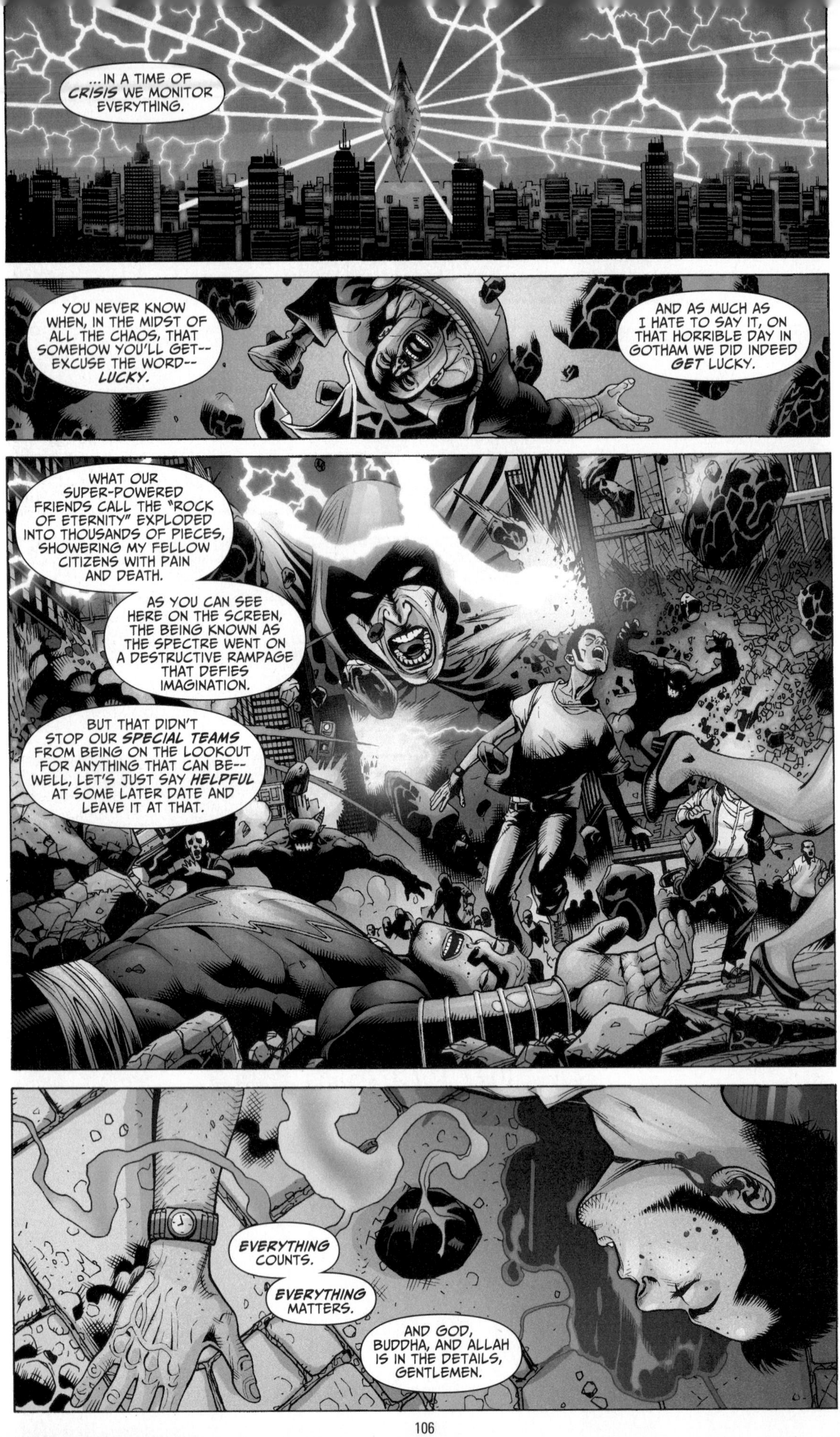

...IN A TIME OF CRISIS WE MONITOR EVERYTHING.
YOU NEVER KNOW WHEN, IN THE MIDST OF ALL THE CHAOS, THAT SOMEHOW YOU'LL GET-- EXCUSE THE WORD-- LUCKY.
AND AS MUCH AS I HATE TO SAY IT, ON THAT HORRIBLE DAY IN GOTHAM WE DID INDEED GET LUCKY.
WHAT OUR SUPER-POWERED FRIENDS CALL THE "ROCK OF ETERNITY" EXPLODED INTO THOUSANDS OF PIECES, SHOWERING MY FELLOW CITIZENS WITH PAIN AND DEATH.
AS YOU CAN SEE HERE ON THE SCREEN, THE BEING KNOWN AS THE SPECTRE WENT ON A DESTRUCTIVE RAMPAGE THAT DEFIES IMAGINATION.
BUT THAT DIDN'T STOP OUR SPECIAL TEAMS FROM BEING ON THE LOOKOUT FOR ANYTHING THAT CAN BE-- WELL, LET'S JUST SAY HELPFUL AT SOME LATER DATE AND LEAVE IT AT THAT.
EVERYTHING COUNTS.
EVERYTHING MATTERS.
AND GOD, BUDDHA, AND ALLAH IS IN THE DETAILS, GENTLEMEN.

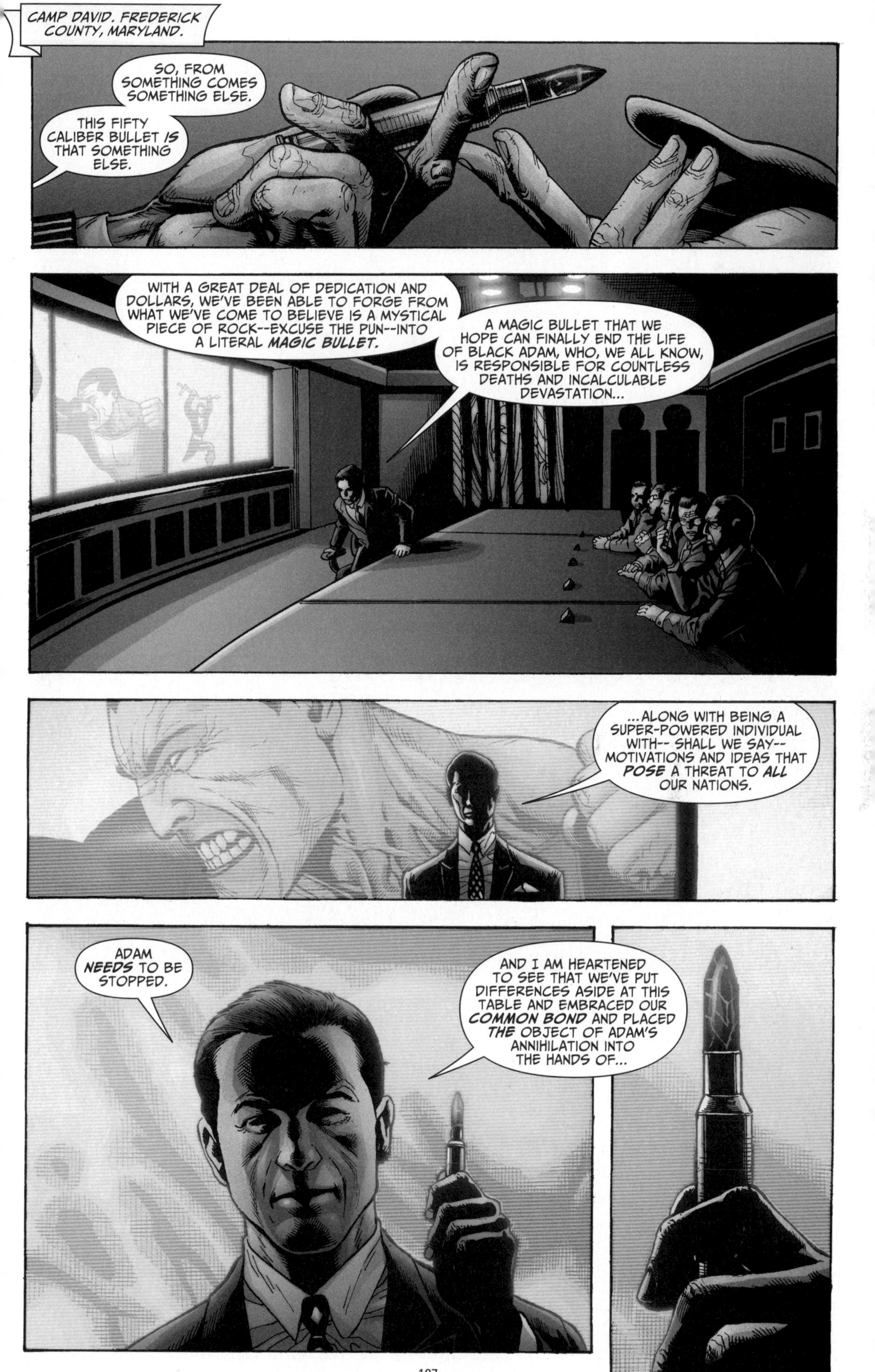

CAMP DAVID. FREDERICK COUNTY, MARYLAND.
SO, FROM SOMETHING COMES SOMETHING ELSE.
THIS FIFTY CALIBER BULLET *IS* THAT SOMETHING ELSE.
WITH A GREAT DEAL OF DEDICATION AND DOLLARS, WE'VE BEEN ABLE TO FORGE FROM WHAT WE'VE COME TO BELIEVE IS A MYSTICAL PIECE OF ROCK--EXCUSE THE PUN--INTO A LITERAL *MAGIC BULLET.*
A MAGIC BULLET THAT WE HOPE CAN FINALLY END THE LIFE OF BLACK ADAM, WHO, WE ALL KNOW, IS RESPONSIBLE FOR COUNTLESS DEATHS AND INCALCULABLE DEVASTATION...
...ALONG WITH BEING A SUPER-POWERED INDIVIDUAL WITH-- SHALL WE SAY-- MOTIVATIONS AND IDEAS THAT *POSE* A THREAT TO *ALL* OUR NATIONS.
ADAM *NEEDS* TO BE STOPPED.
AND I AM HEARTENED TO SEE THAT WE'VE PUT DIFFERENCES ASIDE AT THIS TABLE AND EMBRACED OUR *COMMON BOND* AND PLACED *THE* OBJECT OF ADAM'S ANNIHILATION INTO THE HANDS OF...

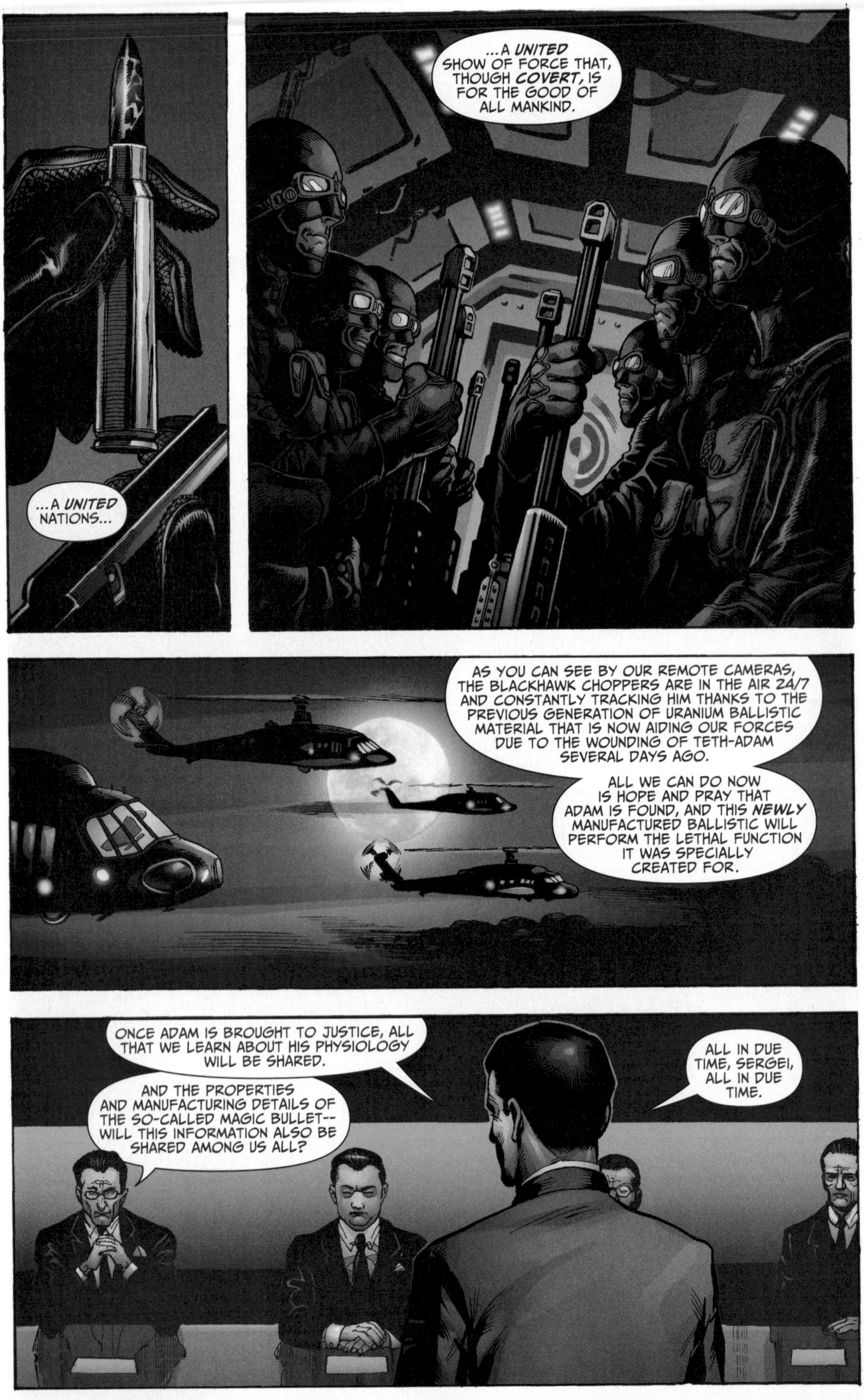

...A UNITED NATIONS...
...A UNITED SHOW OF FORCE THAT, THOUGH COVERT, IS FOR THE GOOD OF ALL MANKIND.
AS YOU CAN SEE BY OUR REMOTE CAMERAS, THE BLACKHAWK CHOPPERS ARE IN THE AIR 24/7 AND CONSTANTLY TRACKING HIM THANKS TO THE PREVIOUS GENERATION OF URANIUM BALLISTIC MATERIAL THAT IS NOW AIDING OUR FORCES DUE TO THE WOUNDING OF TETH-ADAM SEVERAL DAYS AGO.
ALL WE CAN DO NOW IS HOPE AND PRAY THAT ADAM IS FOUND, AND THIS NEWLY MANUFACTURED BALLISTIC WILL PERFORM THE LETHAL FUNCTION IT WAS SPECIALLY CREATED FOR.
ONCE ADAM IS BROUGHT TO JUSTICE, ALL THAT WE LEARN ABOUT HIS PHYSIOLOGY WILL BE SHARED.
AND THE PROPERTIES AND MANUFACTURING DETAILS OF THE SO-CALLED MAGIC BULLET-- WILL THIS INFORMATION ALSO BE SHARED AMONG US ALL?
ALL IN DUE TIME, SERGEI, ALL IN DUE TIME.

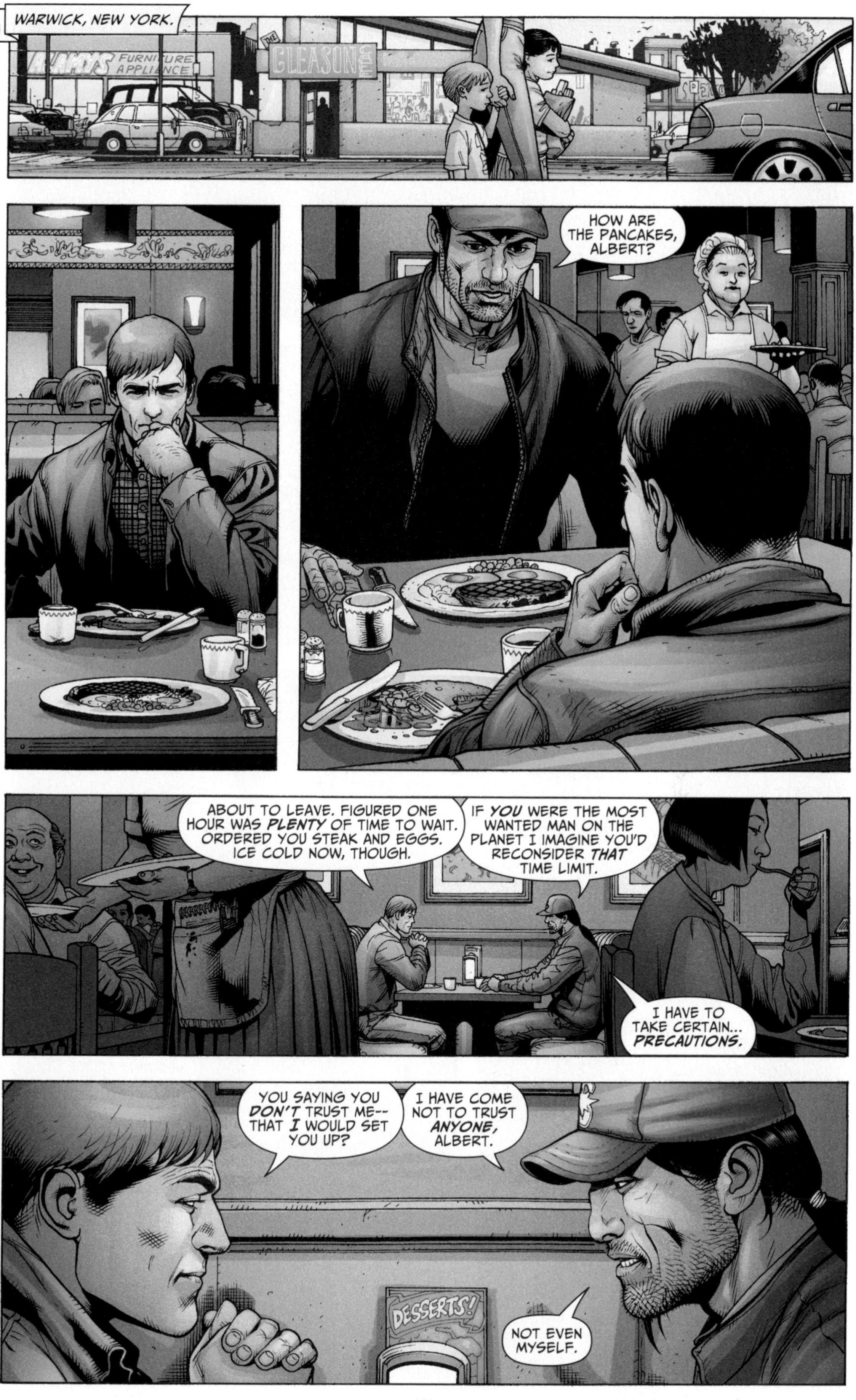
WARWICK, NEW YORK.
FURNITURE APPLIANCE
GLEASON
HOW ARE THE PANCAKES, ALBERT?
ABOUT TO LEAVE. FIGURED ONE HOUR WAS *PLENTY* OF TIME TO WAIT. ORDERED YOU STEAK AND EGGS. ICE COLD NOW, THOUGH.
IF *YOU* WERE THE MOST WANTED MAN ON THE PLANET I IMAGINE YOU'D RECONSIDER *THAT* TIME LIMIT.
I HAVE TO TAKE CERTAIN... ***PRECAUTIONS.***
YOU SAYING YOU *DON'T* TRUST ME-- THAT *I* WOULD SET YOU UP?
I HAVE COME NOT TO TRUST *ANYONE,* ALBERT.
DESSERTS!
NOT EVEN MYSELF.

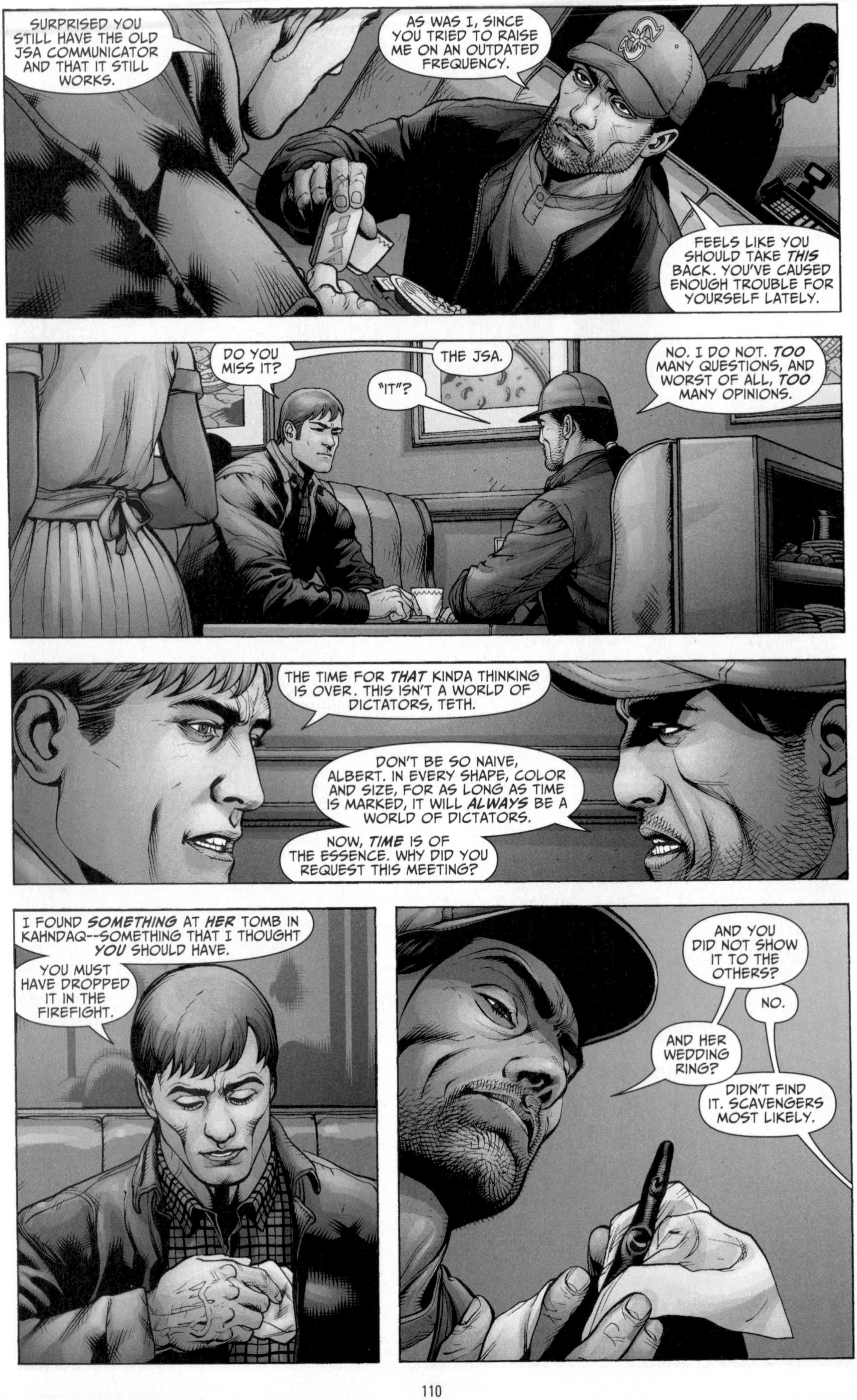
SURPRISED YOU STILL HAVE THE OLD JSA COMMUNICATOR AND THAT IT STILL WORKS.
AS WAS I, SINCE YOU TRIED TO RAISE ME ON AN OUTDATED FREQUENCY.
FEELS LIKE YOU SHOULD TAKE THIS BACK. YOU'VE CAUSED ENOUGH TROUBLE FOR YOURSELF LATELY.
DO YOU MISS IT?
"IT"?
THE JSA.
NO. I DO NOT. TOO MANY QUESTIONS, AND WORST OF ALL, TOO MANY OPINIONS.
THE TIME FOR THAT KINDA THINKING IS OVER. THIS ISN'T A WORLD OF DICTATORS, TETH.
DON'T BE SO NAIVE, ALBERT. IN EVERY SHAPE, COLOR AND SIZE, FOR AS LONG AS TIME IS MARKED, IT WILL ALWAYS BE A WORLD OF DICTATORS.
NOW, TIME IS OF THE ESSENCE. WHY DID YOU REQUEST THIS MEETING?
I FOUND SOMETHING AT HER TOMB IN KAHNDAQ--SOMETHING THAT I THOUGHT YOU SHOULD HAVE.
YOU MUST HAVE DROPPED IT IN THE FIREFIGHT.
AND YOU DID NOT SHOW IT TO THE OTHERS?
NO.
AND HER WEDDING RING?
DIDN'T FIND IT. SCAVENGERS MOST LIKELY.

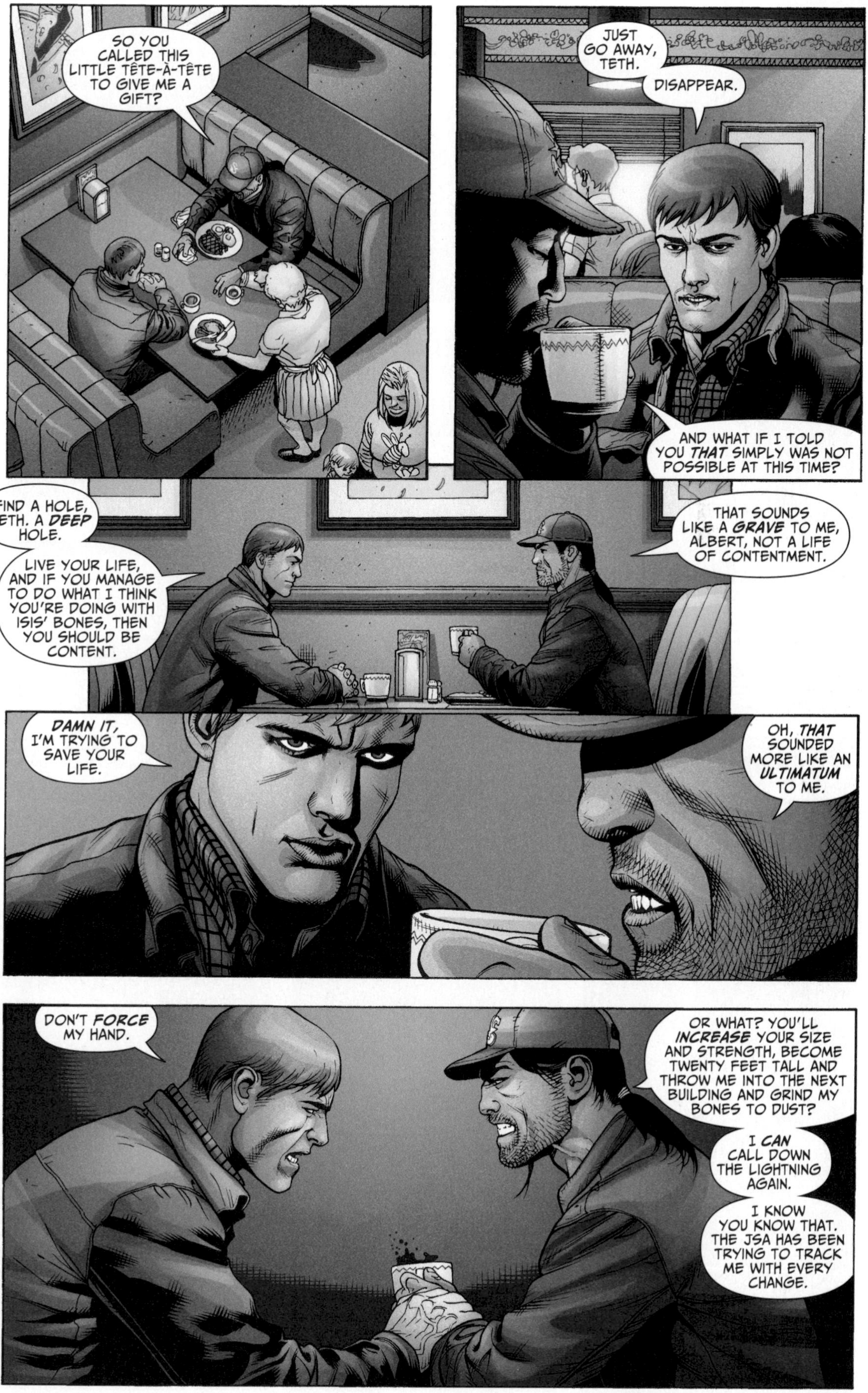
SO YOU CALLED THIS LITTLE TÊTE-À-TÊTE TO GIVE ME A GIFT?
JUST GO AWAY, TETH.
DISAPPEAR.
AND WHAT IF I TOLD YOU THAT SIMPLY WAS NOT POSSIBLE AT THIS TIME?
FIND A HOLE, TETH. A DEEP HOLE.
LIVE YOUR LIFE, AND IF YOU MANAGE TO DO WHAT I THINK YOU'RE DOING WITH ISIS' BONES, THEN YOU SHOULD BE CONTENT.
THAT SOUNDS LIKE A GRAVE TO ME, ALBERT, NOT A LIFE OF CONTENTMENT.
DAMN IT, I'M TRYING TO SAVE YOUR LIFE.
OH, THAT SOUNDED MORE LIKE AN ULTIMATUM TO ME.
DON'T FORCE MY HAND.
OR WHAT? YOU'LL INCREASE YOUR SIZE AND STRENGTH, BECOME TWENTY FEET TALL AND THROW ME INTO THE NEXT BUILDING AND GRIND MY BONES TO DUST?
I CAN CALL DOWN THE LIGHTNING AGAIN.
I KNOW YOU KNOW THAT. THE JSA HAS BEEN TRYING TO TRACK ME WITH EVERY CHANGE.

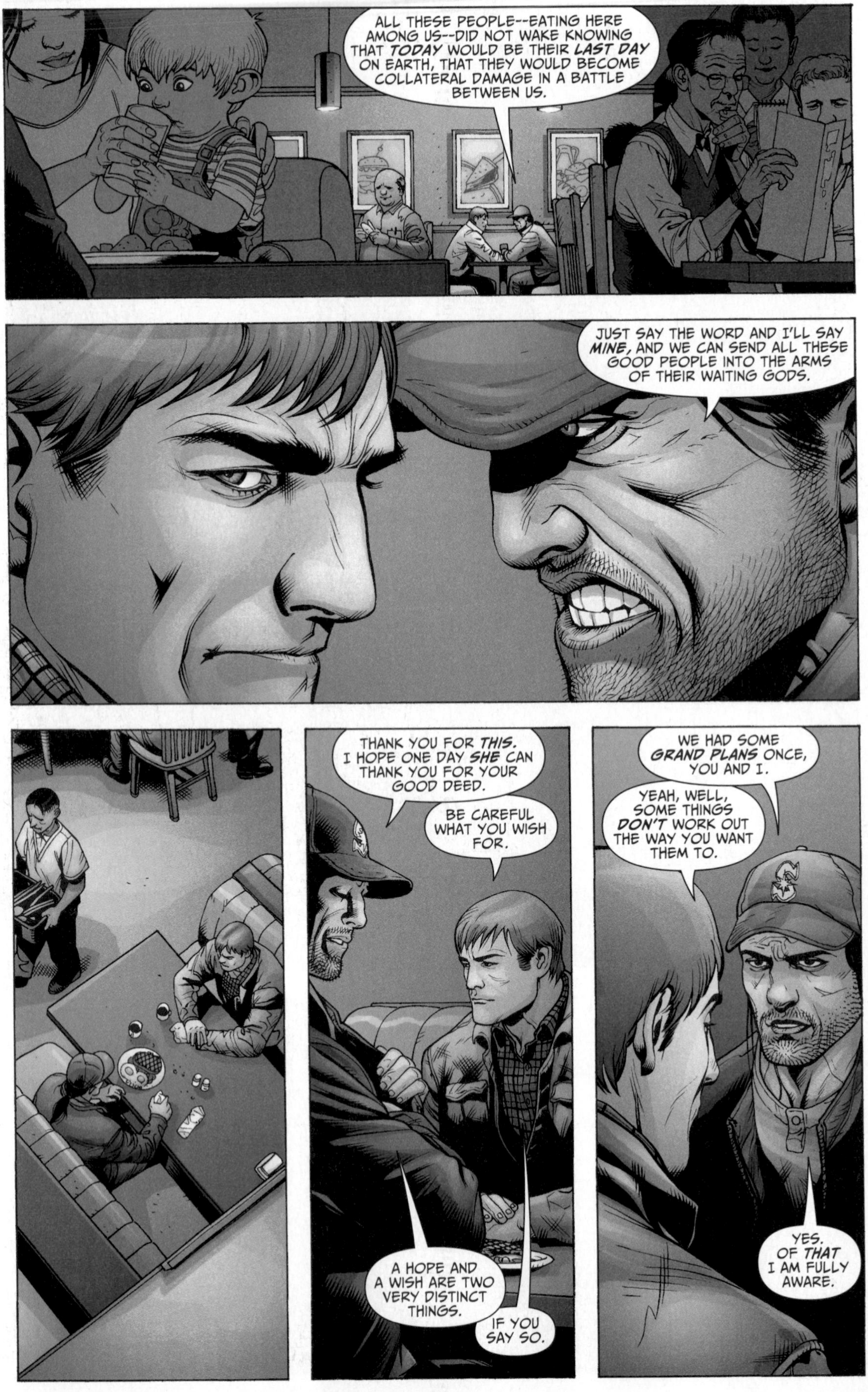
ALL THESE PEOPLE--EATING HERE AMONG US--DID NOT WAKE KNOWING THAT *TODAY* WOULD BE THEIR *LAST DAY* ON EARTH, THAT THEY WOULD BECOME COLLATERAL DAMAGE IN A BATTLE BETWEEN US.
JUST SAY THE WORD AND I'LL SAY *MINE,* AND WE CAN SEND ALL THESE GOOD PEOPLE INTO THE ARMS OF THEIR WAITING GODS.
THANK YOU FOR *THIS.* I HOPE ONE DAY *SHE* CAN THANK YOU FOR YOUR GOOD DEED.
BE CAREFUL WHAT YOU WISH FOR.
A HOPE AND A WISH ARE TWO VERY DISTINCT THINGS.
IF YOU SAY SO.
WE HAD SOME *GRAND PLANS* ONCE, YOU AND I.
YEAH, WELL, SOME THINGS *DON'T* WORK OUT THE WAY YOU WANT THEM TO.
YES. OF *THAT* I AM FULLY AWARE.

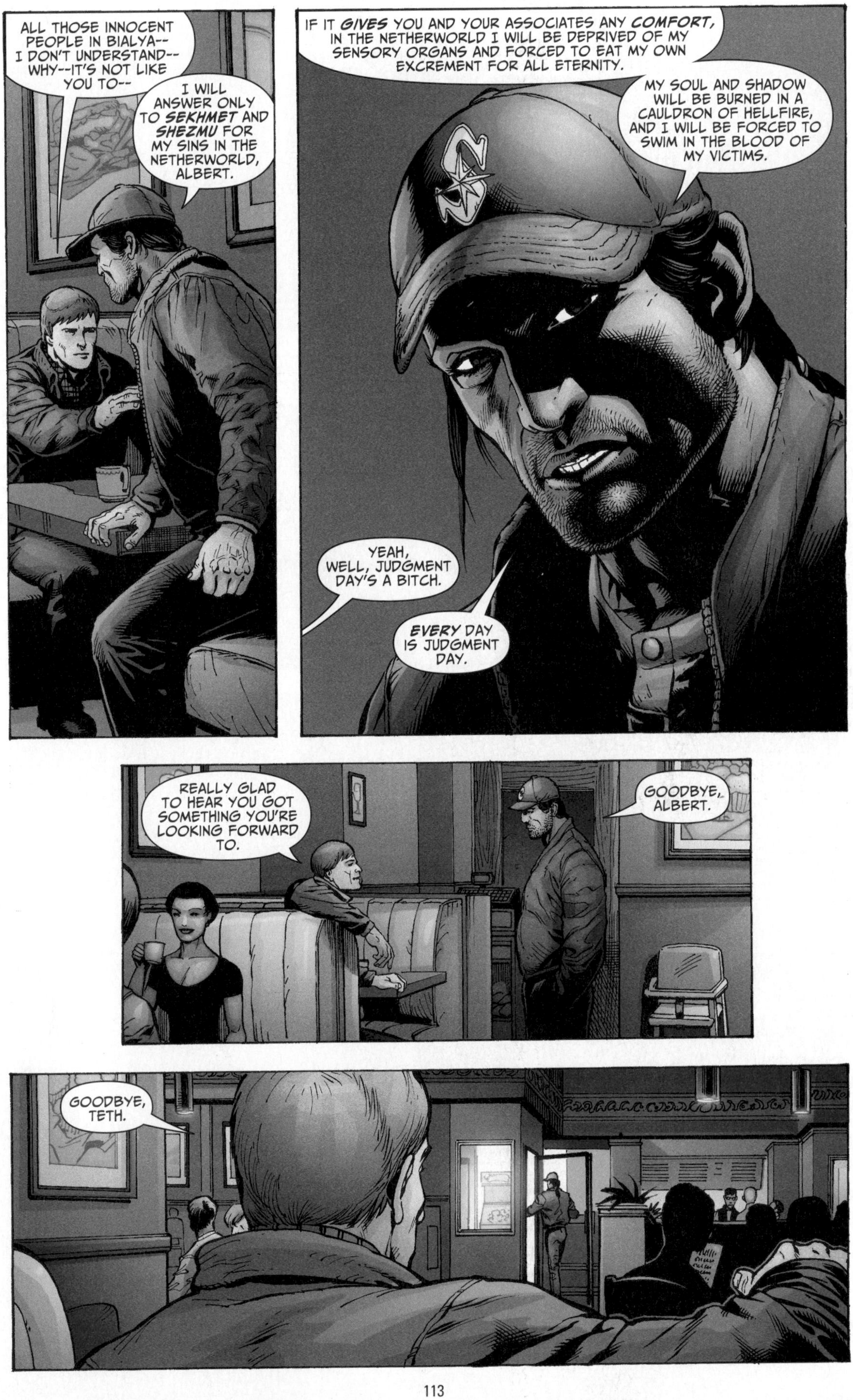
ALL THOSE INNOCENT PEOPLE IN BIALYA-- I DON'T UNDERSTAND-- WHY--IT'S NOT LIKE YOU TO--
I WILL ANSWER ONLY TO SEKHMET AND SHEZMU FOR MY SINS IN THE NETHERWORLD, ALBERT.
IF IT GIVES YOU AND YOUR ASSOCIATES ANY COMFORT, IN THE NETHERWORLD I WILL BE DEPRIVED OF MY SENSORY ORGANS AND FORCED TO EAT MY OWN EXCREMENT FOR ALL ETERNITY.
MY SOUL AND SHADOW WILL BE BURNED IN A CAULDRON OF HELLFIRE, AND I WILL BE FORCED TO SWIM IN THE BLOOD OF MY VICTIMS.
YEAH, WELL, JUDGMENT DAY'S A BITCH.
EVERY DAY IS JUDGMENT DAY.
REALLY GLAD TO HEAR YOU GOT SOMETHING YOU'RE LOOKING FORWARD TO.
GOODBYE, ALBERT.
GOODBYE, TETH.

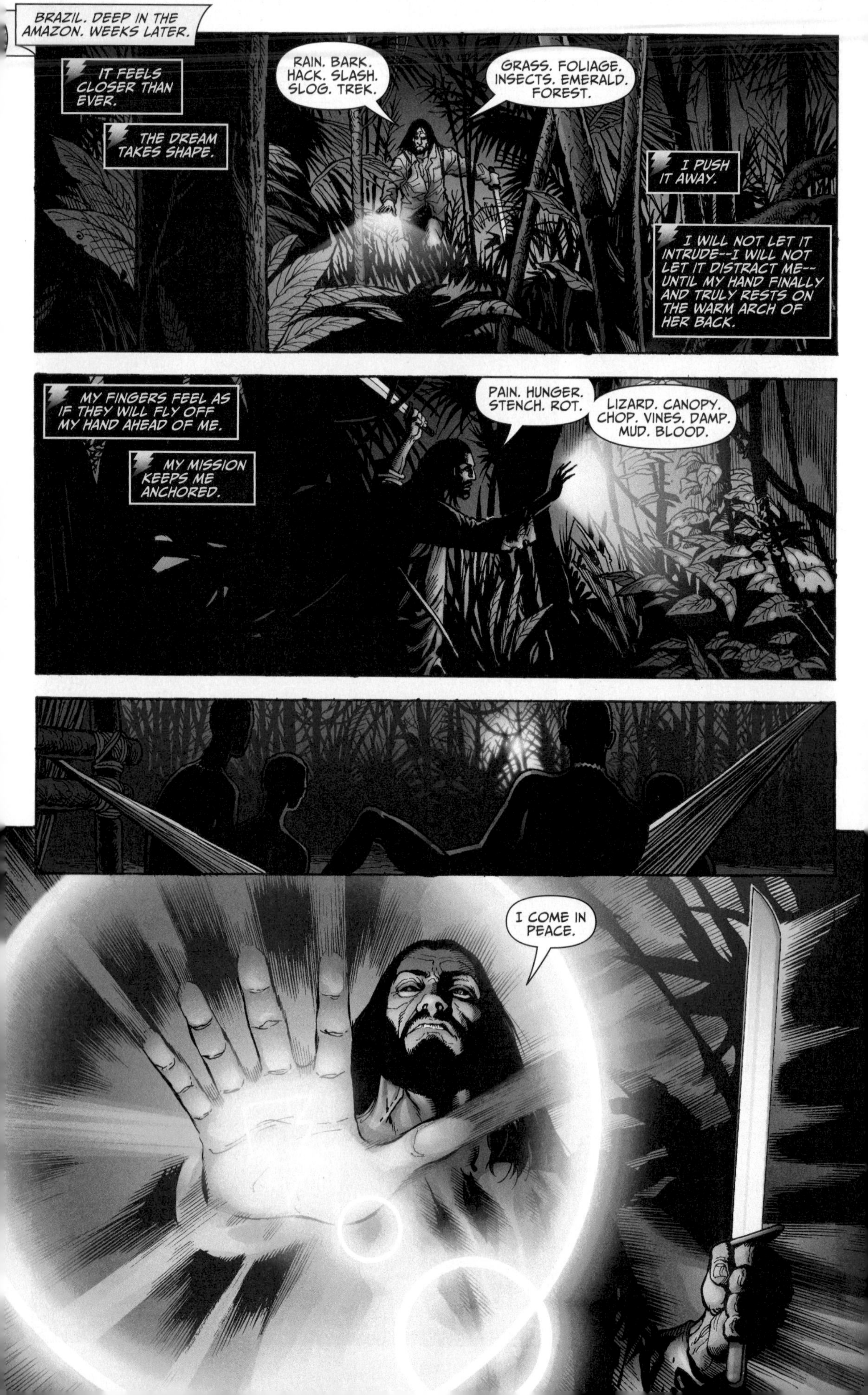
BRAZIL. DEEP IN THE AMAZON. WEEKS LATER.
IT FEELS CLOSER THAN EVER.
THE DREAM TAKES SHAPE.
RAIN. BARK. HACK. SLASH. SLOG. TREK.
GRASS. FOLIAGE. INSECTS. EMERALD. FOREST.
I PUSH IT AWAY.
I WILL NOT LET IT INTRUDE--I WILL NOT LET IT DISTRACT ME--UNTIL MY HAND FINALLY AND TRULY RESTS ON THE WARM ARCH OF HER BACK.
MY FINGERS FEEL AS IF THEY WILL FLY OFF MY HAND AHEAD OF ME.
MY MISSION KEEPS ME ANCHORED.
PAIN. HUNGER. STENCH. ROT.
LIZARD. CANOPY. CHOP. VINES. DAMP. MUD. BLOOD.
I COME IN PEACE.

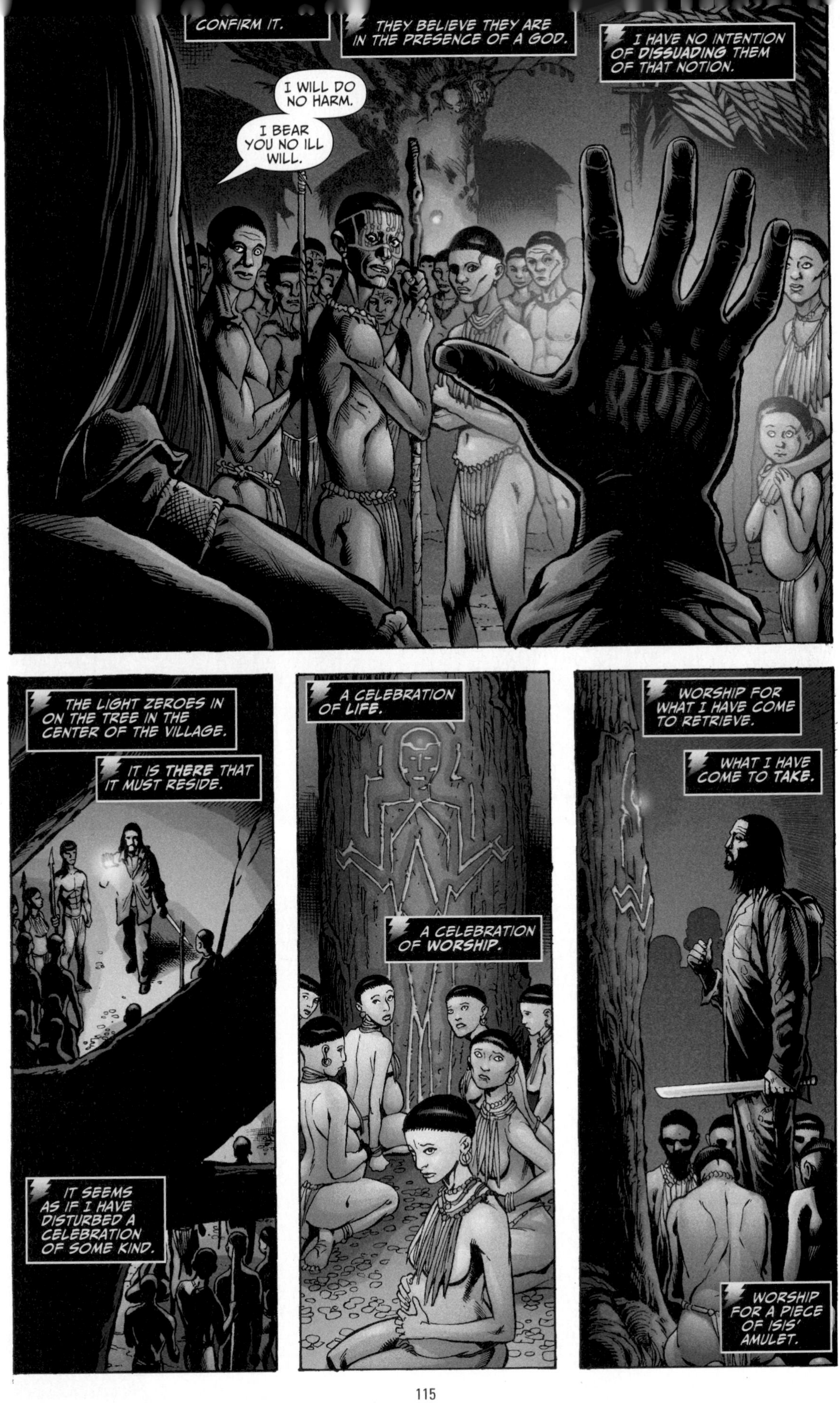
CONFIRM IT.
THEY BELIEVE THEY ARE IN THE PRESENCE OF A GOD.
I HAVE NO INTENTION OF DISSUADING THEM OF THAT NOTION.
I WILL DO NO HARM.
I BEAR YOU NO ILL WILL.
THE LIGHT ZEROES IN ON THE TREE IN THE CENTER OF THE VILLAGE.
IT IS THERE THAT IT MUST RESIDE.
IT SEEMS AS IF I HAVE DISTURBED A CELEBRATION OF SOME KIND.
A CELEBRATION OF LIFE.
A CELEBRATION OF WORSHIP.
WORSHIP FOR WHAT I HAVE COME TO RETRIEVE.
WHAT I HAVE COME TO TAKE.
WORSHIP FOR A PIECE OF ISIS' AMULET.

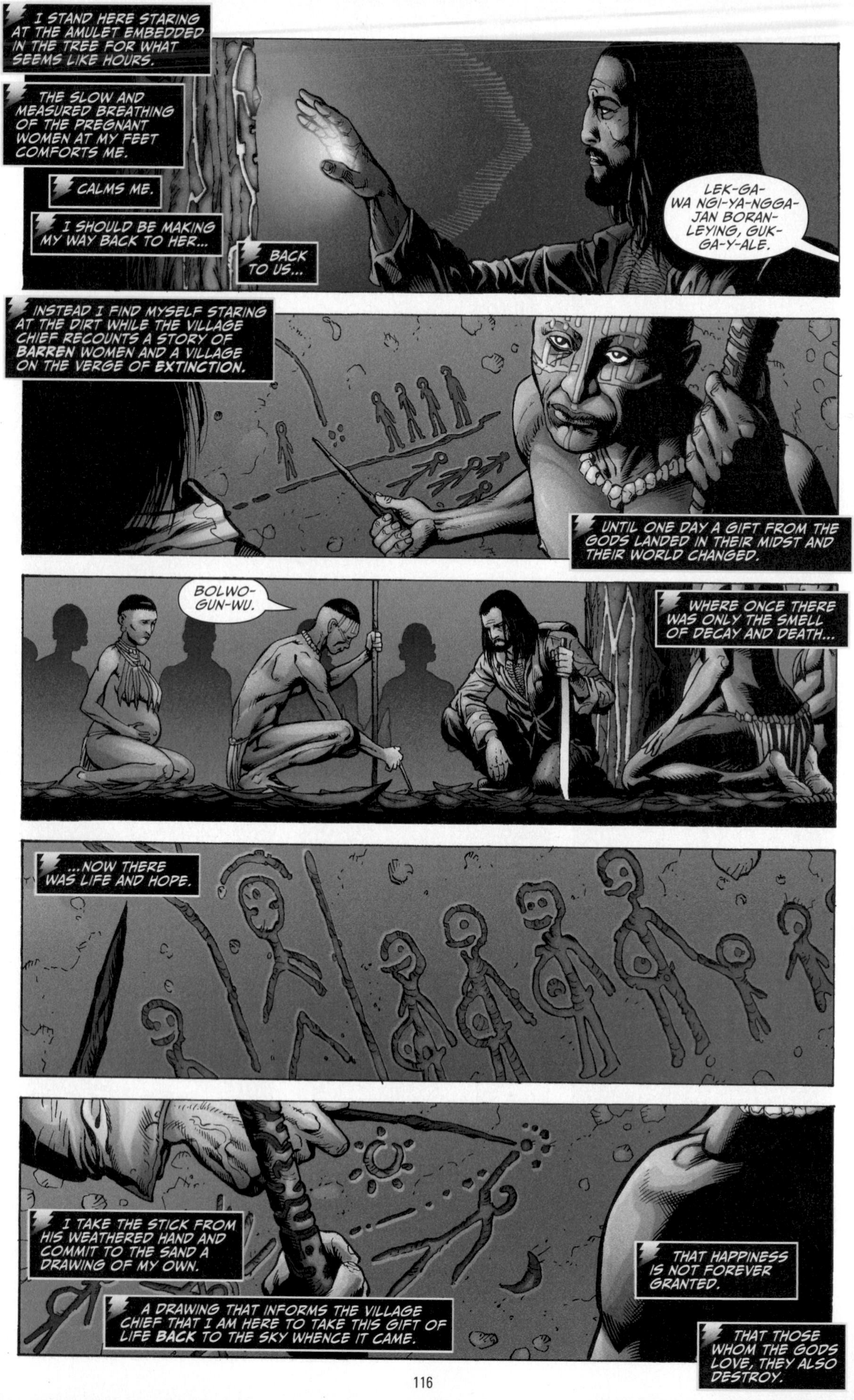
I STAND HERE STARING AT THE AMULET EMBEDDED IN THE TREE FOR WHAT SEEMS LIKE HOURS.
THE SLOW AND MEASURED BREATHING OF THE PREGNANT WOMEN AT MY FEET COMFORTS ME.
CALMS ME.
I SHOULD BE MAKING MY WAY BACK TO HER...
BACK TO US...
LEK-GA-WA NGI-YA-NGGA-JAN BORAN-LEYING, GUK-GA-Y-ALE.
INSTEAD I FIND MYSELF STARING AT THE DIRT WHILE THE VILLAGE CHIEF RECOUNTS A STORY OF BARREN WOMEN AND A VILLAGE ON THE VERGE OF EXTINCTION.
UNTIL ONE DAY A GIFT FROM THE GODS LANDED IN THEIR MIDST AND THEIR WORLD CHANGED.
BOLWO-GUN-WU.
WHERE ONCE THERE WAS ONLY THE SMELL OF DECAY AND DEATH...
...NOW THERE WAS LIFE AND HOPE.
I TAKE THE STICK FROM HIS WEATHERED HAND AND COMMIT TO THE SAND A DRAWING OF MY OWN.
A DRAWING THAT INFORMS THE VILLAGE CHIEF THAT I AM HERE TO TAKE THIS GIFT OF LIFE BACK TO THE SKY WHENCE IT CAME.
THAT HAPPINESS IS NOT FOREVER GRANTED.
THAT THOSE WHOM THE GODS LOVE, THEY ALSO DESTROY.

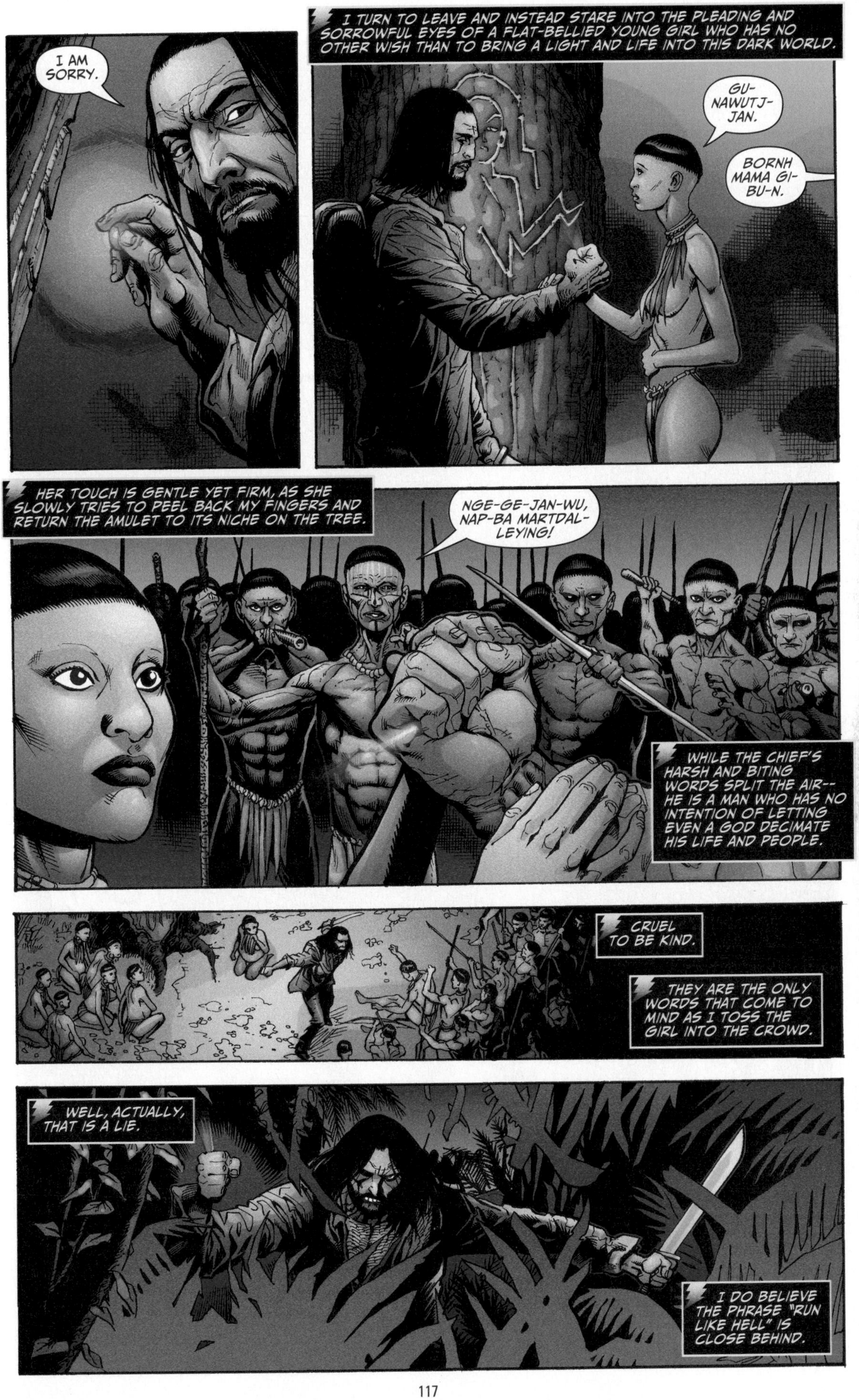
I AM SORRY.
I TURN TO LEAVE AND INSTEAD STARE INTO THE PLEADING AND SORROWFUL EYES OF A FLAT-BELLIED YOUNG GIRL WHO HAS NO OTHER WISH THAN TO BRING A LIGHT AND LIFE INTO THIS DARK WORLD.
GU-NAWUTJ-JAN.
BORNH MAMA GI-BU-N.
HER TOUCH IS GENTLE YET FIRM, AS SHE SLOWLY TRIES TO PEEL BACK MY FINGERS AND RETURN THE AMULET TO ITS NICHE ON THE TREE.
NGE-GE-JAN-WU, NAP-BA MARTDAL-LEYING!
WHILE THE CHIEF'S HARSH AND BITING WORDS SPLIT THE AIR-- HE IS A MAN WHO HAS NO INTENTION OF LETTING EVEN A GOD DECIMATE HIS LIFE AND PEOPLE.
CRUEL TO BE KIND.
THEY ARE THE ONLY WORDS THAT COME TO MIND AS I TOSS THE GIRL INTO THE CROWD.
WELL, ACTUALLY, THAT IS A LIE.
I DO BELIEVE THE PHRASE "RUN LIKE HELL" IS CLOSE BEHIND.

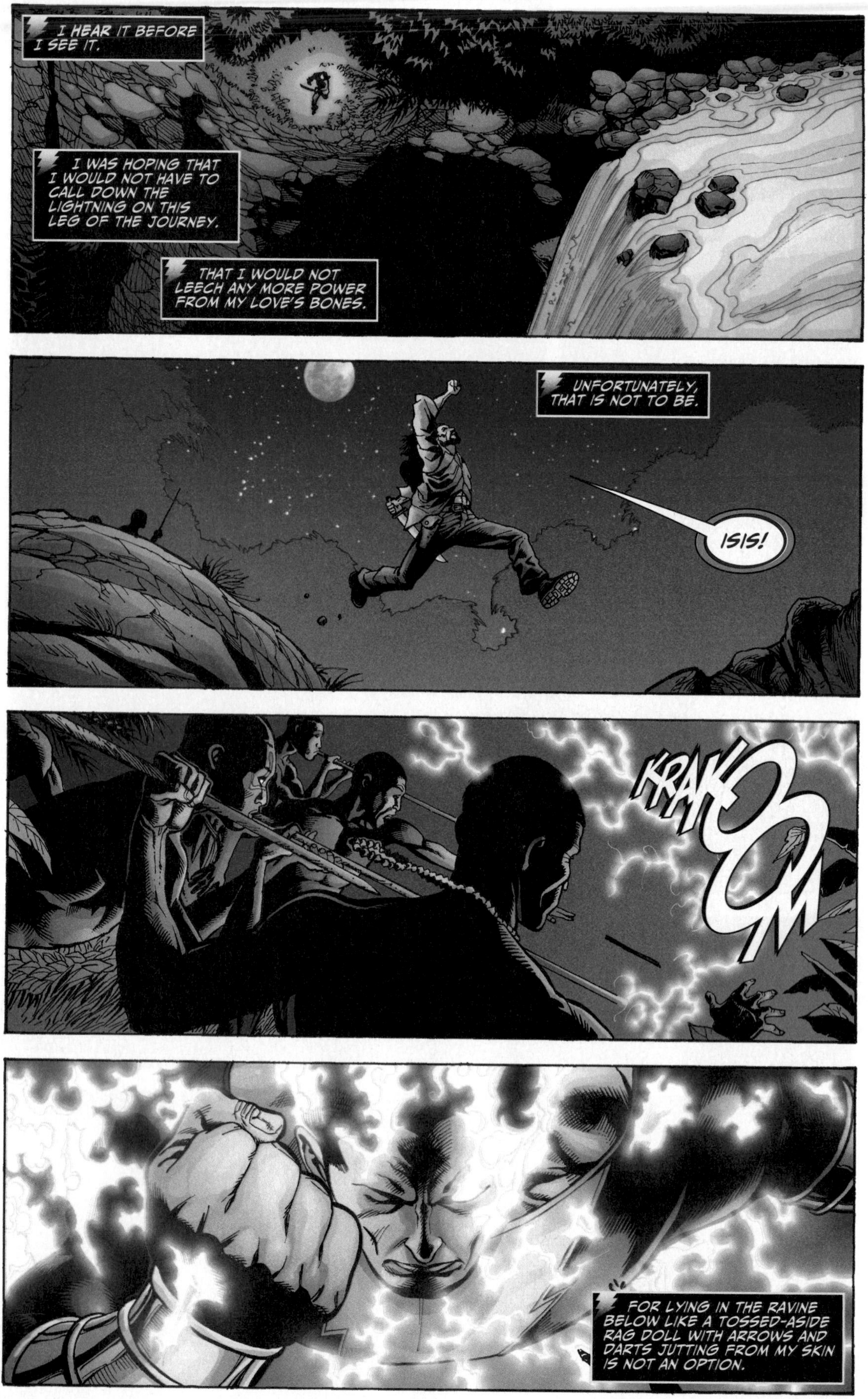
I HEAR IT BEFORE I SEE IT.
I WAS HOPING THAT I WOULD NOT HAVE TO CALL DOWN THE LIGHTNING ON THIS LEG OF THE JOURNEY.
THAT I WOULD NOT LEECH ANY MORE POWER FROM MY LOVE'S BONES.
UNFORTUNATELY, THAT IS NOT TO BE.
ISIS!
KRAKOOM
FOR LYING IN THE RAVINE BELOW LIKE A TOSSED-ASIDE RAG DOLL WITH ARROWS AND DARTS JUTTING FROM MY SKIN IS NOT AN OPTION.

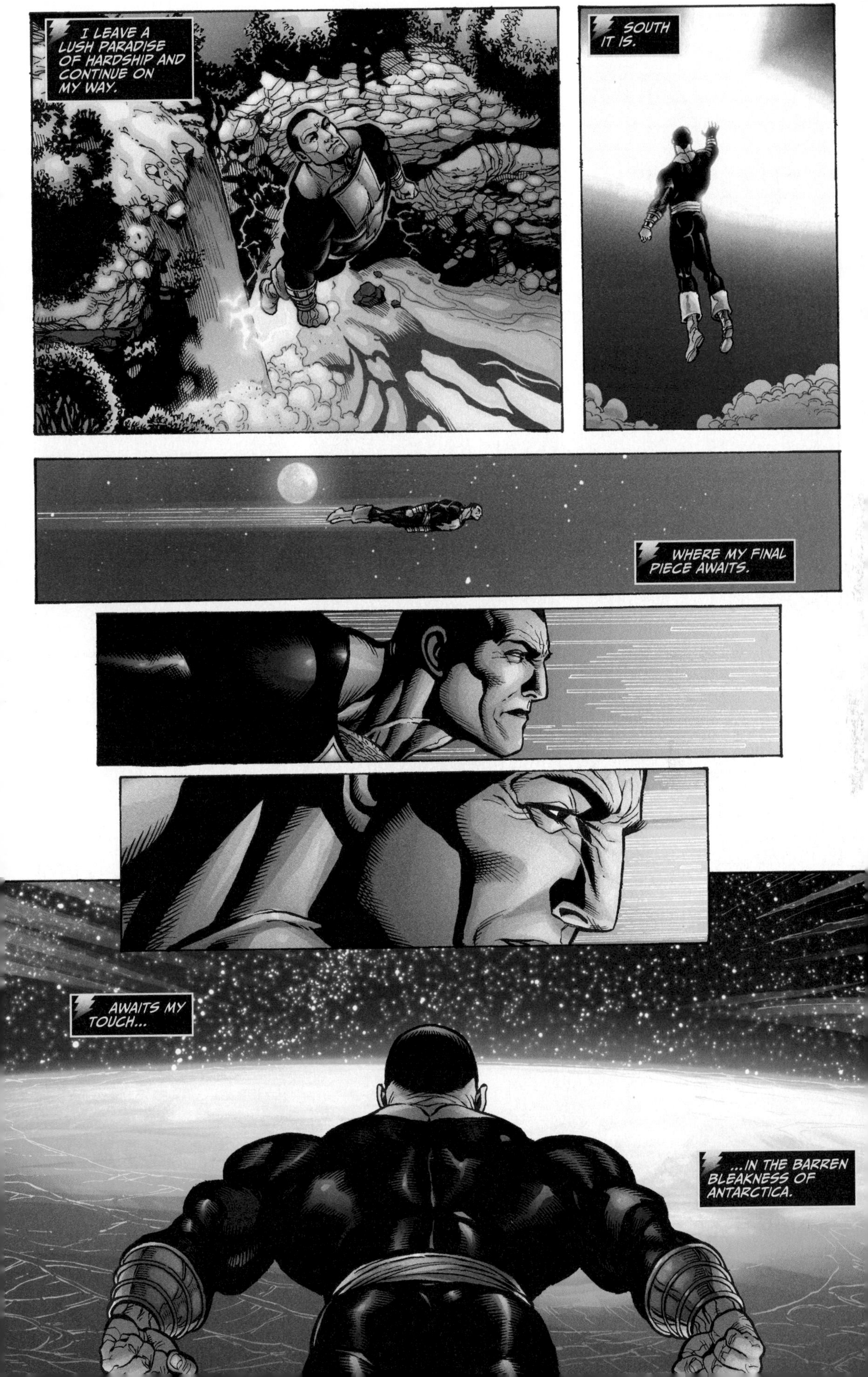
I LEAVE A LUSH PARADISE OF HARDSHIP AND CONTINUE ON MY WAY.
SOUTH IT IS.
WHERE MY FINAL PIECE AWAITS.
AWAITS MY TOUCH...
...IN THE BARREN BLEAKNESS OF ANTARCTICA.

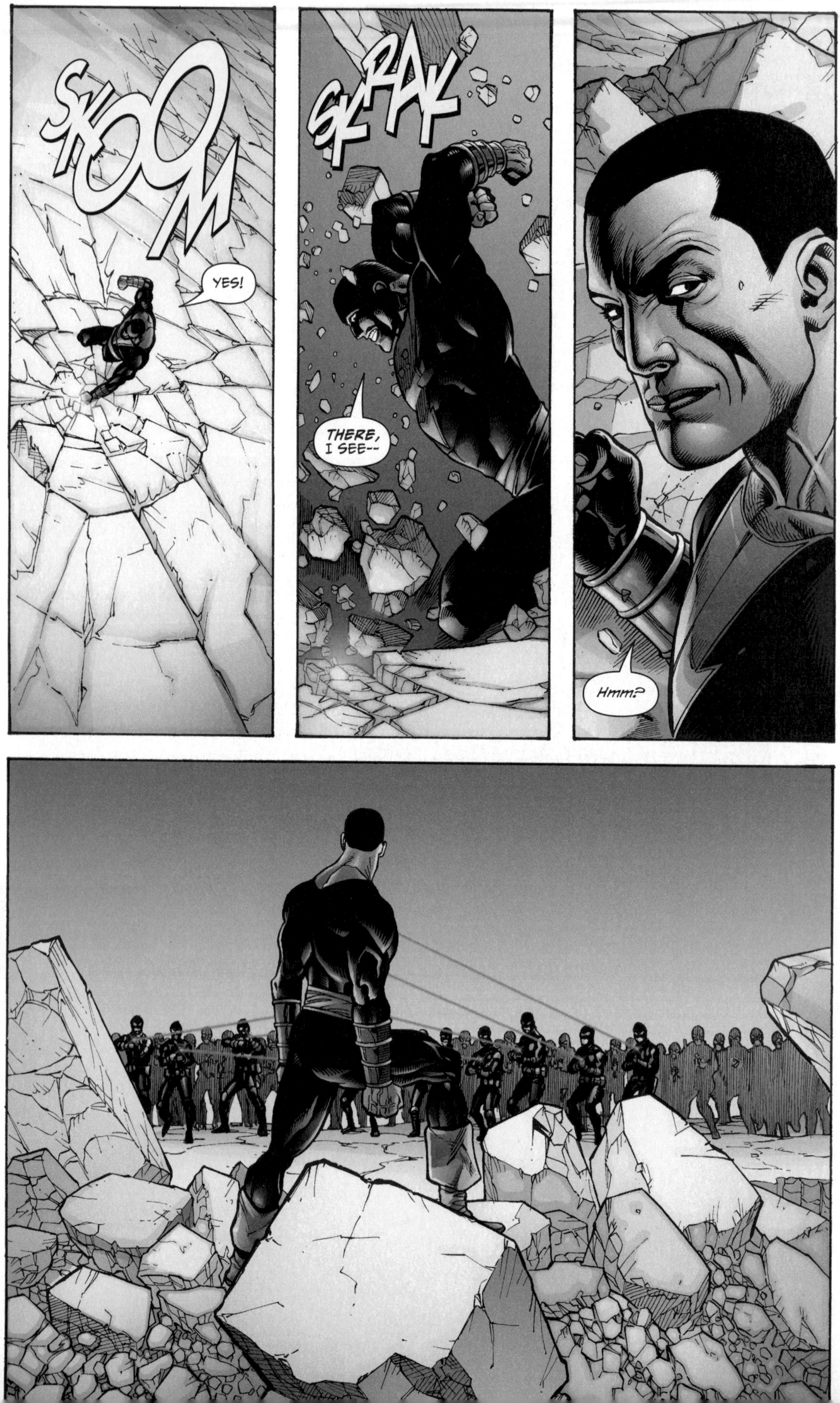
SKOOM
YES!
SKRAK
THERE, I SEE--
Hmm?

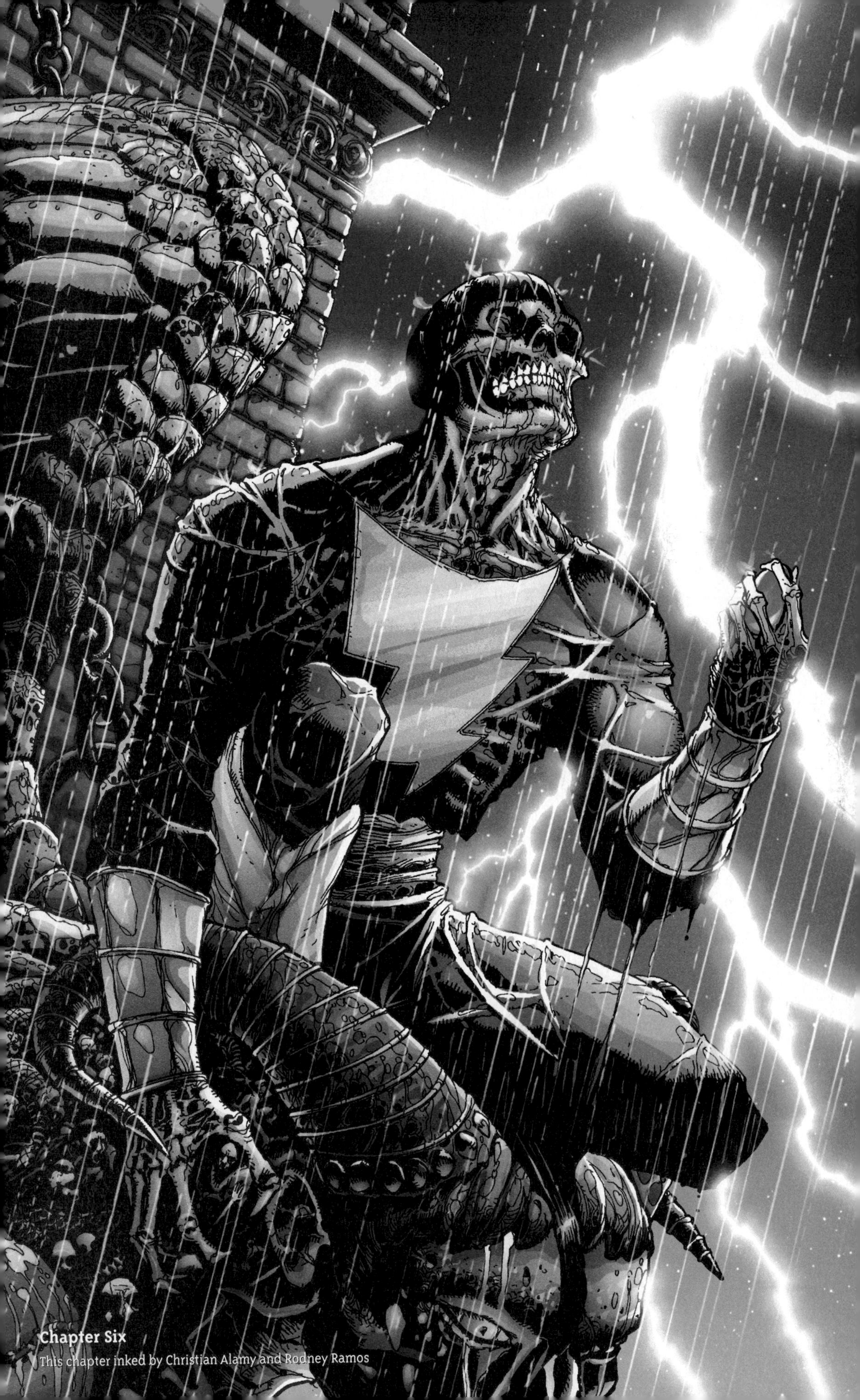

Chapter Six

This chapter inked by Christian Alamy and Rodney Ramos

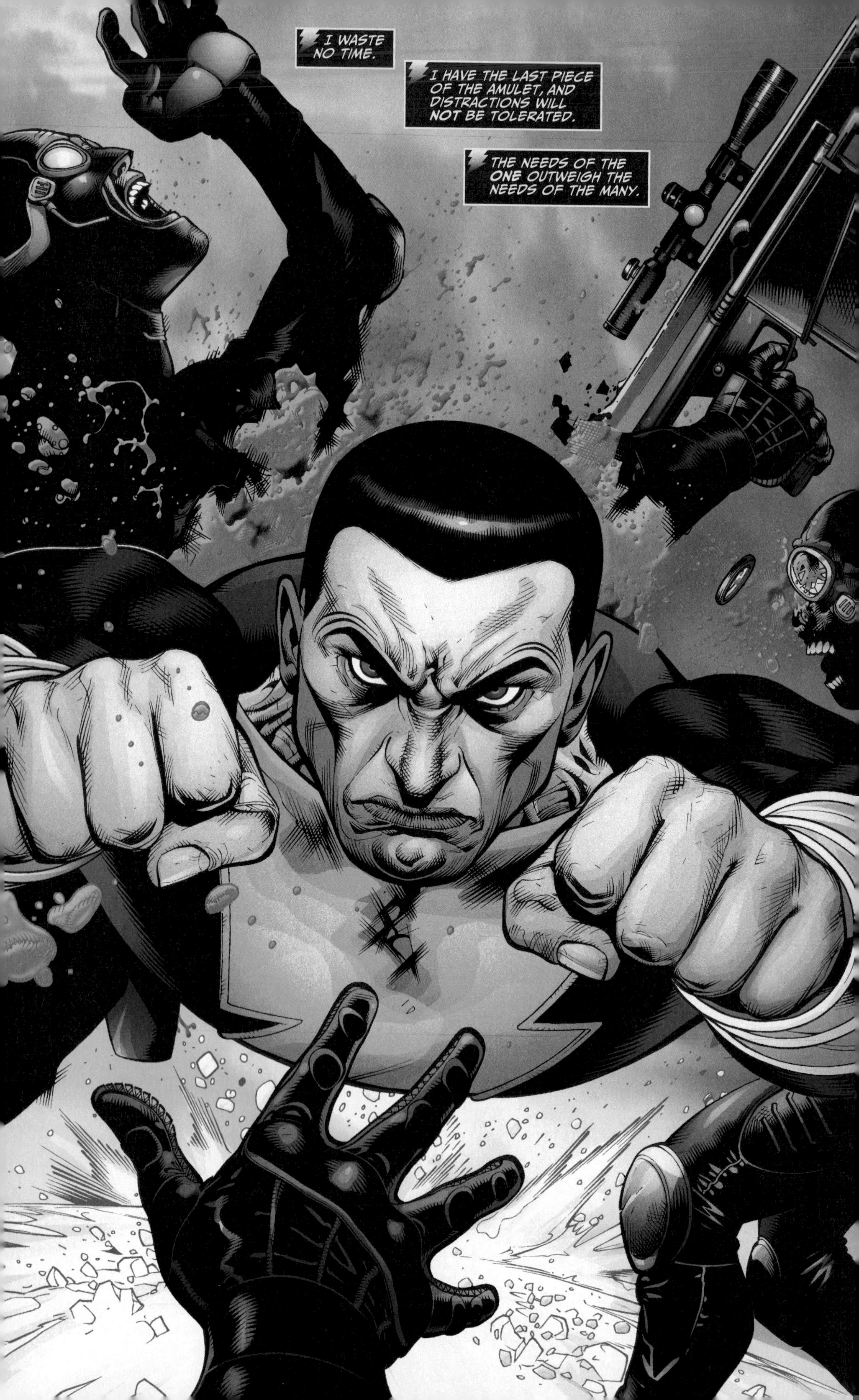
I WASTE NO TIME.
I HAVE THE LAST PIECE OF THE AMULET, AND DISTRACTIONS WILL NOT BE TOLERATED.
THE NEEDS OF THE ONE OUTWEIGH THE NEEDS OF THE MANY.

ACTIONS SPEAK LOUDER THAN WORDS.

AND IT IS TIME TO DISSUADE THESE FOOLS OF HOPE.

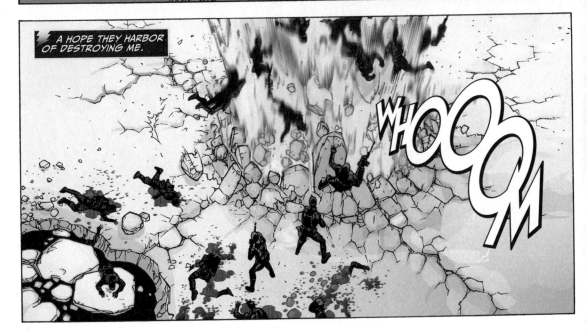

A HOPE THEY HARBOR OF DESTROYING ME.

WHOOOM

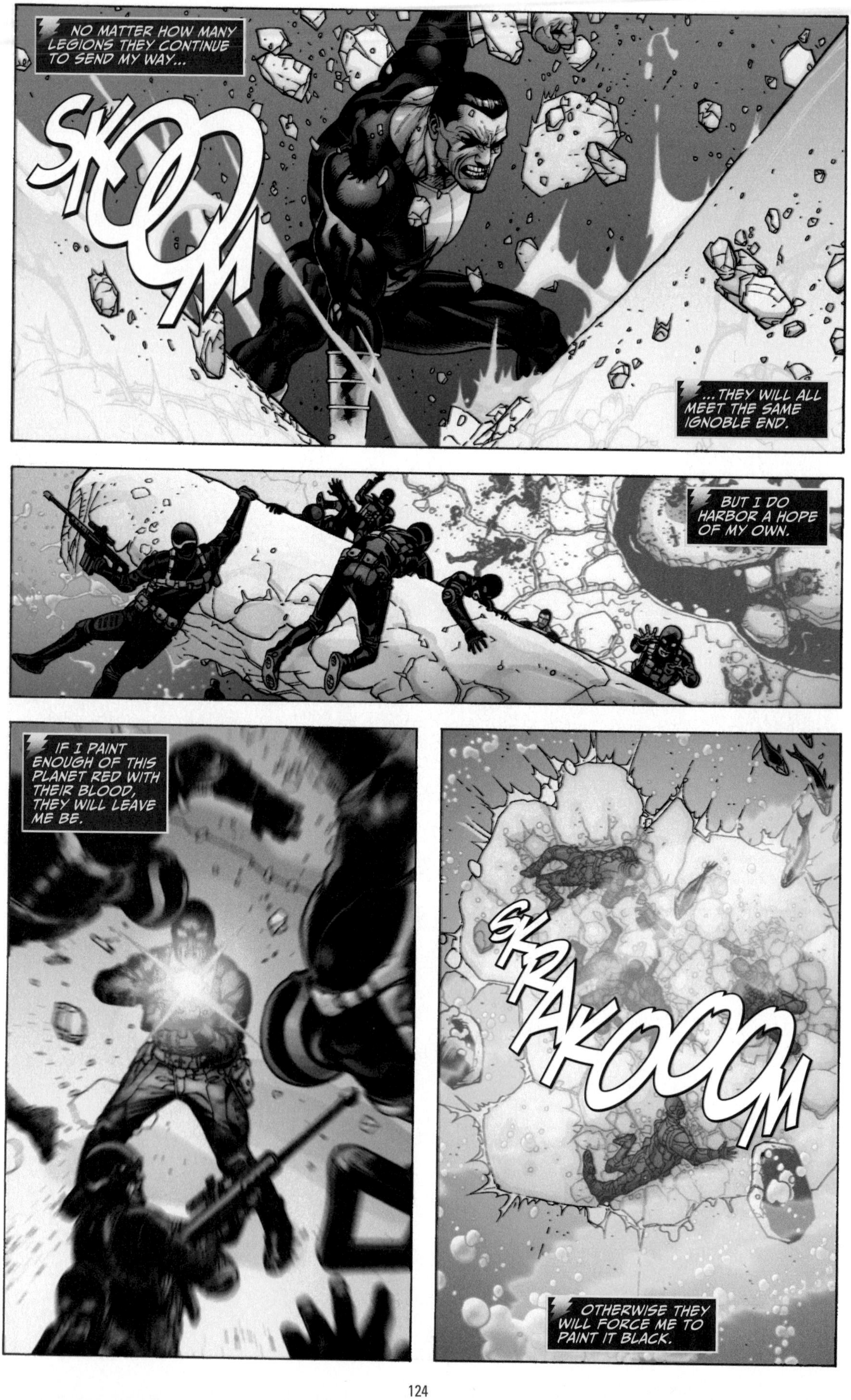
NO MATTER HOW MANY LEGIONS THEY CONTINUE TO SEND MY WAY...
SKOOM
...THEY WILL ALL MEET THE SAME IGNOBLE END.
BUT I DO HARBOR A HOPE OF MY OWN.
IF I PAINT ENOUGH OF THIS PLANET RED WITH THEIR BLOOD, THEY WILL LEAVE ME BE.
SKRAKOOOM
OTHERWISE THEY WILL FORCE ME TO PAINT IT BLACK.

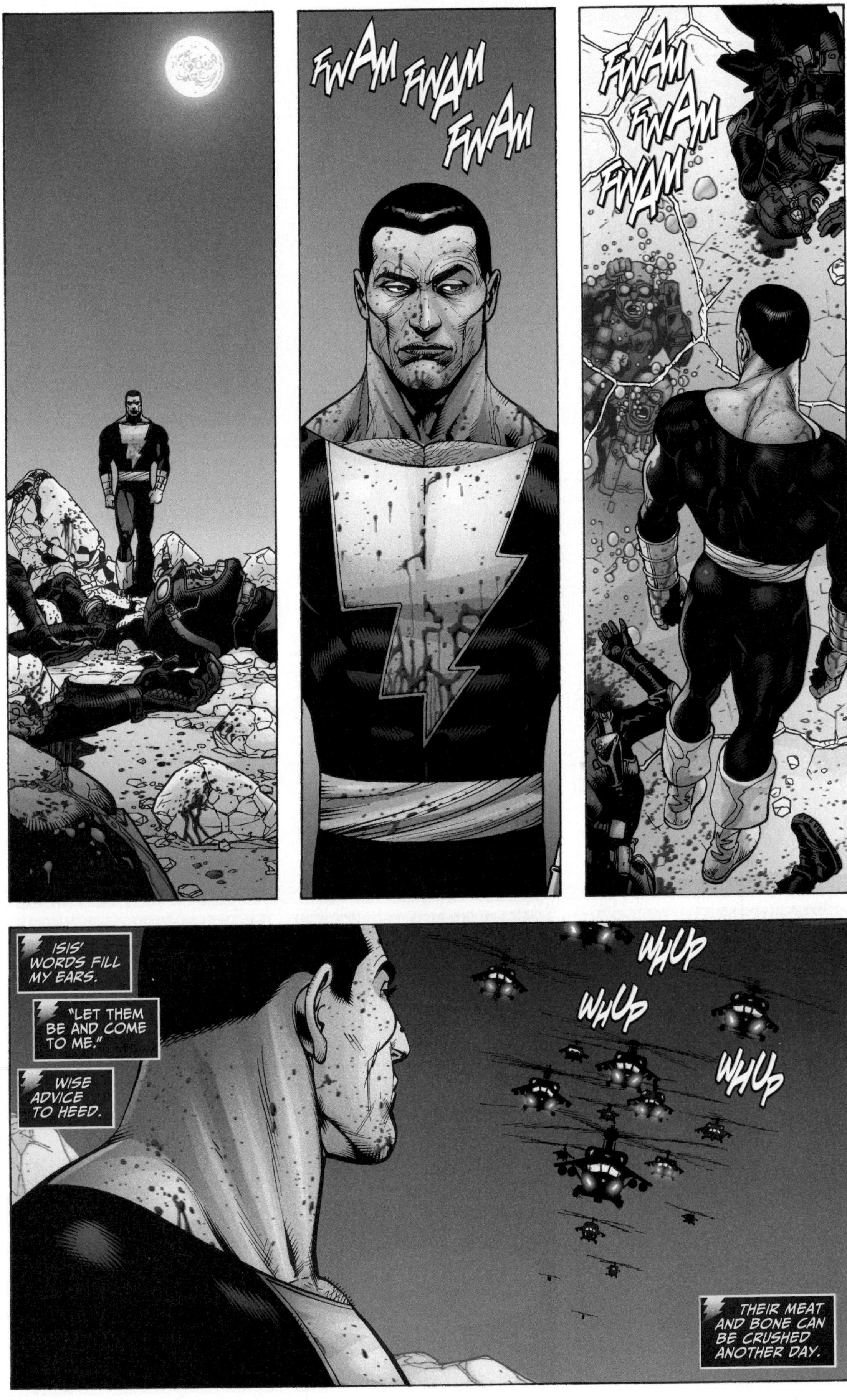
FWAM FWAM
FWAM
FWAM
FWAM
FWAM
ISIS' WORDS FILL MY EARS.
"LET THEM BE AND COME TO ME."
WISE ADVICE TO HEED.
WHUP
WHUP
WHUP
THEIR MEAT AND BONE CAN BE CRUSHED ANOTHER DAY.

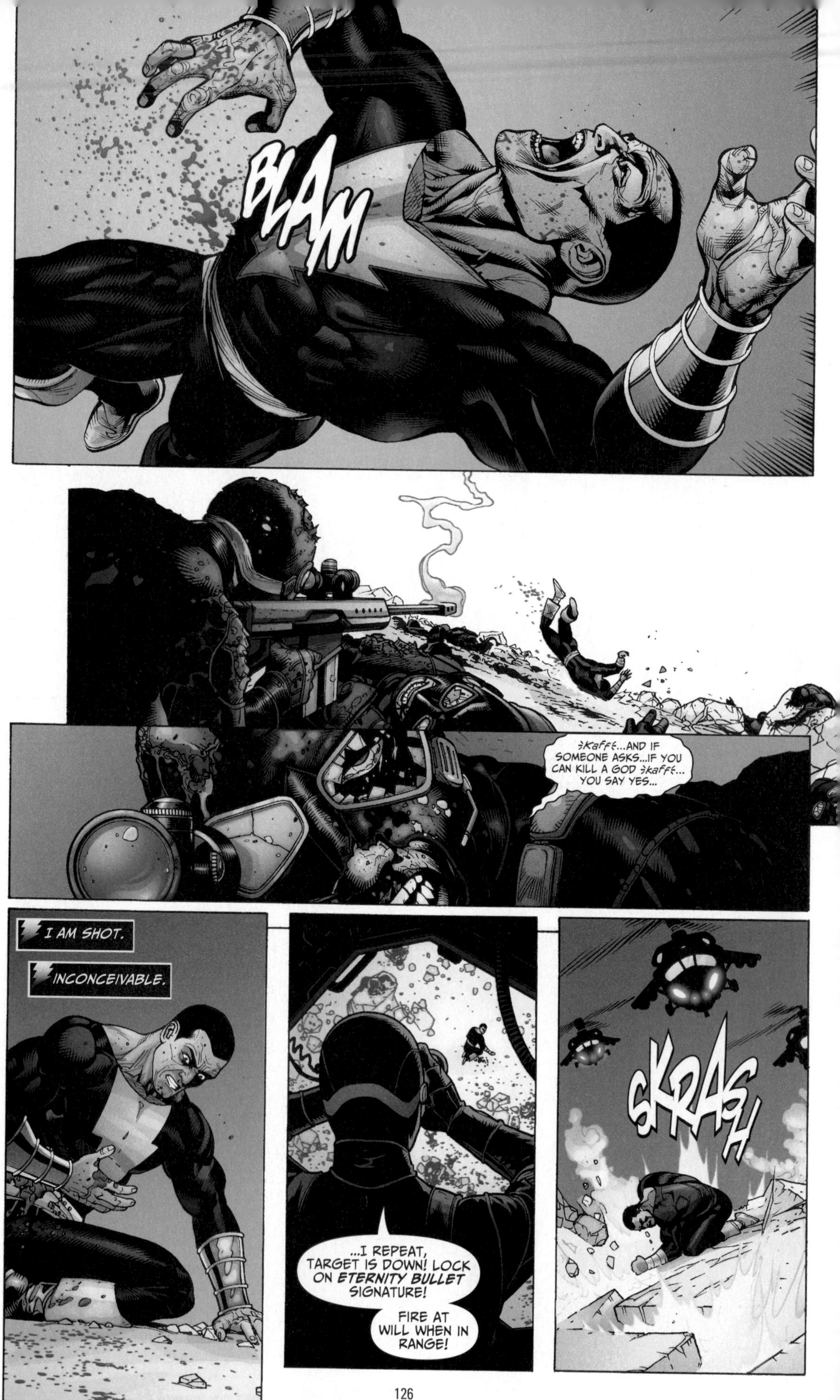
BLAM
ꟹKAFFꟹ...AND IF SOMEONE ASKS...IF YOU CAN KILL A GOD ꟹKAFFꟹ... YOU SAY YES...
I AM SHOT.
INCONCEIVABLE.
...I REPEAT, TARGET IS DOWN! LOCK ON ETERNITY BULLET SIGNATURE!
FIRE AT WILL WHEN IN RANGE!
SKRASH

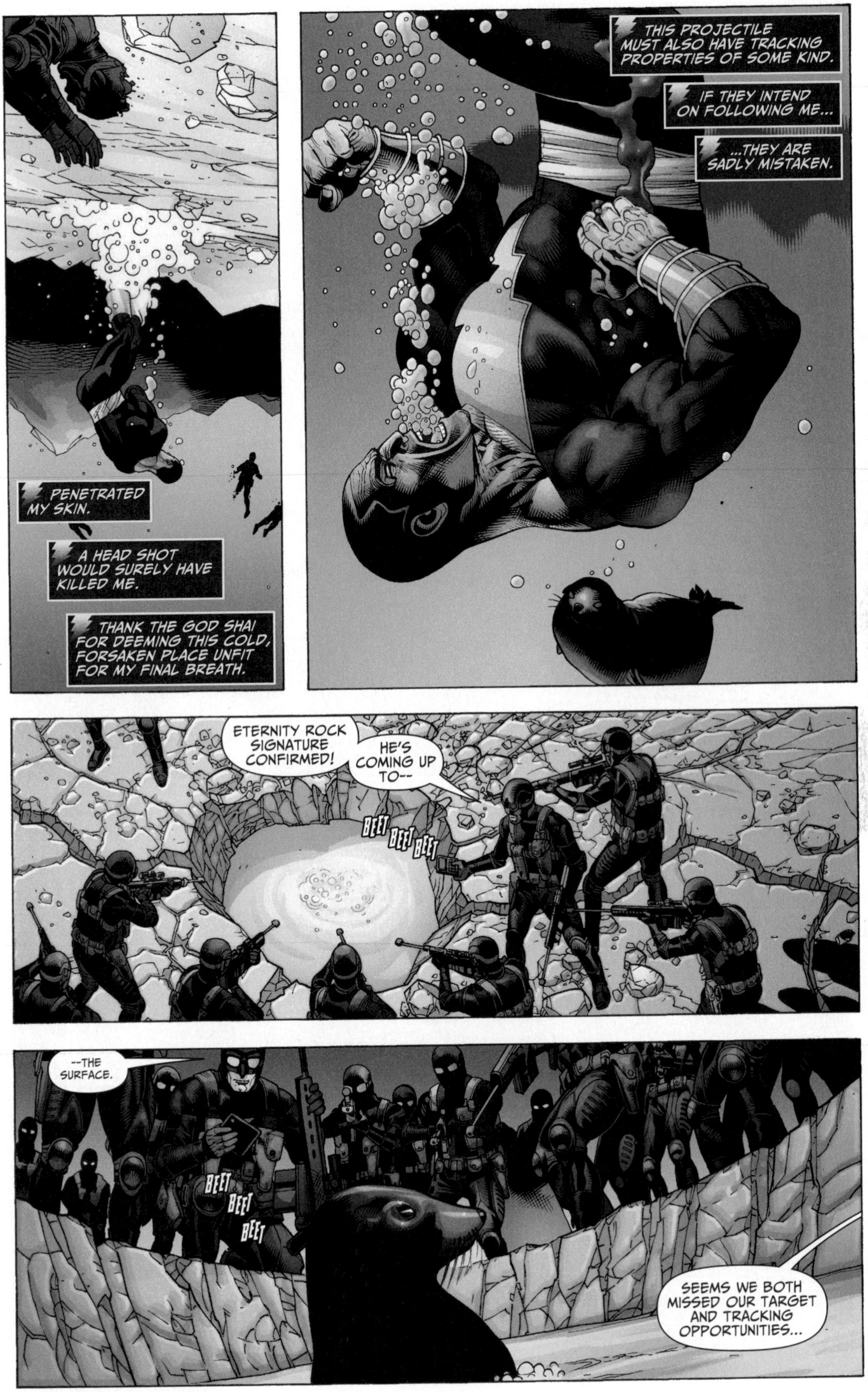
PENETRATED MY SKIN.
A HEAD SHOT WOULD SURELY HAVE KILLED ME.
THANK THE GOD SHAI FOR DEEMING THIS COLD, FORSAKEN PLACE UNFIT FOR MY FINAL BREATH.
THIS PROJECTILE MUST ALSO HAVE TRACKING PROPERTIES OF SOME KIND.
IF THEY INTEND ON FOLLOWING ME...
...THEY ARE SADLY MISTAKEN.
ETERNITY ROCK SIGNATURE CONFIRMED!
HE'S COMING UP TO--
BEET BEET BEET
--THE SURFACE.
BEET BEET BEET
SEEMS WE BOTH MISSED OUR TARGET AND TRACKING OPPORTUNITIES...

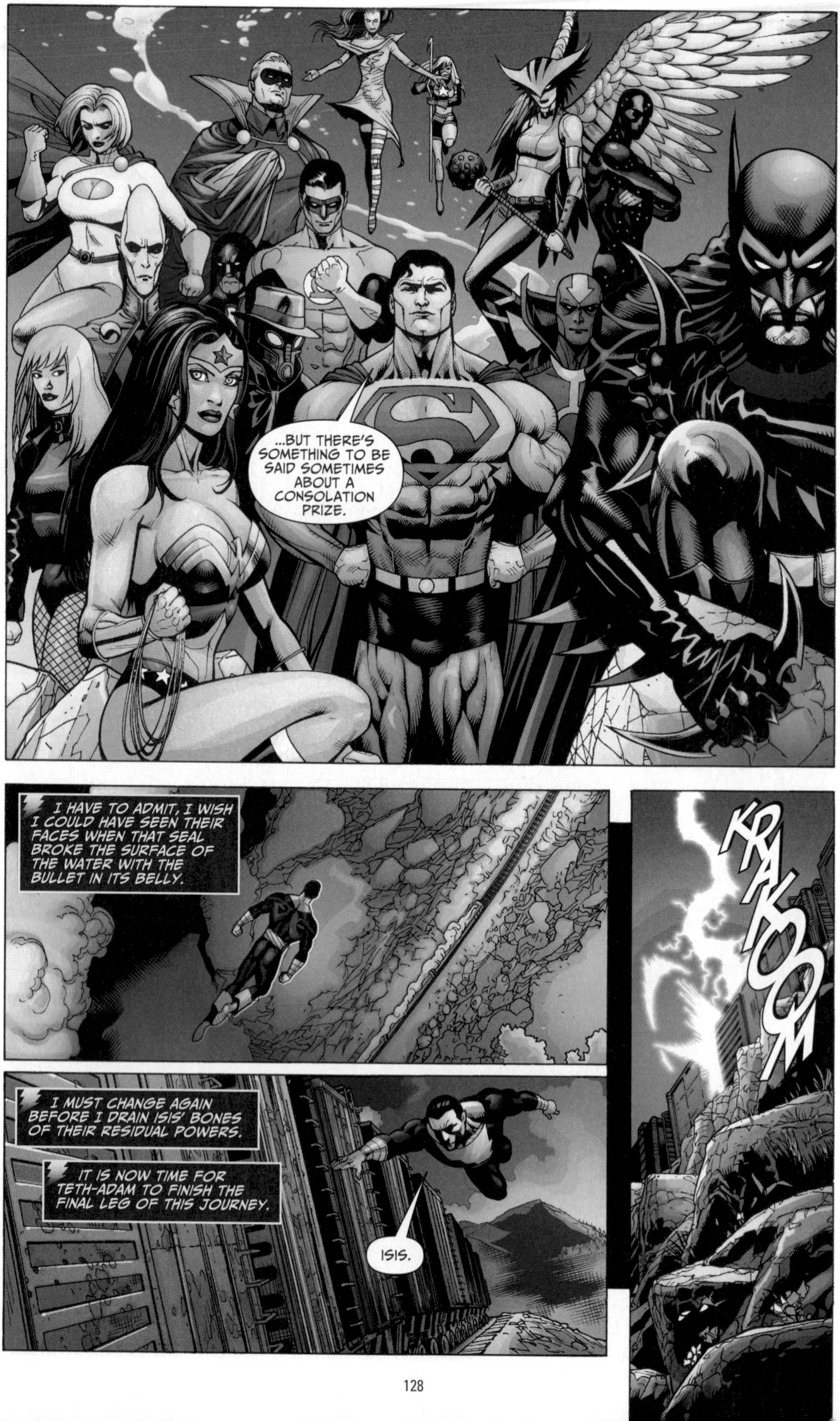
...BUT THERE'S SOMETHING TO BE SAID SOMETIMES ABOUT A CONSOLATION PRIZE.
I HAVE TO ADMIT, I WISH I COULD HAVE SEEN THEIR FACES WHEN THAT SEAL BROKE THE SURFACE OF THE WATER WITH THE BULLET IN ITS BELLY.
I MUST CHANGE AGAIN BEFORE I DRAIN ISIS' BONES OF THEIR RESIDUAL POWERS.
IT IS NOW TIME FOR TETH-ADAM TO FINISH THE FINAL LEG OF THIS JOURNEY.
ISIS.
KRAKOOM

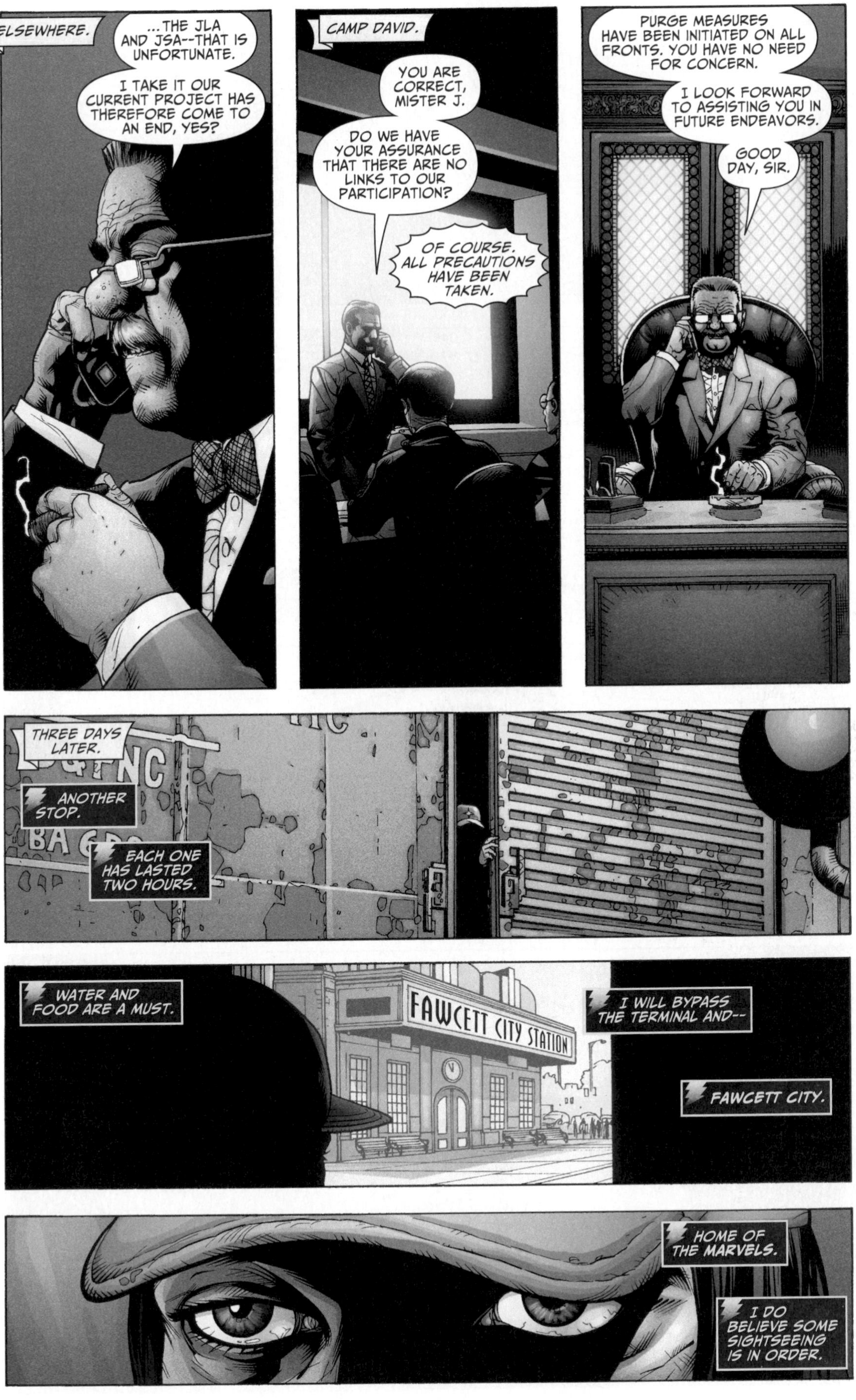
ELSEWHERE.
...THE JLA AND JSA--THAT IS UNFORTUNATE.
I TAKE IT OUR CURRENT PROJECT HAS THEREFORE COME TO AN END, YES?
CAMP DAVID.
YOU ARE CORRECT, MISTER J.
DO WE HAVE YOUR ASSURANCE THAT THERE ARE NO LINKS TO OUR PARTICIPATION?
OF COURSE. ALL PRECAUTIONS HAVE BEEN TAKEN.
PURGE MEASURES HAVE BEEN INITIATED ON ALL FRONTS. YOU HAVE NO NEED FOR CONCERN.
I LOOK FORWARD TO ASSISTING YOU IN FUTURE ENDEAVORS.
GOOD DAY, SIR.
THREE DAYS LATER.
ANOTHER STOP.
EACH ONE HAS LASTED TWO HOURS.
WATER AND FOOD ARE A MUST.
FAWCETT CITY STATION
I WILL BYPASS THE TERMINAL AND--
FAWCETT CITY.
HOME OF THE MARVELS.
I DO BELIEVE SOME SIGHTSEEING IS IN ORDER.

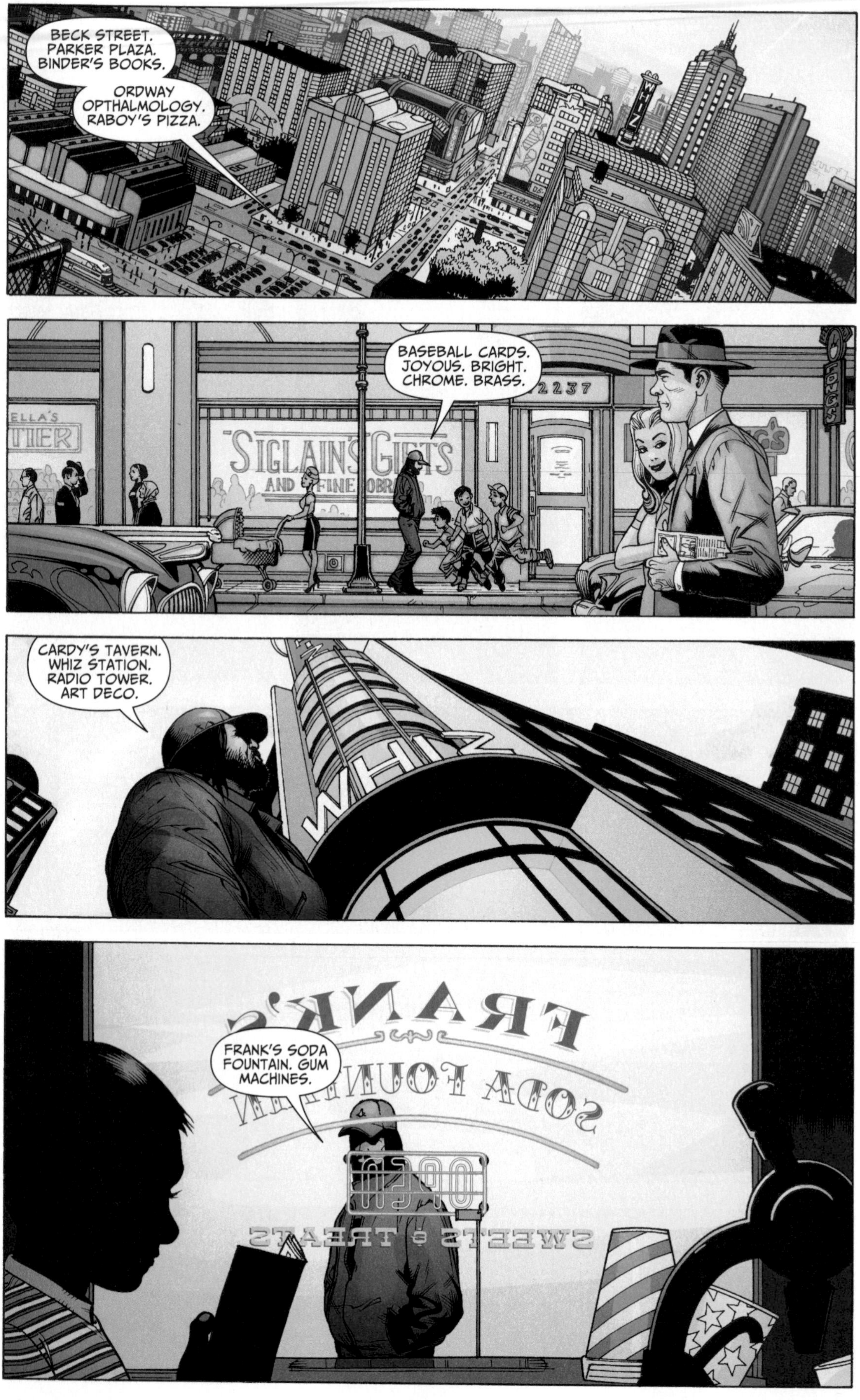
BECK STREET. PARKER PLAZA. BINDER'S BOOKS.
ORDWAY OPTHALMOLOGY. RABOY'S PIZZA.
WHIZ
BASEBALL CARDS. JOYOUS. BRIGHT. CHROME. BRASS.
2237
SIGLAIN'S GIFTS
FONGS
CARDY'S TAVERN. WHIZ STATION. RADIO TOWER. ART DECO.
WHIZ
FRANK'S SODA FOUNTAIN. GUM MACHINES.

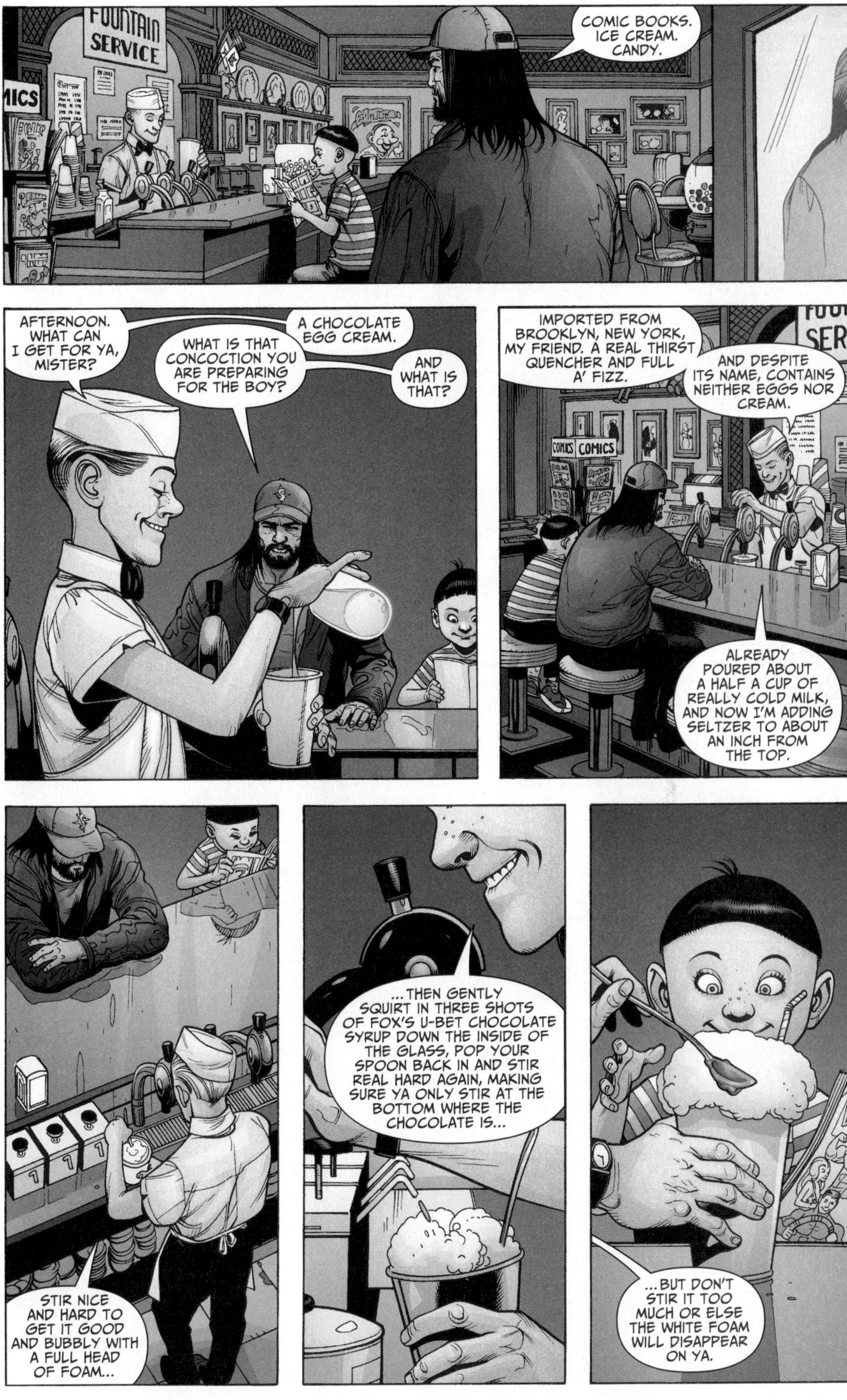
FOUNTAIN SERVICE
MICS
COMIC BOOKS. ICE CREAM. CANDY.
AFTERNOON. WHAT CAN I GET FOR YA, MISTER?
WHAT IS THAT CONCOCTION YOU ARE PREPARING FOR THE BOY?
A CHOCOLATE EGG CREAM.
AND WHAT IS THAT?
IMPORTED FROM BROOKLYN, NEW YORK, MY FRIEND. A REAL THIRST QUENCHER AND FULL A' FIZZ.
AND DESPITE ITS NAME, CONTAINS NEITHER EGGS NOR CREAM.
COMICS COMICS
ALREADY POURED ABOUT A HALF A CUP OF REALLY COLD MILK, AND NOW I'M ADDING SELTZER TO ABOUT AN INCH FROM THE TOP.
STIR NICE AND HARD TO GET IT GOOD AND BUBBLY WITH A FULL HEAD OF FOAM...
...THEN GENTLY SQUIRT IN THREE SHOTS OF FOX'S U-BET CHOCOLATE SYRUP DOWN THE INSIDE OF THE GLASS, POP YOUR SPOON BACK IN AND STIR REAL HARD AGAIN, MAKING SURE YA ONLY STIR AT THE BOTTOM WHERE THE CHOCOLATE IS...
...BUT DON'T STIR IT TOO MUCH OR ELSE THE WHITE FOAM WILL DISAPPEAR ON YA.

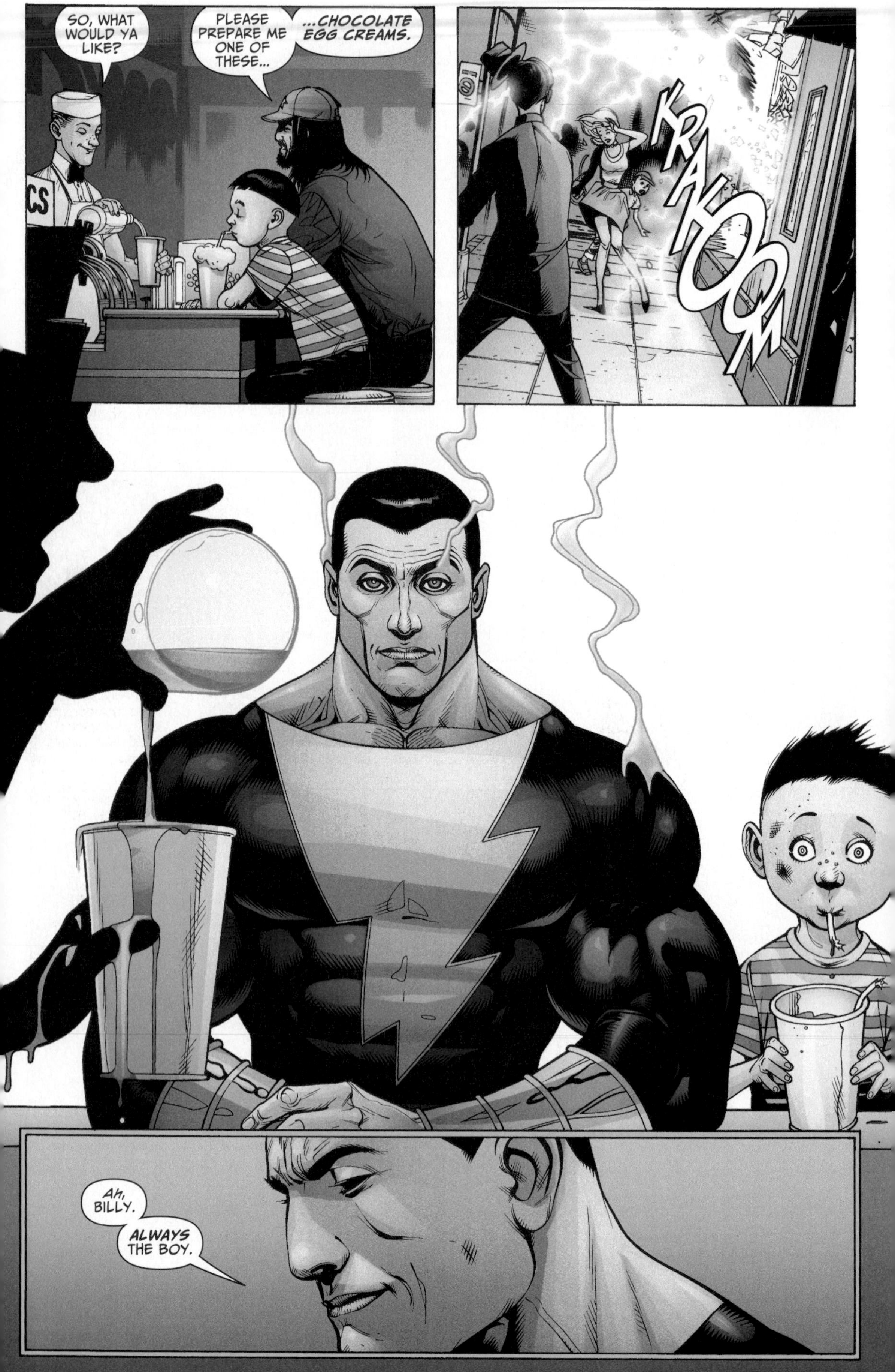
SO, WHAT WOULD YA LIKE?
PLEASE PREPARE ME ONE OF THESE...
...CHOCOLATE EGG CREAMS.
KRAKOOM
AH, BILLY.
ALWAYS THE BOY.

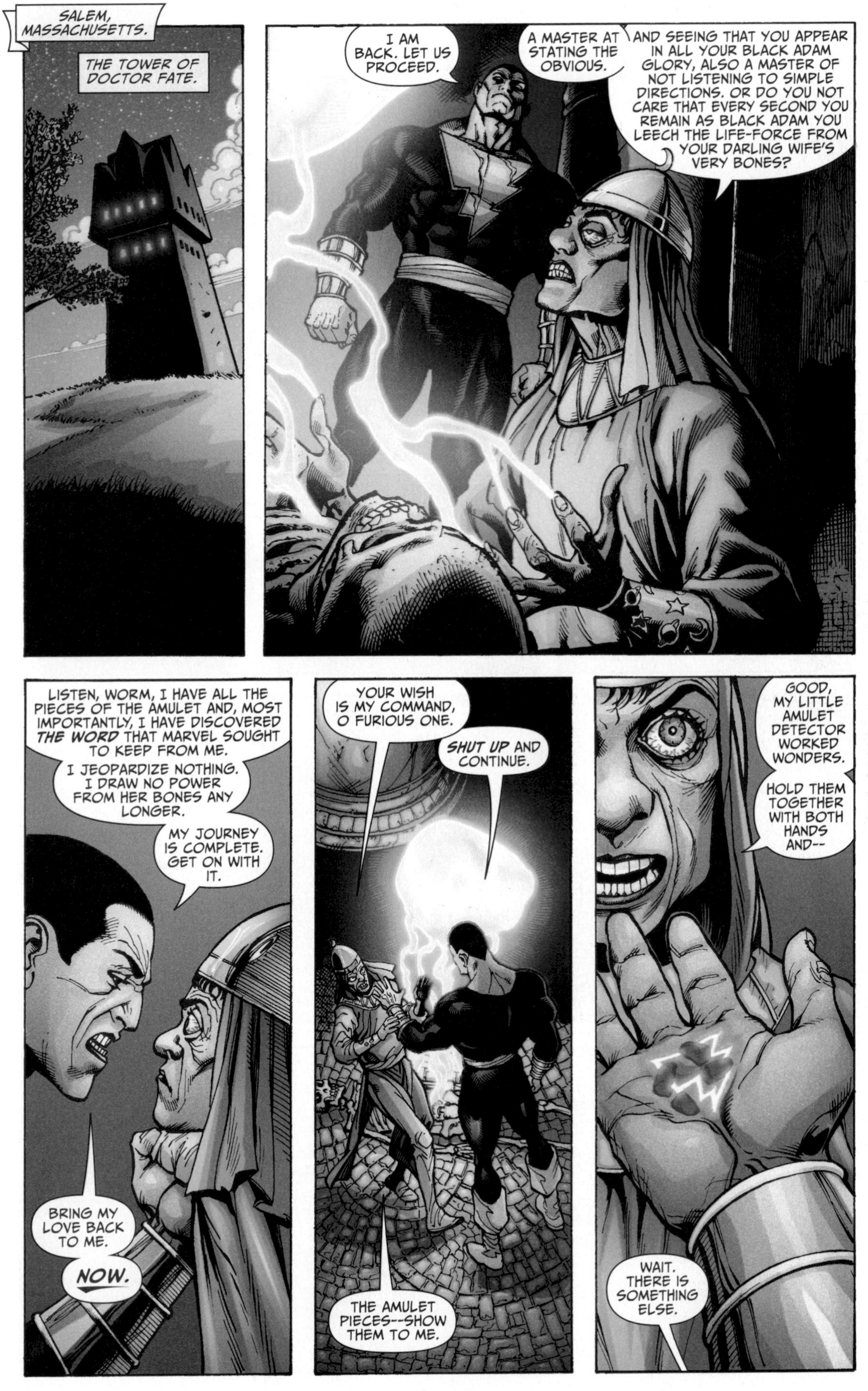
SALEM, MASSACHUSETTS.
THE TOWER OF DOCTOR FATE.
I AM BACK. LET US PROCEED.
A MASTER AT STATING THE OBVIOUS.
AND SEEING THAT YOU APPEAR IN ALL YOUR BLACK ADAM GLORY, ALSO A MASTER OF NOT LISTENING TO SIMPLE DIRECTIONS. OR DO YOU NOT CARE THAT EVERY SECOND YOU REMAIN AS BLACK ADAM YOU LEECH THE LIFE-FORCE FROM YOUR DARLING WIFE'S VERY BONES?
LISTEN, WORM, I HAVE ALL THE PIECES OF THE AMULET AND, MOST IMPORTANTLY, I HAVE DISCOVERED THE WORD THAT MARVEL SOUGHT TO KEEP FROM ME.
I JEOPARDIZE NOTHING. I DRAW NO POWER FROM HER BONES ANY LONGER.
MY JOURNEY IS COMPLETE. GET ON WITH IT.
BRING MY LOVE BACK TO ME.
NOW.
YOUR WISH IS MY COMMAND, O FURIOUS ONE.
SHUT UP AND CONTINUE.
THE AMULET PIECES--SHOW THEM TO ME.
GOOD, MY LITTLE AMULET DETECTOR WORKED WONDERS.
HOLD THEM TOGETHER WITH BOTH HANDS AND--
WAIT. THERE IS SOMETHING ELSE.

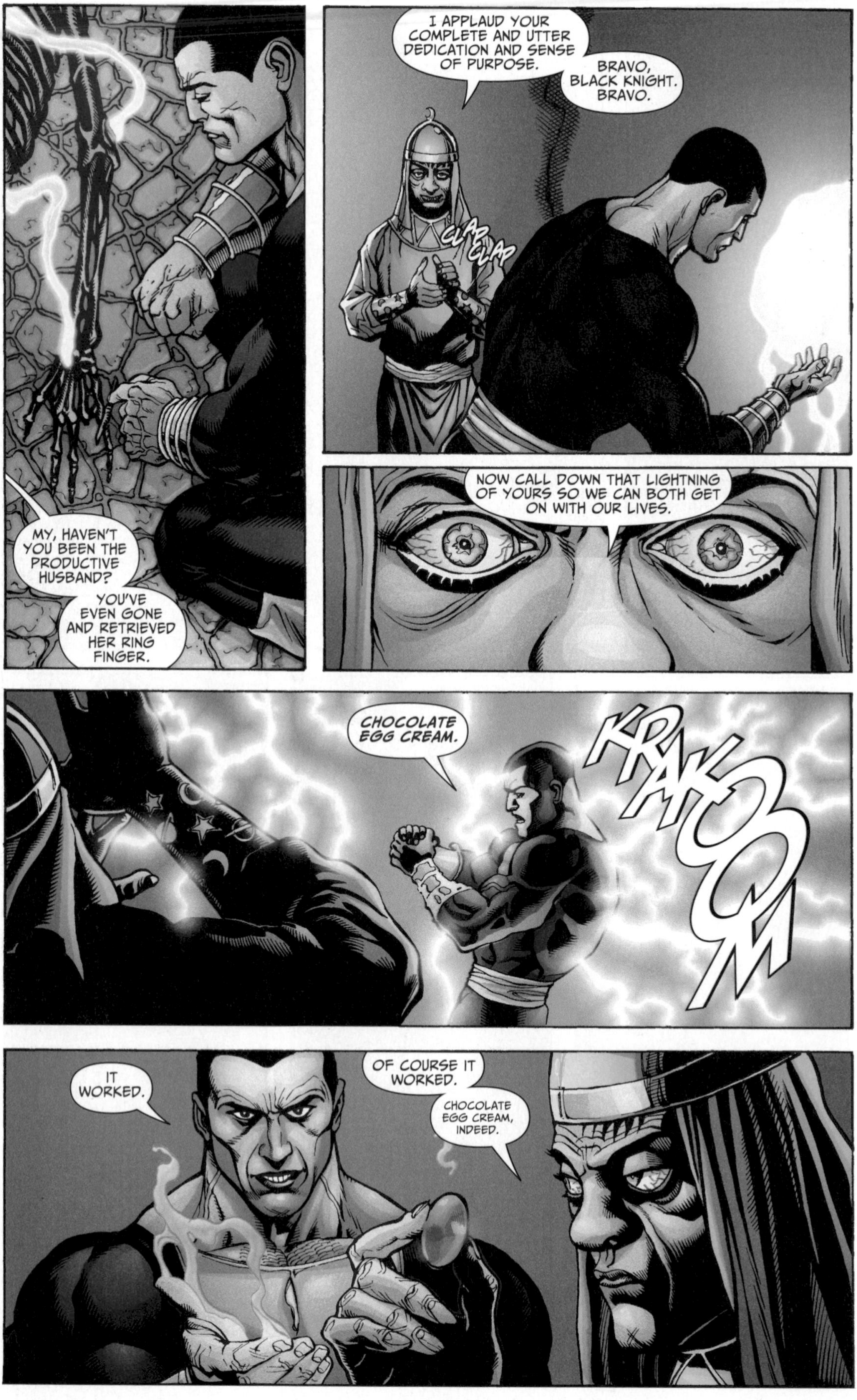
MY, HAVEN'T YOU BEEN THE PRODUCTIVE HUSBAND?
YOU'VE EVEN GONE AND RETRIEVED HER RING FINGER.
I APPLAUD YOUR COMPLETE AND UTTER DEDICATION AND SENSE OF PURPOSE.
BRAVO, BLACK KNIGHT. BRAVO.
CLAP CLAP
NOW CALL DOWN THAT LIGHTNING OF YOURS SO WE CAN BOTH GET ON WITH OUR LIVES.
CHOCOLATE EGG CREAM.
KRAKOOM
IT WORKED.
OF COURSE IT WORKED.
CHOCOLATE EGG CREAM, INDEED.

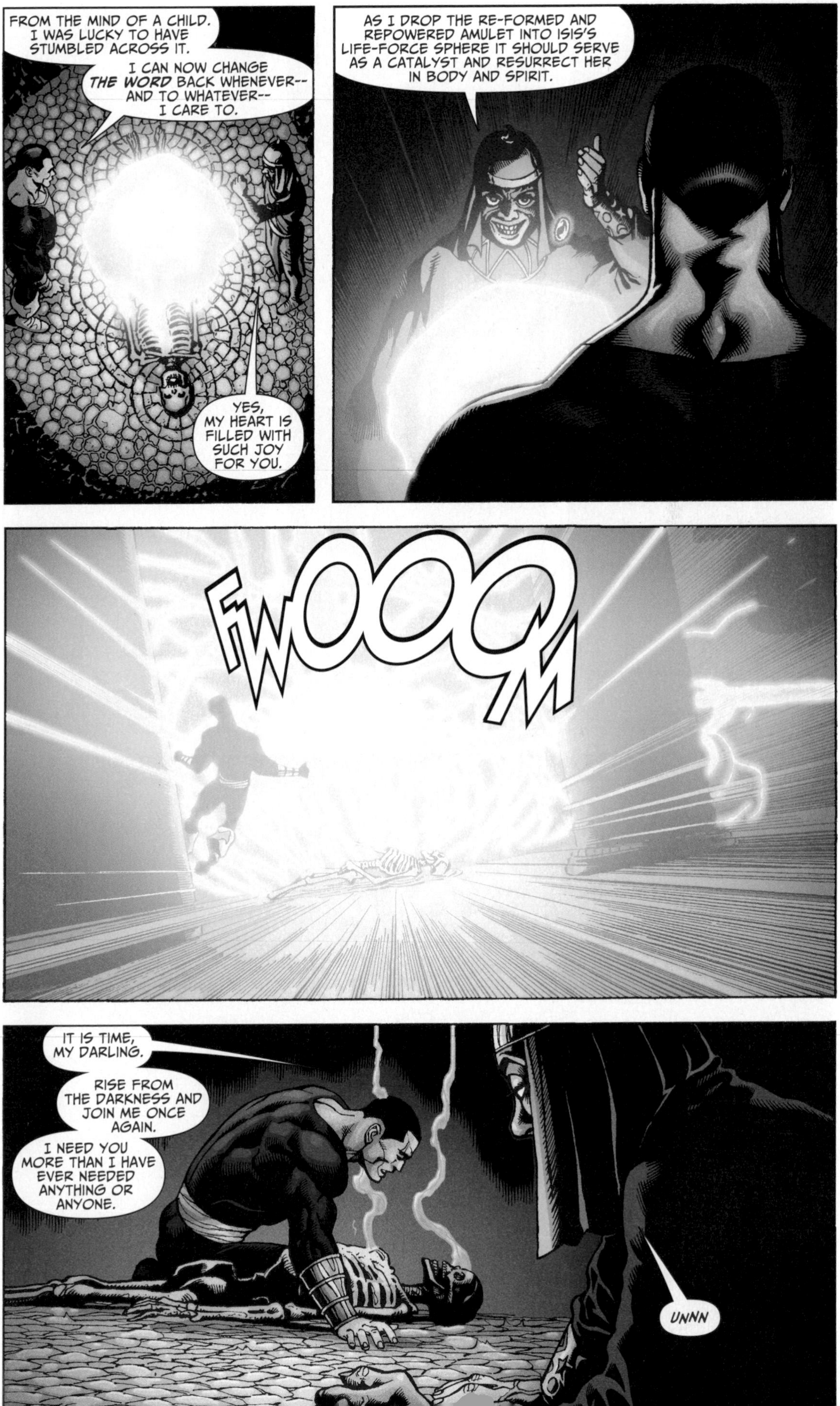
FROM THE MIND OF A CHILD. I WAS LUCKY TO HAVE STUMBLED ACROSS IT.
I CAN NOW CHANGE *THE WORD* BACK WHENEVER-- AND TO WHATEVER-- I CARE TO.
YES, MY HEART IS FILLED WITH SUCH JOY FOR YOU.
AS I DROP THE RE-FORMED AND REPOWERED AMULET INTO ISIS'S LIFE-FORCE SPHERE IT SHOULD SERVE AS A CATALYST AND RESURRECT HER IN BODY AND SPIRIT.
FWOOOM
IT IS TIME, MY DARLING.
RISE FROM THE DARKNESS AND JOIN ME ONCE AGAIN.
I NEED YOU MORE THAN I HAVE EVER NEEDED ANYTHING OR ANYONE.
UNNN

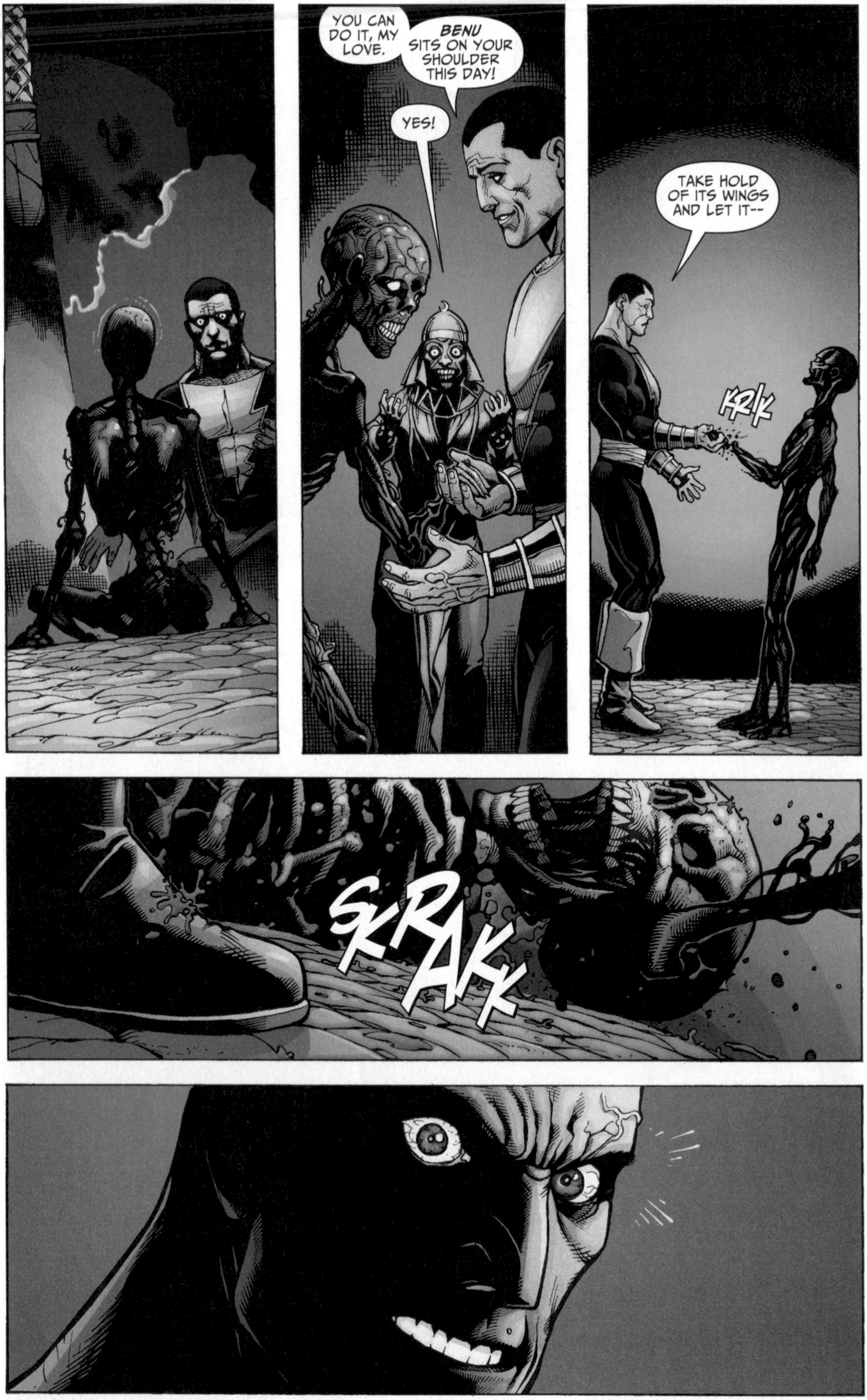
YOU CAN DO IT, MY LOVE.
BENU SITS ON YOUR SHOULDER THIS DAY!
YES!
TAKE HOLD OF ITS WINGS AND LET IT--
KRIK
SKRAKK

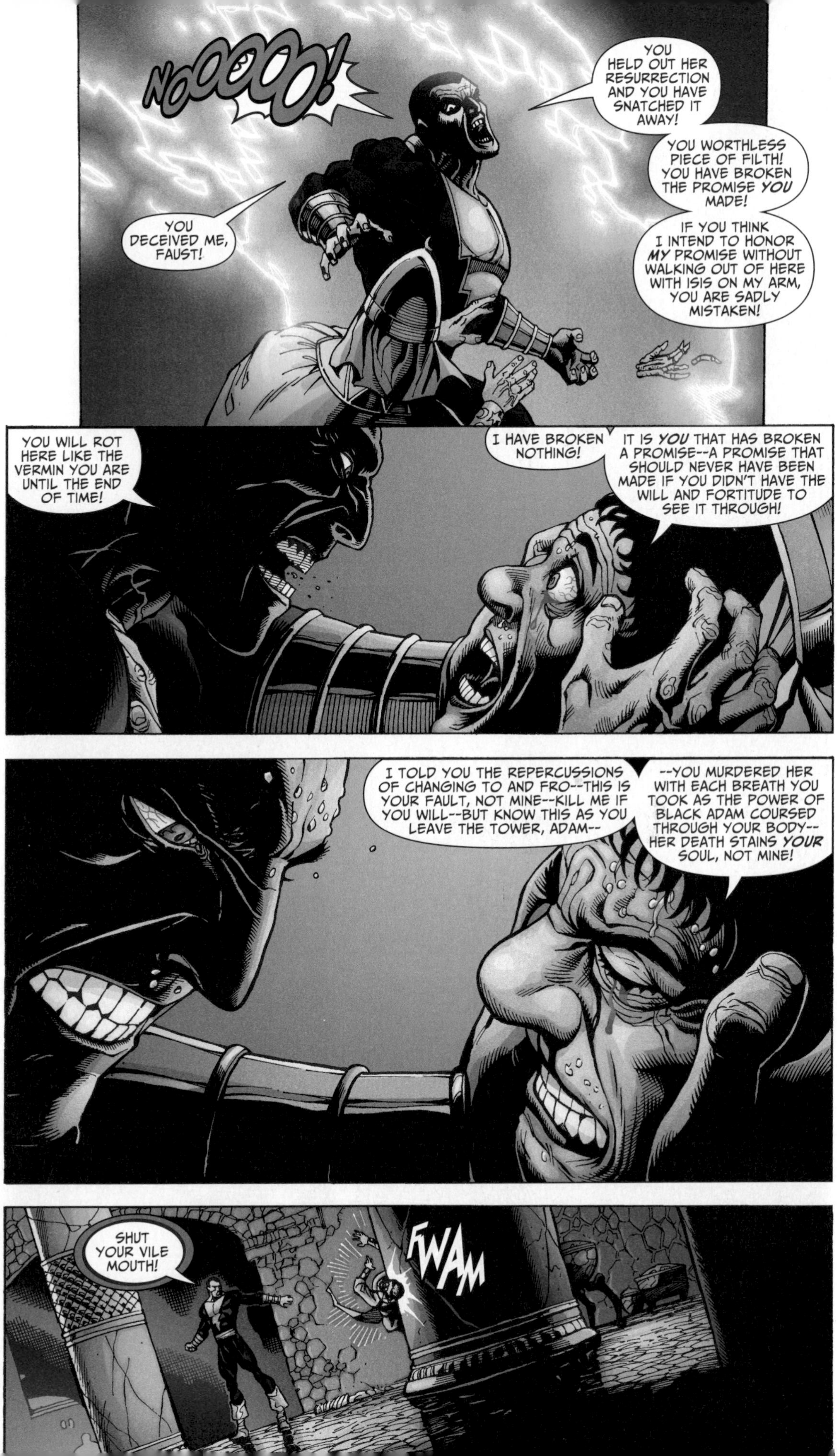
NOOOOO!
YOU DECEIVED ME, FAUST!
YOU HELD OUT HER RESURRECTION AND YOU HAVE SNATCHED IT AWAY!
YOU WORTHLESS PIECE OF FILTH! YOU HAVE BROKEN THE PROMISE YOU MADE!
IF YOU THINK I INTEND TO HONOR MY PROMISE WITHOUT WALKING OUT OF HERE WITH ISIS ON MY ARM, YOU ARE SADLY MISTAKEN!
YOU WILL ROT HERE LIKE THE VERMIN YOU ARE UNTIL THE END OF TIME!
I HAVE BROKEN NOTHING!
IT IS YOU THAT HAS BROKEN A PROMISE--A PROMISE THAT SHOULD NEVER HAVE BEEN MADE IF YOU DIDN'T HAVE THE WILL AND FORTITUDE TO SEE IT THROUGH!
I TOLD YOU THE REPERCUSSIONS OF CHANGING TO AND FRO--THIS IS YOUR FAULT, NOT MINE--KILL ME IF YOU WILL--BUT KNOW THIS AS YOU LEAVE THE TOWER, ADAM--
--YOU MURDERED HER WITH EACH BREATH YOU TOOK AS THE POWER OF BLACK ADAM COURSED THROUGH YOUR BODY--HER DEATH STAINS YOUR SOUL, NOT MINE!
SHUT YOUR VILE MOUTH!
FWAM

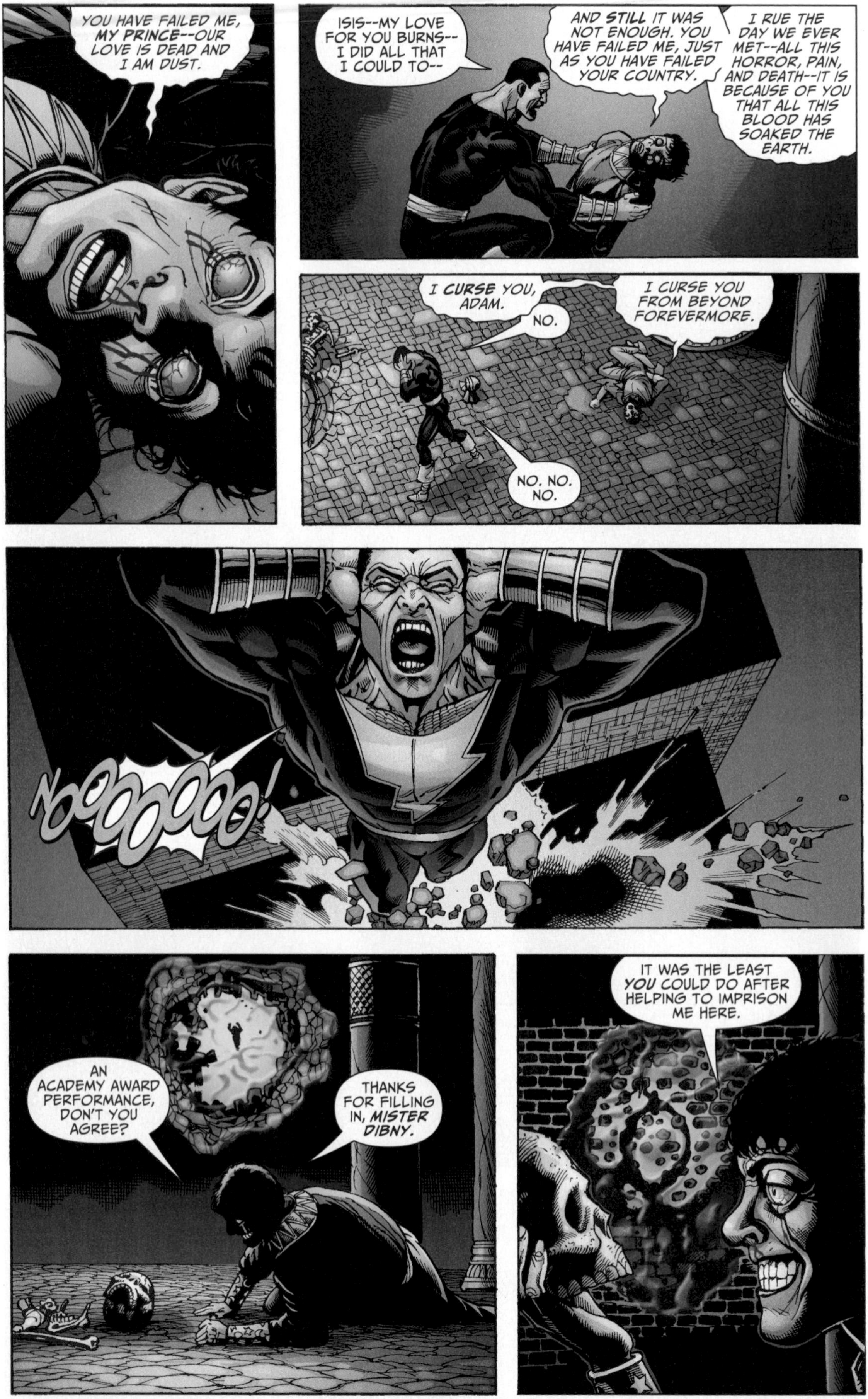

YOU HAVE FAILED ME, MY PRINCE--OUR LOVE IS DEAD AND I AM DUST.
ISIS--MY LOVE FOR YOU BURNS--I DID ALL THAT I COULD TO--
AND STILL IT WAS NOT ENOUGH. YOU HAVE FAILED ME, JUST AS YOU HAVE FAILED YOUR COUNTRY.
I RUE THE DAY WE EVER MET--ALL THIS HORROR, PAIN, AND DEATH--IT IS BECAUSE OF YOU THAT ALL THIS BLOOD HAS SOAKED THE EARTH.
I CURSE YOU, ADAM.
NO.
I CURSE YOU FROM BEYOND FOREVERMORE.
NO. NO. NO.
NOOOOOOO!
AN ACADEMY AWARD PERFORMANCE, DON'T YOU AGREE?
THANKS FOR FILLING IN, MISTER DIBNY.
IT WAS THE LEAST YOU COULD DO AFTER HELPING TO IMPRISON ME HERE.

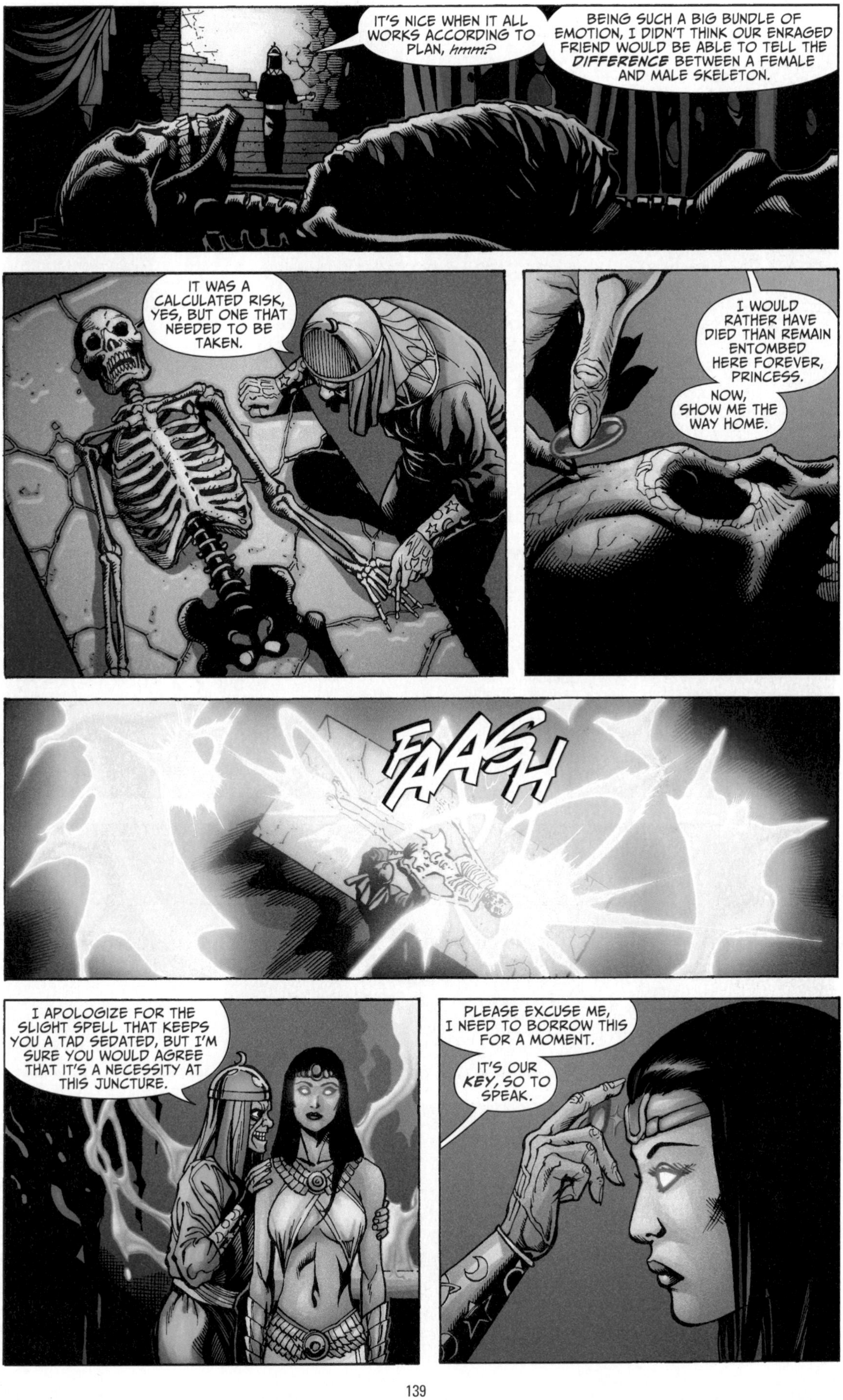
IT'S NICE WHEN IT ALL WORKS ACCORDING TO PLAN, *hmm?*
BEING SUCH A BIG BUNDLE OF EMOTION, I DIDN'T THINK OUR ENRAGED FRIEND WOULD BE ABLE TO TELL THE ***DIFFERENCE*** BETWEEN A FEMALE AND MALE SKELETON.
IT WAS A CALCULATED RISK, YES, BUT ONE THAT NEEDED TO BE TAKEN.
I WOULD RATHER HAVE DIED THAN REMAIN ENTOMBED HERE FOREVER, PRINCESS.
NOW, SHOW ME THE WAY HOME.
FAASH
I APOLOGIZE FOR THE SLIGHT SPELL THAT KEEPS YOU A TAD SEDATED, BUT I'M SURE YOU WOULD AGREE THAT IT'S A NECESSITY AT THIS JUNCTURE.
PLEASE EXCUSE ME, I NEED TO BORROW THIS FOR A MOMENT.
IT'S OUR ***KEY,*** SO TO SPEAK.

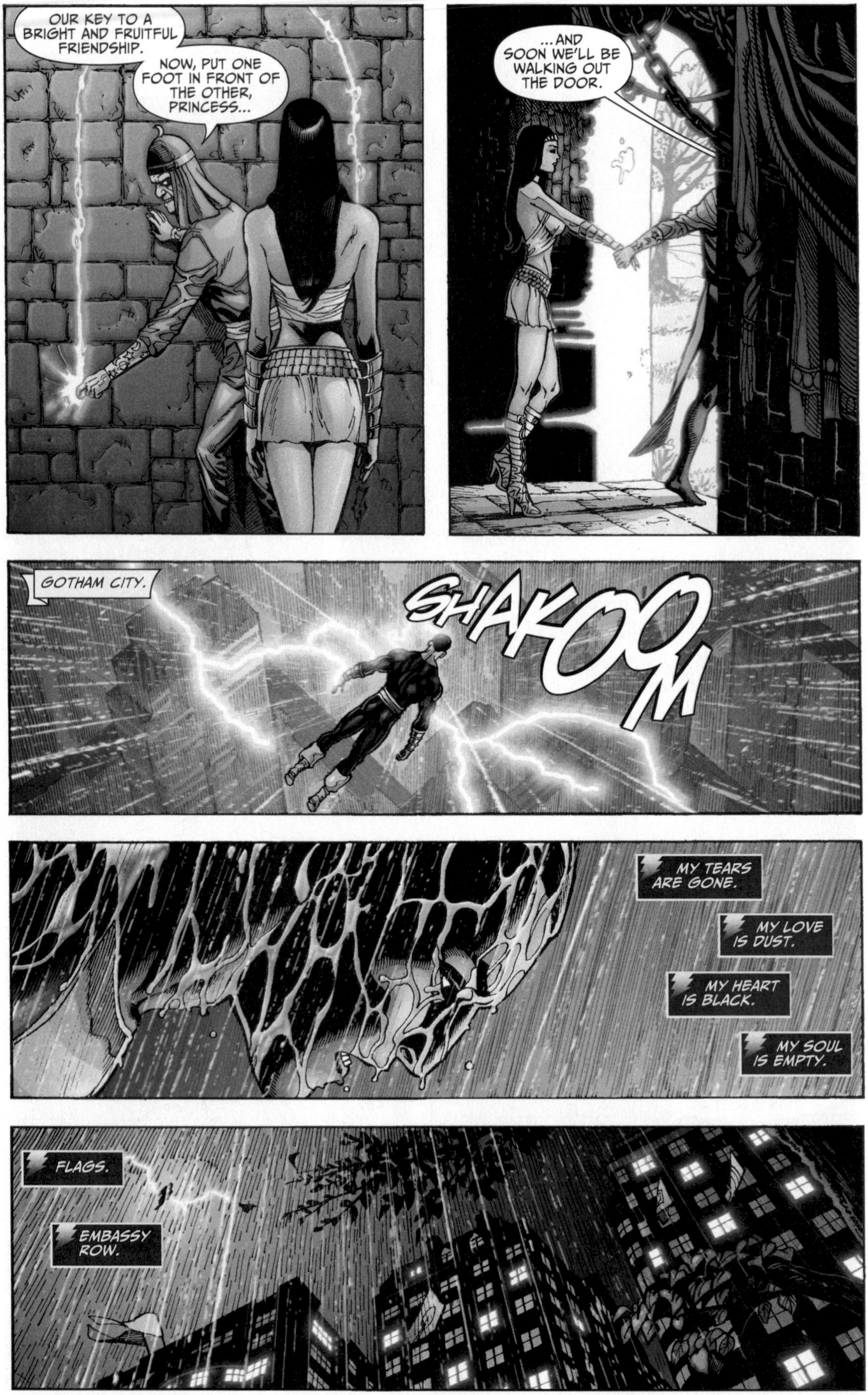
OUR KEY TO A BRIGHT AND FRUITFUL FRIENDSHIP.
NOW, PUT ONE FOOT IN FRONT OF THE OTHER, PRINCESS...
...AND SOON WE'LL BE WALKING OUT THE DOOR.
GOTHAM CITY.
SHAKOOOM
MY TEARS ARE GONE.
MY LOVE IS DUST.
MY HEART IS BLACK.
MY SOUL IS EMPTY.
FLAGS.
EMBASSY ROW.

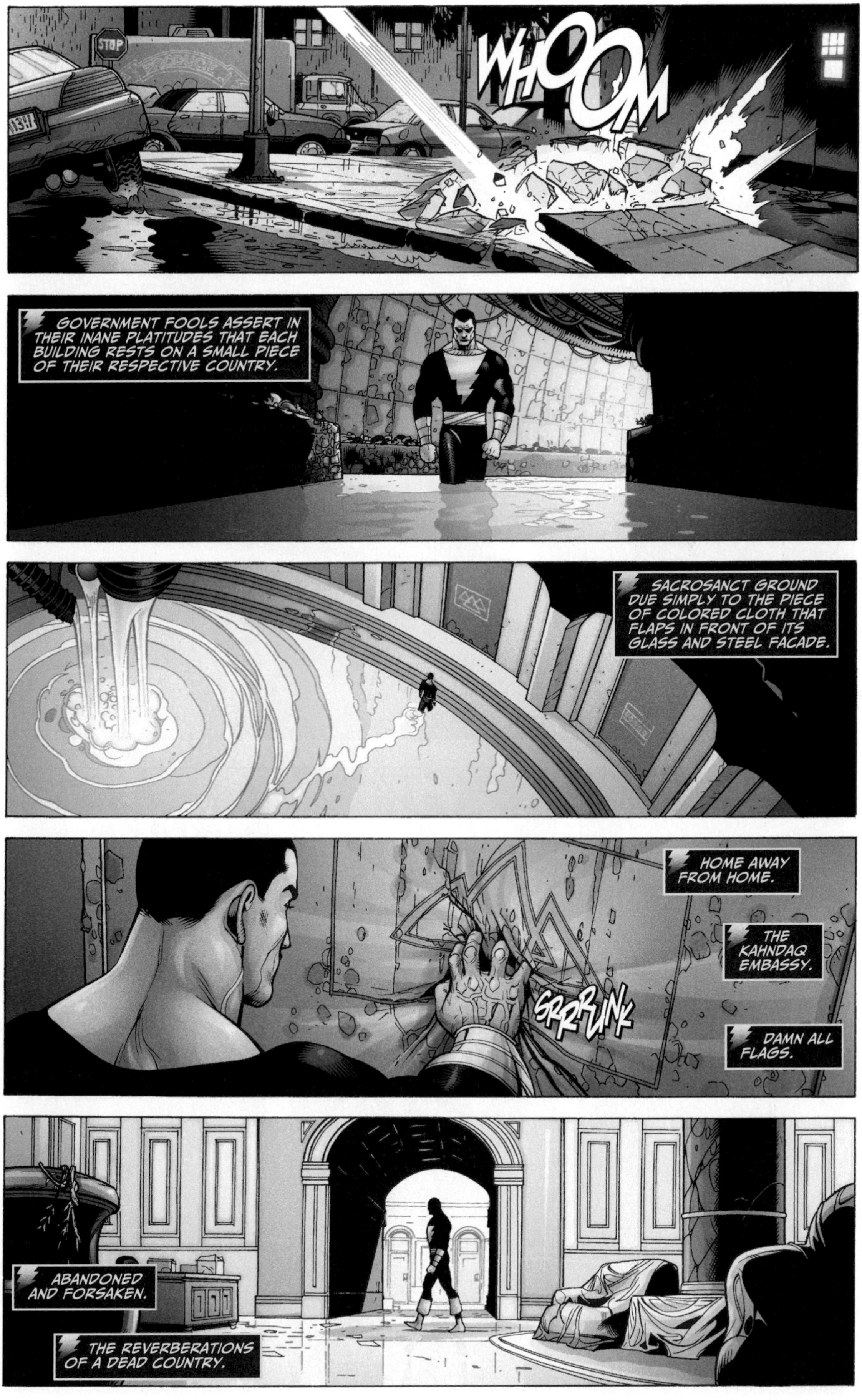
WHOOOM
GOVERNMENT FOOLS ASSERT IN THEIR INANE PLATITUDES THAT EACH BUILDING RESTS ON A SMALL PIECE OF THEIR RESPECTIVE COUNTRY.
SACROSANCT GROUND DUE SIMPLY TO THE PIECE OF COLORED CLOTH THAT FLAPS IN FRONT OF ITS GLASS AND STEEL FACADE.
HOME AWAY FROM HOME.
THE KAHNDAQ EMBASSY.
SRRRUNK
DAMN ALL FLAGS.
ABANDONED AND FORSAKEN.
THE REVERBERATIONS OF A DEAD COUNTRY.

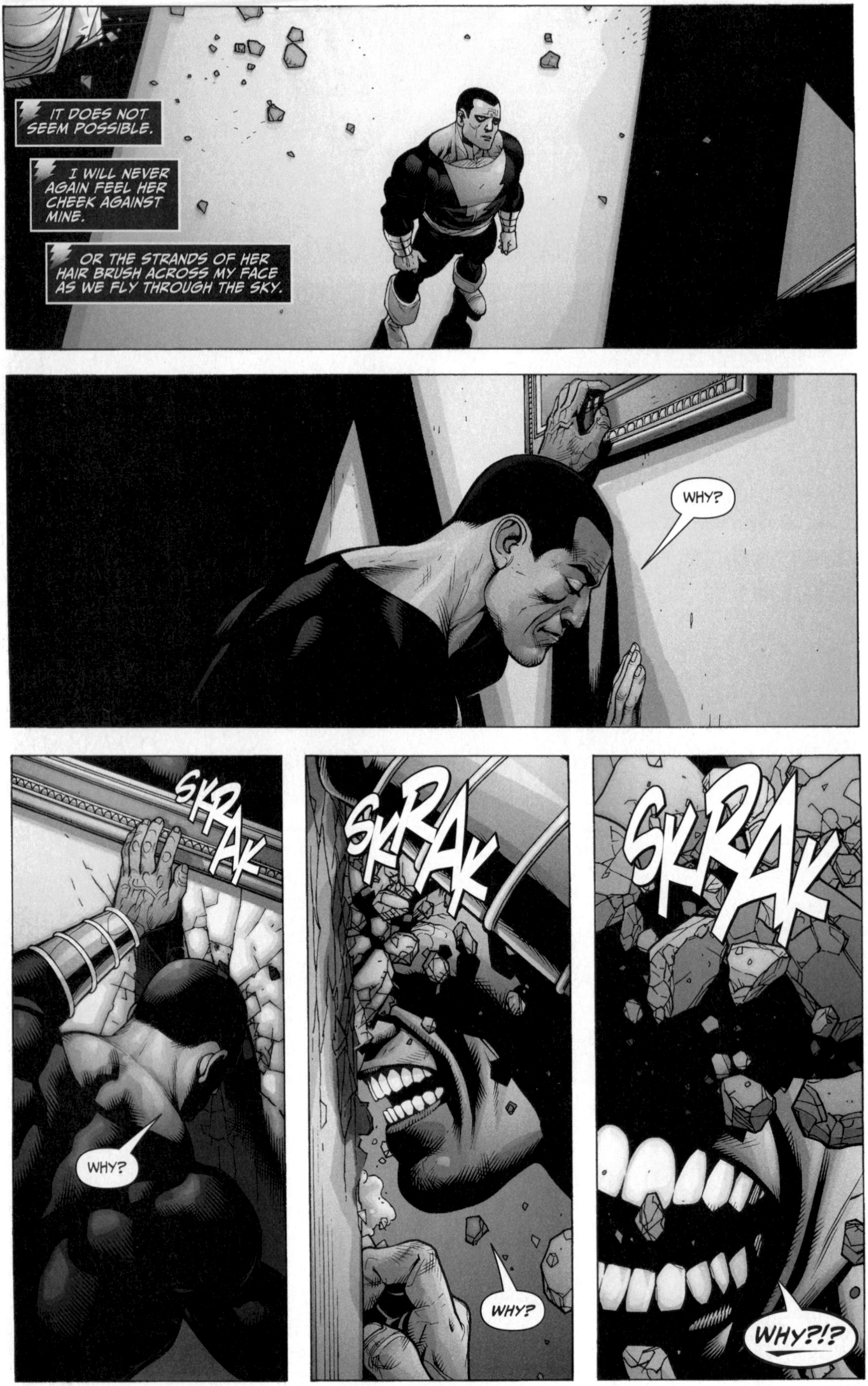
IT DOES NOT SEEM POSSIBLE.
I WILL NEVER AGAIN FEEL HER CHEEK AGAINST MINE.
OR THE STRANDS OF HER HAIR BRUSH ACROSS MY FACE AS WE FLY THROUGH THE SKY.
WHY?
SKRAK
WHY?
SKRAK
WHY?
SKRAK
WHY?!?

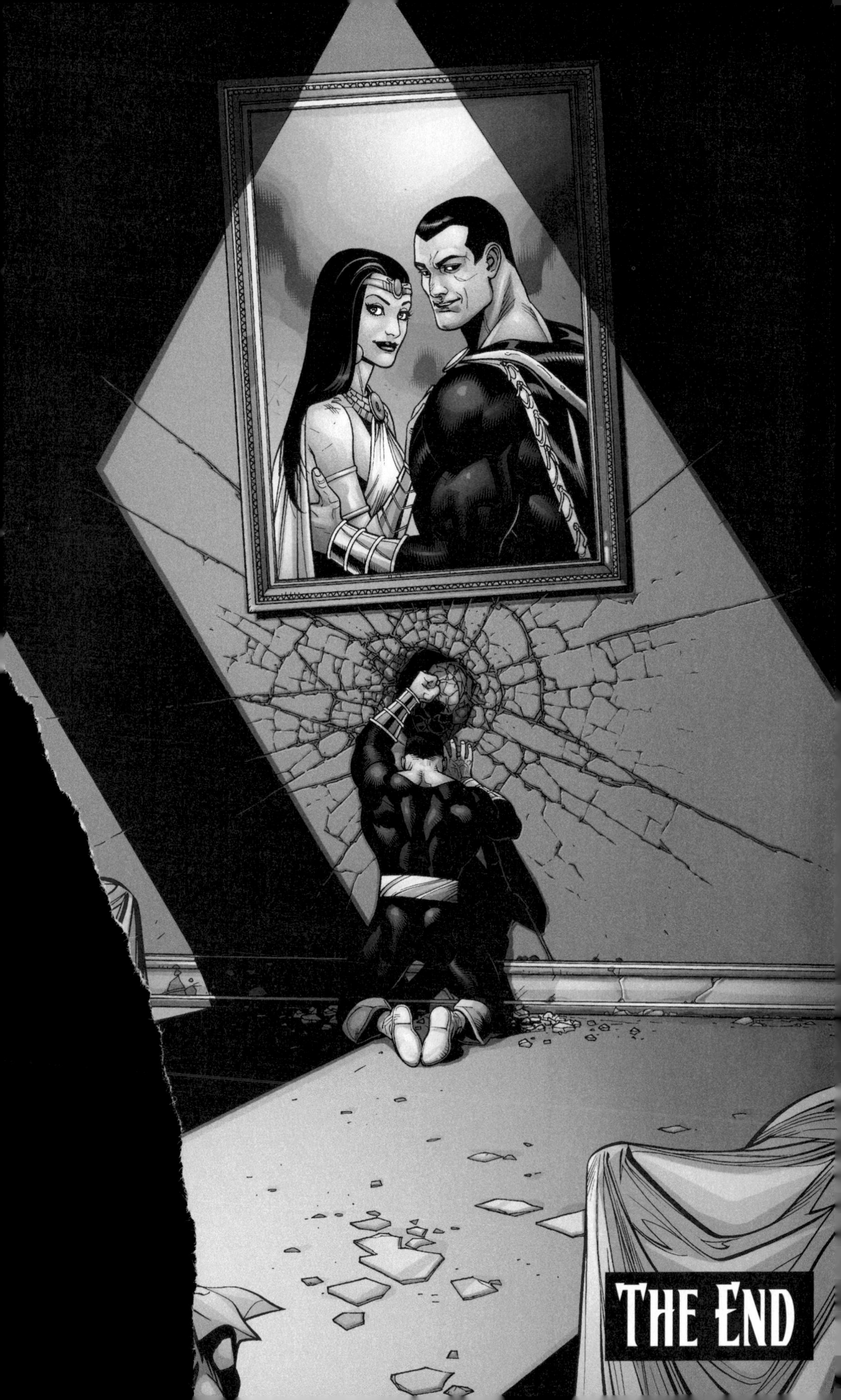
THE END

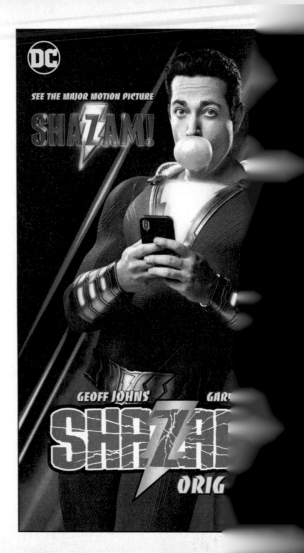